MANAGING THE LEGAL FACTOR

AN ANTICIPATORY THINKING APPROACH TO PREVENTATIVE LAW

HOW TO EFFECTIVELY MANAGE THE LEGAL RISKS OF COMMERCIAL TRANSACTIONS

SPECIAL BSL 485 SUPPLEMENT

NEW AND UPDATED

BY
MARTIN E. SEGAL

MANAGING
THE
LEGAL FACTOR

SPECIAL BSL 485 SUPPLEMENT

6th EDITION
MARTIN E. SEGAL
© 2017
All Rights Reserved

NEW AGE PUBLISHING CO.
P.O. BOX 01-1549
MIAMI, FL 33101
newagepub2003@yahoo.com

MANAGING THE LEGAL FACTOR

SPECIAL BSL 485 SUPPLEMENT

TABLE OF CONTENTS

MANAGING THE LEGAL FACTOR
BSL 485 SUPPLEMENT
INTRODUCTION

We know that skillful managerial decisions in planning, negotiating and implementing commercial transactions are crucial to business success. A key component of these decisions is their legal implications.

Managing the legal factor is one of the essential components of proper corporate governance. It requires analysis of potential liability resulting from interactions of the parties in the business marketplace

Most disputes in the business marketplace are either CONTRACT claims (per the main text) or non-contract wrongs known as TORT claims. Liability is either direct due to the acts on non-acts of the defendant, or indirect liability from the acts of others under the law of AGENCY. The ability to shield oneself from personal liability, every bit as important as the financial nuts and bolts of a commercial transaction, is a critical aspect of FORMS OF DOING BUSINESS. The need for business expansion and raising of capital from the investing public involves SECURITIES REGULATION. Financial reverses may require protection of BANKRUPTCY laws. The manner in which business is conducted using principles of BUSINESS ETHICS may have important implications throughout the legal spectrum. Awareness of the rapidly changing legal arena seen in LEGAL TRENDS is also critical to business success. The APPENDIX OF CHAPTER CASE DIGESTS presents recent cases, section-by-section, to update our material, courtesy of www.swlearning.com/blaw/cases/new_case_updates.html.

Our analysis process also requires cultivation of anticipatory thinking, so that a preventive law strategy of risk management can be achieved. The optimum result of managing the legal factor is not necessarily just putting out business fires, which in most companies is the main focus of legal concerns. Of equal importance is avoiding, preventing and minimizing the impact of the business law time bombs that were the cause of those fires. We discuss the anticipatory thinking approach in the main text Chapter 1A. Its principles are applicable to all business transactions.

Contract and Sales concepts are the main focus of the main text, presented in Chapters 1 through 4, where one party seeks to enforce their agreement and the other party seeks to avoid its legal consequences. This contract dance steps its way through creation, enforcement, defenses to validity, issues of written or verbal form, rights of third party outsiders and legal excuses for non-performance.

Special rules for sales of goods, based upon the statutory provisions of the Uniform Commercial Code (UCC), including major differences between domestic UCC transactions and international CISG transactions, imperfect title disputes and risk of loss rules are presented in main text Chapter 5A.

Special rules governing product liability disputes, including fault-based negligence, no-fault strict liability and contract warranty claims are discussed in main text Chapter 5B. Special legal rules for doing e-business in the cyber-marketplace are examined in main text Chapter 5C. The legal system that provides the underlying framework for resolution of disputes, whether they are contract or tort, is discussed in the main text Chapter 6. Legal Trends Facing Business Managers are discussed in main text Chapter 7.

This supplement begins in Section I with analysis of the variety of INTENTIONAL TORTS that often adversely impact business managers and entrepreneurs. They involve unlawful interference with someone's rights - called torts against persons, torts against property and torts against business. They also include the Contract Torts: (1) breach of the duty of good faith and fair dealing, and (2) interference with an advantageous contract, both of which are discussed in the main text. We also discuss some special rules governing the unintentional tort of negligence that impact many everyday commercial business transactions.

In Section II AGENCY we discuss vicarious liability. While a party who breaches a contract or commits a tort is always directly liable, a principal with deep financial pockets is often sued not for his own acts but for those of his agents under a theory of indirect liability.

Since potential direct and indirect contract/tort liability underlies the structuring, negotiating, and implementing of all business decisions, the key to financial success may lie in Section III FORMS OF DOING BUSINESS. Here we discuss advantages and disadvantages of the different ways to transact business. This includes common law sole proprietorship and general partnership, as well as statutory limited liability through LP, LLP, LLC, and the Corporation.

Section IV SECURITIES REGULATION explores the main laws implemented by the federal government to try to protect the investing public.

Though we hope our managerial efforts will succeed in avoiding or defusing liability claims, adverse financial results sometimes occur. If so, we must be familiar with the legal protections discussed in Section V BANKRUPTCY LAWS, including the sweeping changes made by the 2005 Bankruptcy Abuse Act.

Section VI discusses BUSINESS ETHICS, analyzing its historical theories, examples of famous ethical disputes, and practical management strategies to better assure positive results.

Section VII updates LEGAL TRENDS, originally discussed in the text's Chapter 7 material.

Section VIII updates CHAPTER CASE DIGESTS of court decisions.

I.   INTENTIONAL TORTS

" New and nameless torts are being recognized constantly, and the progress of the common law is marked by many cases of first impression, in which the court has struck out boldly to create a new cause of action . . . The law of torts is anything but static, and the limits of its development are never set."
Prosser, Torts, Section 1 (4th Ed. 1971)

As we begin our discussion of intentional torts, remember that the plaintiff has the burden of proving the tort's existence by the usual burden of proof – a preponderance of the evidence. In addition to *liability*, the plaintiff must also prove legal *damages* were suffered. But courts will often infer some type of nominal damages so that the main aspect of proving plaintiff's case is liability – the existence of the claimed tort.

In many of these cases the plaintiff requests an award of punitive damages in addition to being compensated for actual loss, since the defendant's intentional conduct carries a higher degree of culpability due to its willful nature. The more malicious, reckless and outrageous the complained acts, the higher the likelihood that the defendant will be punished with these additional damages.

The current legal trend widens areas of potential liability, especially in torts. The legal waters are constantly being tested by plaintiffs for new or expanded claims. And if they are successful, business defendants usually pass on the increased costs to their customers in the form of higher prices for goods sold.

Also notice from the cases that follow how the same set of facts creating a dispute may result in a legal claim for multiple torts. This is practically accomplished in lawsuits by suing for alternative relief, and hoping to hit the target on one or more separate counts.

A. Interference With Personal Rights

1. ASSAULT – defendant causes the plaintiff to be in reasonable fear of immediate bodily harm, even though there is no physical contact. The acts complained of must be unauthorized threats of present, rather than future harm.

> Example: George is a 6 foot, 265 pound bodybuilder who gets into an argument with 5 foot, 145 pound Alan. If Alan look up, draws back his fist, and threatens to break George's nose, we probably don't have assault because of a lack of the required "reasonable apprehension of bodily harm." But what if George claimed assault because the height differential brought Alan's extended fist in proximity with George's genitals, and he was fearful of serious injury? Or what if Alan stood on a ladder when he made the threat? The result would probably be different.

However, what if the roles were reversed and George was the aggressor? It would be reasonable for Alan to be fearful because of the threat (liability), and if he suffered a nervous reaction plus some outward physical symptoms (damages), the tort would arise.

2. BATTERY – defendant's conduct involves unauthorized and harmful physical contact. This is known as the impact rule – a touching of the plaintiff without his consent, which results in some damages. The dollar amount of recoverable damages will depend upon the severity of the contact.

The unauthorized contact may be direct touching by the defendant, or indirect touching such as striking the defendant with a thrown object. Although the defendant is usually aware of the battery, it isn't legally necessary. A sleeping plaintiff can recover for the tort so long as the facts of the unauthorized contact are proven.

Example: Bill, Sarah and Jane work at Burger Queen. Bill and Sarah anger their supervisor who pushes Bill and throws a burger patty at Sarah. Part of it hits her in the face and part hits Jane. All parties may claim battery. Bill recovers for direct impact and Sarah can recover under the indirect impact rule. Jane recovers under the rule of transferred intent, since Sarah's intentional act is deemed directed to its victim.

A related case: In *Manning v. Grimsley, 643 F.2d 20 (1st Cir. 1981)*, Ross Grimsley, a pitcher for the Baltimore Orioles baseball team, was warming up at Fenway Park for a game with the Boston Red Sox by throwing a ball from the pitcher's mound to a plate in the bullpen located near the right field bleachers where plaintiff and other spectators loudly heckling the pitcher were seated.

On several occasions Grimsley looked directly at the hecklers. Then he lifted his arm as if to throw the ball to his catcher, but suddenly turned at a 90 degree angle and threw the ball at the hecklers in the stands. The ball penetrated the protective screening, missed the hecklers he was aiming at, and struck the plaintiff. Plaintiff sued for battery, the trial court directed a verdict for defendant, and this was reversed on appeal.

The court said, "We, unlike the district judge, are of the view that . . . the jury could reasonably have inferred that Grimsley intended (1) to throw the ball in the direction of the hecklers, (2) to cause them imminent apprehension of being hit, and (3) to respond to conduct presently affecting his ability to warm up ...."

The court's wording indicates that a claim for the torts of assault and battery would be available. If the spectator who was struck was not a heckler, he would still be able to recover for battery under the transferred intent doctrine.

Note: Assault and Battery are more commonly known as crimes. Sometimes the same acts of a defendant will result in criminal charges brought by the State and a civil lawsuit for money damages brought by the victimized party plaintiff. Remember the O.J. Simpson drama? He was acquitted of the 1st degree murder charges brought against him by the State of California, but a money judgment was later entered against him in the "wrongful death" civil action brought by Fred Goldman, father of one of the persons he allegedly murdered, based on the same set of facts.

3.   FALSE IMPRISONMENT – defendant restrains or confines plaintiff without consent or legal grounds. This usually occurs in situations where the defendant mistakenly believes the plaintiff is shoplifting or is otherwise engaged in committing a crime.

There usually is forced confinement, such as by locking the defendant in a room. However, there may also be implied confinement through the threat of force or false statement of legal authority to restrain.

In these latter cases, no actual physical barriers impede the plaintiff from leaving, but it is reasonably understood why he does not choose to leave.

Example: Spin Records has a store on the University campus, and its security guard is posted at the front door to prevent theft by inspecting the back packs of student customers when they leave the store. Harry is suspected of stealing merchandise as he leaves the store. When the guard yells, "Stop at once," Harry freezes in place and is searched. When nothing is found, he sues for the tort.

Since Harry properly obeyed the instructions to stop, he is legally detained even though there is no physical confinement. The falsity of the suspected grounds for the search, and the sustaining of nominal damages by Harry completes the tort.

Historically, false imprisonment created significant problems for businesses selling goods to the public. If a customer was detained in any way and falsely accused of theft, no matter how understandable the mistake, the tort would be proper. The business community was between the proverbial rock and a hard place. If patrons were never detained for suspected stealing, theft would increase and profits would fall. If customers were aggressively detained, liability losses would escalate.

Two events occurred that have dramatically reduced in-store theft:

- Legislators responded to the theft predicament of retailers by passing "merchant detainer" laws in all states creating a "shopkeeper's privilege" to do what would formerly constitute false imprisonment so long as the merchant satisfies the *reasonableness* standard of care in determining grounds to detain, and the manner, method and time of the confinement.

- Technology created the computer chip sensors that are attached to store merchandise and emit loud noises if the articles are removed from the store without being disabled at time of payment.

A related case: In *Wal-Mart Stores, Inc. v. Goodman, 789 So.2d 166 (Ala .2000)*, plaintiff went shopping in a Wal-Mart store with her two young daughters.

Goodman says – she brought with her for exchange a cordless phone she had previously bought at another Wal-Mart store. She delivered the boxed phone and sales receipt to the customer service desk while she looked for a replacement. She was unable to find one she liked, retrieved her phone and sales receipt, made other purchases, checked out and left the store. She was stopped outside by Wal-Mart security and accused of stealing the phone. Even though she offered to show the original receipt, she was detained and handcuffed in front of her children, the police were called, and she was arrested for theft based upon the criminal charges filed by Wal-Mart.

Wal-Mart says – Goodman was seen to take the boxed telephone from the electronics department and concealed it in her shopping bags with her other purchases. When stopped outside the store, she first claimed she had purchased all the items, and then changed her story to say that she was returning the phone for exchange. She did show a purchase receipt dated 7 days earlier. It had the same product code, but was disregarded because the customer service desk said she had not attempted to return anything.

Goodman was acquitted and then sued Wal-Mart for tort damages, including a count of false imprisonment. Wal-Mart claimed it had acted reasonably under the merchant protection statute. The jury disagreed, awarded her $200,000 in compensatory damages and added another $3 million in punitive damages. On appeal, the punitive damages were reduced from their excessive ratio of 15:1 to an amount of $600,000, a 3:1 ratio.

Note: Wal-Mart is the world's biggest retailer and is sued more often than any American entity other than the U.S. government, with over 5,000 lawsuits filed against it every year. There are websites created by plaintiff's attorneys and disgruntled customers sharing litigation strategy, complaints and related current information. The retailer's litigation problems were aggravated by their long-standing policy of refusing to settle claims or the lawsuits filed to enforce them.

This hard-line approach essentially dared potential plaintiffs to pursue their cases all the way to a final decision by judge or jury, and ran counter to the claims policy of most other large companies to settle quickly and cut their losses. Playing hard ball proved so expensive in legal fees and damaging to their reputation that new management has instituted a separate division for effective claim management that now encourages early settlement and prompt resolution of claims without litigation.

Critics wonder whether Wal-Mart is serious about its new "kinder and friendlier" image. What do you think? How would you handle the legal claims in your business?

4. **EMOTIONAL DISTRESS** – the defendant's *outrageous* conduct causes plaintiff to suffer some degree of mental, emotional and/or physical upset, ranging from mild discomfort all the way to a serious illness. Notice these descriptive words for the actionable nature of the defendant's conduct and the plaintiff's reaction to it:

- Defendant's act – willful, malicious, reckless, disgraceful, extreme, atrocious, intolerable, beyond the boundaries of human decency.

- Plaintiff's reaction – anxiety, worry, fear, shame, embarrassment, disgrace, anger, rage, pain, headache, stomach ache, heart palpitations, nausea, disease.

Punitive damages are often demanded in these cases due to the extreme nature of the actionable conduct, as reflected by the words that describe the actions of the defendant and the reactions of the plaintiff. No physical contact is required. This is a departure from the "impact rule" which for many years prohibited any recovery for mere emotional distress, except for assault, without a corresponding physical touching.

There is also a wide disparity in the state courts deciding these cases. Since the requirement of "outrageous conduct" is a matter of opinion, and resulting emotional distress is difficult to diagnose and quantify – the possibility of fraud exists. The proof spectrum runs from legal requirements of actual physical injury or illness that is substantiated by expert medical testimony all the way to almost any form of alleged emotional discomfort.

Example: Steve and Delia are getting divorced, despite his strong objections. He is angry and wants to get even. While sitting in the park, he notices Delia's dog running by itself. Steve knows how much she loves the dog, calls her on his cell phone and falsely tells her he just saw her dog get hit by a car. She has a severe emotional upset, and then sues him for the tort.

Pretend you are the judge in this case. Is Steve's conduct outrageous? Is Delia's reaction reasonable? What boundaries would you personally impose on the liability and damages aspects of this tort?

A related case: In *Roach v. Stern, 675 N.Y.S.2d 133 (1998),* topless dancer Deborah Roach, aka Debbie Tay frequently guested on shock-jock Howard Stern's nationally syndicated cable television show. After her death from a drug overdose and cremation, her sister Driscoll gave a portion of the remains to her friend Hayden. Hayden then appeared on Stern's show with a box containing them and the parties played with them.

"Stern at one point donned rubber gloves and held up certain bone fragments while he guessed whether they came from Tay's skull or ribs." He also made a number of crude and obscene comments about them.

Plaintiff sued for the tort of emotional distress, and the trial court granted defendant's motion to dismiss. Even though it felt the conduct complained of was "vulgar and disrespectful," it was not outrageous. On appeal, the ruling was reversed.

"Although the defendants contend that the conduct at issue was not particularly shocking, in light of Stern's reputation for vulgar humor and Tay's actions during her guest appearances on his program, a jury might reasonably conclude that the manner in which Tay's remains were handled, for entertainment purposes and against the express wishes of her family, went beyond the bounds of decent behavior."

There is also a separate area of recovery for negligent infliction of emotional distress. In *Air Crash Disaster -Estrada v. Aeronaves de Mexico, 967 F.2d 1421 (9th Cir. 1992),* plaintiff went shopping at a nearby store, leaving her husband and three children at home. On her return she saw, heard and felt a large explosion caused by the collision of defendant's airliner with a private aircraft and its crashing into her house. She did not witness the plane crash, only its after-effects where she saw her house consumed by a fire. Her family perished in that fire. She suffered a severe emotional trauma and successfully sued.

"A plaintiff may recover damages for emotional distress caused by observing the negligently inflicted injury of a third person if, but only if, said plaintiff: (1) is closely related to the injury victim; (2) is present at the scene of the injury-producing event at the time it occurs and is then aware that it is causing injury to the victim; and (3) as a result suffers serious emotional distress – a reaction beyond that which would be anticipated in a disinterested witness and which is not an abnormal response to the circumstances."

"Estrada's emotional distress did not stem merely from the knowledge that her husband and children had died. Estrada understandably experienced great emotional distress as a result of watching helplessly as flames engulfed her home and burned her family to death."

But in the case of *Golstein v. West Coast Cancer Foundation, 223 Cal.App.3d 1415 (Cal. App. 1990),* plaintiff was denied recovery in her action for negligent infliction of emotional distress caused by her son being given a fatal overdose of radiation during treatment for a curable cancer. She had not witnessed the overdose and was unaware her son was being overexposed. A similar result was *Jones v. City of Houston, (2009 WL 2634226, Tex. App.),* where the siblings of a drowned child who watched rescue teams recover the lifeless body weren't at the original accident scene.

"... to recover damages for emotional distress caused by observing the negligently inflicted injury of a third person, the plaintiff must experience a contemporaneous sensory awareness of the causal connection between the negligent conduct and the resulting injury."

This confusion has been somewhat clarified by two recent emotional distress cases. In *Diaz v. NBC Universal, Inc., (2008 WL 465235, S.D.N.Y.)*, the court dismissed a group suit for defamation and emotional distress brought on behalf of 400 New York DEA agents claimed to have violated drug laws in the movie "American Gangster."

In *Eskin v. Bartee, (2008 WL 3504934, Sup. Ct. Tenn)* , the family of a boy seriously injured in an auto accident who arrived at the scene afterwards were allowed to sue for emotional distress even though they hadn't witnessed the event. The court recited the 4-pronged recovery test *as:* (1) death or serious injury, (2) intimate personal relationship, (3) severe emotional injury, and (4) observation of the accident scene. But the latter requirement was lessened if the after – observed scene remained the same.

Note: Plaintiffs continue trying to expand liability for emotional distress:
- Nervous airline passengers claim that severe air turbulence caused them emotional and physical upsets. The airlines defend on assumption of the risk of known and foreseeable dangers, claiming bumpy flights may occur, especially in "clear air turbulence." But what if the airline ignores weather warnings or directions to re-route flights? What about long tarmac delays where passengers aren't allowed to leave the plane? What do you think?

- Obesity lawsuits are filed against deep – pocket fast food defendants such as KFC, Burger King, McDonald's and Taco Bell, claiming "you made me fat." But what if nutritional content of the food is falsified? What do you think?

- investors who lost substantial monies in Wall Street scandals have sued brokerage houses and investment banks on various fraud and negligence theories, claiming emotional distress damages. What do you think?

    5. DEFAMATION– the defendant's unauthorized, unprivileged, and untrue written (libel) or verbal (slander) statement of fact is communicated to another and injures the plaintiff's personal reputation. If this occurs in a business context, concerning plaintiff's products, services, property or business reputation, the tortuous economic damage is called trade libel, product disparagement, or injurious falsehood.

    The essential elements of the tort must be proven by the plaintiff and may also serve as a legal defense if they are absent from the facts of a particular dispute:

    1. plaintiff didn't consent to the defamatory statements before they were made or ratify them after the fact. If plaintiff authorizes the statement, the right to sue for damages is lost.

2. the defamatory statements carried no "absolute privilege" such as statements made in governmental legislative or judicial proceedings, or a "qualified privilege" accorded the media when it reports defamatory material and then promptly issues a retraction upon request. Statutes of many states also create another qualified privilege in cases of requested job references for departing employees. So long as the employer acts makes a good faith effort to verify the truth of its report, it is not liable for inadvertent false statements. Even so, most employers these days facing a job reference request will only verify dates of employment and job titles for fear of potential tort liability.

3. the defamatory statements were not true, whether or not the defendant believed them to be. True statements are not actionable.

4. the defamatory statements were present facts, not opinions or predictions about the future. Only factual statements may harm one's reputation.

5. the defamatory statement was "published," meaning that a third party saw or heard the defamatory statement. Plaintiff cannot sue for defamatory statements uttered in a closed room.

6. the statement harmed plaintiff's reputation. The same derogatory statement made about a pimp or a pope would have a different result.

7. if the plaintiff is someone "in the public eye," their celebrity or well-known status prevents them from a recovery for alleged defamatory statements unless they prove the defendant acted "with malice." This means the defendant acted willfully, maliciously and recklessly, which incidentally is the same legal test for punitive damages.

Example: Senator Fred is feuding with Senator Gwen in the State Legislature because she is the swing vote on his bill and won't vote for it. He calls her "a known communist" during debate, even though he has no evidence of that fact. After the session is over, and he is interviewed by the press back at his office he repeats the statement. Gwen sues Fred for slander.

Let's analyze the dispute. The statement is an intentional published assertion of an untrue fact, and is not authorized by Gwen. The utterance during the congressional session is privileged but its later repetition is not. If uttered in the 1950's era of the Cold War the statement would certainly be defamatory. But in the year 2004 it would barely be noticed. Since Gwen is probably considered to be a public figure, the requirement of "malice" seems satisfied by the personal vendetta nature of Fred's repeated statements. Gwen wins.

A related case: In *Leidholdt v. Larry Flynt Publications, 860 F.2d 890 (9th Cir. 1988)*, plaintiff, who was a founding member of the organization "Women Against Pornography", was called among other terms - "a sexual fascist", sexually repressed", and "a pus bloated walking sphincter" in a regular column of defendant's Hustler Magazine called, Asshole of the Month. The column criticized anti-pornographers in graphic terms, and the particular article included a photograph of plaintiff's face superimposed over a naked man's buttocks.

Plaintiff sued for various torts, including defamation by libel. The trial court granted defendant's motion to dismiss her claim for failure to state a cause of action and the appellate court affirmed.

"The threshold question before us is ... whether the Hustler article constitutes the expression of an opinion rather than of allegedly factual statements." The pornographic content of the magazine and the lampooning nature of the column "will telegraph to the reader that the article presents opinions, not allegations of fact. . .

Even apparent facts must be allowed as opinion 'when the surrounding circumstances of a statement are those of a heated political debate, where certain remarks are necessarily understood as ridicule or vituperation, or both, but not as descriptive of factual matters.'"

A similar result was reached in the case of *Polygram Records, Inc. v. Rege, 170 Cal.App.3d 543(Cal. App. 1985)*, where Rege, a wine distributor, unsuccessfully brought an action for trade libel and personal defamation against entertainer Robin Williams and his record company for his comedy routine that allegedly disparaged Rege Wine.

"The torts of injurious falsehood and defamation protect different interests and have different origins; the action for defamation protects the personal reputation of the injured party and arose from the old actions for libel and slander; the action for injurious falsehood protects economic interests of the injured party against pecuniary loss, and arose as an action on the case for the special damage resulting from the publication."

"The complaint fails to state a cause of action because (1) the joke, told as part of a comedy performance, cannot under the circumstances be reasonably understood as any serious or literal statement of fact and is fully protected speech under the First amendment, (2) Rege's claim that the joke is defamatory because it purportedly associated his products with black consumers should be rejected as a matter of law."

11

6. INVASION OF PRIVACY – the defendant's intrusive behavior violates plaintiff's personal rights of solitude and freedom from unauthorized disclosure of private information, whether true or untrue.

According to Prosser on Torts, "Invasion of Privacy is not one tort, but a complex of four. The law of privacy comprises four distinct kinds of invasion of four different interests of the plaintiff, which are tied together by the common name, but otherwise have almost nothing in common except that each represents an interference with the right of the plaintiff to be let alone."

- Intrusion into one's seclusion and private affairs – including unauthorized wiretaps, searches, viewing of private letters, files and/or emails, and related types of personal espionage.

- Public disclosure of private facts – including one's personal finances, private history, and related confidential information.

- While disclosure of public information, such as a criminal conviction, is usually not actionable, if a long passage of time has occurred from when the facts were initially reported and current disclosure would be personally damaging, the information may now be protected.

- Placing someone in a "false light" – such as falsely creating the impression that objectionable acts or beliefs belong to another. This can include signing someone else's name to an offensive sign, memo, letter or e-communication. (Note: Florida used to allow a separate "false light" tort, but it now is part of defamation. *Jews for Jesus, Inc. v. Rapp, (2008 WL 4659375, Sup. Ct. Fla.)*

7. RIGHT OF PUBLICITY - although a public figure or celebrity forfeits their right of privacy, their name, likeness, image, signature sayings and the like are valuable proprietary assets. They may not be used without their consent and/or payment to them of a negotiated royalty. This includes their estate if deceased.

The right of publicity has properly evolved into a separate tort, distinct from invasion of privacy. While the latter tort involves violation of the plaintiff's desire to be left alone, well-known personalities want to be in the public eye. Therefore the essence of the publicity tort is to protect the celebrity's financial interest in the unauthorized commercial exploitation of his identity.

This is clearly reflected in the following three cases concerning image piracy, voice piracy and popular phrase piracy:

A related case (image/name piracy): In *White v. Samsung Electronics, 971 F.2d 1395 (1992),* celebrity Vanna White, hostess of the long-running television show "Wheel of Fortune", was the subject of defendant's ad campaign, called "the Vanna White ad", depicting her as a robot in the "longest-running game show, 2012 A.D." She never consented to the ad, was not paid for use of her name and image, and sued for the common law tort of right of publicity.

The trial court granted summary judgment against her and she appealed. In reversing and holding that she had pleaded claims that had the right to be heard by a jury, the appellate court said:

"The right of publicity has developed to protect the commercial interest of celebrities in their identities. The theory of the right is that a celebrity's identity can be valuable in the promotion of products, and the celebrity has an interest that may be protected from the unauthorized commercial exploitation of that identity."

A second related case (voice piracy): In *Waits v. Frito-Lay, Inc., 978 F.2d 1093 (9th Cir. 1992),* defendant decided to introduce a new Doritos snack food corn chip product and hired an ad agency to develop a marketing campaign. The agency wrote a commercial that mimicked one of raspy-voiced singer Tom Waits' songs. Since he refused to do the commercial, the agency hired a musician-impressionist. The entertainer imitated plaintiff's distinctive voice in a commercial broadcast nationwide. Waits sued for voice misappropriation and false endorsement and received a jury award of $375,000 compensatory and $2 million punitive damages.

The court cited the landmark prior California case that established the protectability of a distinctive voice (*Bette Midler v. Ford Motor Co.,849 F.2d 460 (9th Cir. 1988)* and allowed damages for unauthorized use:

"The *Midler* tort is a species of violation of the "right of publicity," the right of a person whose identity has commercial value – most often a celebrity – to control the commercial use of that identity. We recognized in *Midler* that when voice is a sufficient indicia of a celebrity's identity, the right to publicity protects against its imitation for commercial purposes without the celebrity's consent."

A third related case (popular phrase/intro theft): In *Johnny Carson v. Here's Johnny Portable Toilets, Inc., 698 F.2d 8312 (6th Cir. 1983),* defendant adopted in its business name the popular phrase that was used nightly to introduce the plaintiff on his top-rated network television late show, and also preceded his numerous appearances in night clubs and theatres around the country. He had also licensed its use in the marketing of various products. Defendant adopted and used its company name without plaintiff's permission.

The court reversed a trial court decision for defendant, and extended right of publicity protection to plaintiff beyond just his name or likeness. It stated:

"We believe that, on the contrary, the district court's conception of the right of publicity is too narrow. The right of publicity, as we have stated, is that a celebrity has a protected pecuniary interest in the commercial exploitation of his identity. If the celebrity's identity is commercially exploited, there has been an invasion of his right whether or not his 'name or likeness' is used."

(The court also discussed other famous cases where a celebrity's nickname - "The Greatest", boxer Muhammad Ali, and "Crazylegs", football star Elroy Hirsch – were also legally protected.)

8. **ABUSE OF LEGAL PROCESS** – the plaintiff files criminal charges or a civil lawsuit against the defendant without any probable cause or reasonable grounds for recovery so that it may be considered to be a "malicious prosecution" when the case is dismissed.

Example: Stanley has the only hardware store in a small town. When James opens a competing business, Stanley is furious and convinces his brother, a lawyer, to sue James for a number of false claims so that the time, expense and stress of defending the lawsuit will drive James out of business.

James would probably answer the complaint by raising this tort defense and counterclaiming for money damages which could include an award of punitive damages, due to the fabrication of a case against him.

In the *Wal-Mart Stores, Inc. v. Goodman* case previously discussed in the false imprisonment section, Goodman also had sued for malicious prosecution, which was deemed to be a question to be decided by the jury.

"In order for a claim of malicious prosecution to be submitted to a jury, the trial court must determine that the plaintiff has presented substantial evidence of the following elements: (1) that the present defendant instituted a prior judicial proceeding against the present plaintiff; (2) that in instituting the prior proceeding the present defendant acted without probable cause and with malice; (3) that the prior proceeding ended in favor of the present plaintiff; and (4) that the present plaintiff was damaged as a result of the prior proceeding."

Note: This tort is one of the most important leveling mechanisms in our legal system. The scales of justice are constantly re-balanced by it when large companies and powerful individuals file frivolous lawsuits to attempt to intimidate weaker adversaries. The "malice" aspect of the tort usually justifies an award of punitive damages in addition to the actual losses suffered by the plaintiff.

It serves as a hopeful deterrent to the spread of apparently baseless lawsuits that seem to constantly test the limits of legal liability, such as:

- Claims for obesity made by patrons of fast food restaurants
- Claims for casino losses made by addicted gamblers
- Claims for emotional distress caused by "reality TV" programs
- Claims for new trials due to alleged incompetent counsel

B. Interference With Property Rights

1. **TRESPASS** – defendant, without authorization, interferes with plaintiff's right to the exclusive right to use and enjoy his real estate. The damages can include compensation for loss of land value and loss of use and possession of one's land.

The tort usually arises in the following situations:

- Defendant enters or remains on the land
- Defendant causes a third party or object to remain on the land
- Defendant fails to remove something he has a legal duty to remove

Actual physical damage to the land is not required. Nor does it matter that the intruder acts without actual knowledge of trespass. In addition, a trespass may be committed to the owner's sub-surface rights below the property or air rights above it.

Example: Travis is the absentee owner of vacant land on which he posts "no trespassing" signs. Zachary, a local contractor, disregards the signs and uses the land as a parking lot for some of his trucks, dumps debris in a waste pit he excavates, and builds a shed in which he stores some of his building materials.

2. **NUISANCE** – defendant does not enter or possess plaintiff's land, but interferes with use and enjoyment of it through excessive noise, emission of unpleasant odors, pollution of its water, discharge of smoke, dust and gas, manufacture or discharge of noxious chemicals, and related invasive acts.

Example: Jed's apple orchard adjoins Mary's vacant land. Jed violates local zoning laws and converts some of his property to a sausage factory where he raises and slaughters hogs, and processes their pork by-products.

3. **CONVERSION** – defendant, without consent, takes away, uses or fails to return plaintiff's tangible personal property. This is also seen as a trespass to personalty. The crime of larceny has the same elements, and carries sanctions that escalate based upon the value of the property unlawfully converted.

Example: Bernard, a Miami resident, buys a new Mercedes automobile as a surprise gift for his son who lives in Jacksonville. It will be delivered by his friend Alice who will then visit her parents who are local residents. Contrary to their agreement, she drives it to Montreal for a vacation, and then refuses to return the car when she comes back to Miami three weeks later.

A related case: In *4WD Parts Center, Inc. (4WD) v. Mackendrick (Mack), 579 S.E.2d 772 (Ga. App. 2003)*, the parties contracted for customization of Mack's 1972 Chevy truck. The job was to take 3-4 months for a total price of $12,000 which Mack paid in advance. After many complaints about inaction, he finally received the truck back as a total loss one year later. Many of its parts were missing, the motor was not usable, the brakes were inoperable and the truck bed was rusted out. Mack sued and was awarded $12,000 for breach of contract and $14,000 for conversion of his vehicle.

"It is axiomatic that a single act or course of conduct may constitute not only a breach of contract but an independent tort as well, if in addition to violating a contract obligation it also violates a duty owed to plaintiff created by contract, express or implied."

C. Interference with Business Rights

The distinction between private/personal torts and business torts is academic rather than pragmatic, because as we have seen the same set of facts in a particular dispute can be actionable for a multitude of torts. But it is helpful nevertheless to separately discuss various so-called business torts that commonly arise in commercial transactions.

1. UNFAIR COMPETITION – the defendant goes beyond legal, vigorous competition sales, mark-downs and loss-leaders to engage in illegal predatory business practices whose avowed purpose is to economically destroy plaintiff's business, including:

- Palming off – defendant falsely passes off its products as those of a better known, well-financed and broadly advertised rival. The defendant copies the plaintiff's distinctive product design, packaging, logo, trademarks and distinctive ads causing consumer confusion and to gain competitive advantage.

- Product Disparagement – also called "trade libel", defendant intends to harm the plaintiff's products, services, and reputation by publishing false, commercially damaging information.

16

- **False Advertising** – defendant publishes untruthful and/or misleading comparative ads in interstate commerce to gain a competitive advantage. Section 43(a) of the Federal Lanham Act prohibits this practice and allows injunctive relief and recovery of money damages.

- **Business Fraud** – This is the same cause of action as the defense to contract enforcement we previously discussed in chapter 15 (page 252), where the defendant's deception invalidates plaintiff's acceptance of a business contract.

  Car dealers are often involved in these disputes. A typical case is *Forshey v. Carr Chevrolet, Inc., 965 P.2d 440 (Or. 1998),* where plaintiff bought a used Chevrolet Suburban truck paying cash and trade-in of his two older autos. All of the documents contained "as-is" clauses disclaiming all sales warranties. A short time after the purchase, plaintiff noticed and verified significant problems that had not existed before. The truck's VIN number was removed, the engine had been replaced, the odometer was tampered with, and the emission control equipment was missing. Forshey then discovered from a title search that the vehicle had previously been stolen. When the dealer refused to cancel the transaction, plaintiff sued for business fraud and recovered $11,496 in compensatory damages and $300,000 in punitive damages.

  "It is a good idea to require (in used automobile sales) disclosure of material defects to allow a buyer to purchase something with as much information about that product as possible."

  "An as-is clause saves a seller from being liable for normal features – that is, the engine fails because of honestly disclosed miles – but does not save a seller who concealed facts from the buyer and who has engaged in fraud."

Note: When legal, medical and accounting firms raid other firms in their professions to hire away key partners and their client relationships, a claim of "unfair competition" is sometimes made. This is based upon an alleged breach of fiduciary duty that is the basis of the contract tort of good faith and fair dealing. What do you think?

2. **INTELLECTUAL PROPERTY RIGHTS (IPR's)** – the defendant infringes plaintiff's registered patents, copyrights or trademarks. This is an economically significant and expanding area of intangible personal property protection . As the world of business has become more high-tech, the commercial success or failure of a company's goods or services is closely linked to its inventions, secret processes, distinctive product marketing and overall creativity in attracting the consumer. If legal protection was not available there would be chaos in the marketplace as competitors misappropriated the most profitable items.

Student Research Assignment: Using your favorite Internet search engine, print out a current listing of Federal laws regulating Patents, Copyrights and Trademarks

The common procedure for authorized usage of protected inventions, creative works and distinctive products is to request permission from the registered owner and pay a mutually agreed licensing fee for usage, commonly called a royalty.

A. Basics of Patents -

- inventions that are useful, unique and non-obvious – utility, plant, design
- abstract ideas (Einstein's Theory), scientific principles (Newton's Law) and isolated computer programs (1-Click ordering) are not patentable
- exclusively governed by federal law (Federal Patent Act of 1952) – applications filed with U.S. Patent & Trademark office in Washington, D.C., disputes heard in federal court
- registration procedure is complicated, expensive, time-consuming – not allowed if invention was in "public use" for more than one year
- registration application requires public disclosure of invention details
- registration logo – "patent pending" or registered U.S. patent number
- grants a limited monopoly to make, use or sell the invention for 20 years (utility, plant) or 14 years (design) from filing date – may not be renewed
- legal remedy is action for infringement – "cease and desist", injunctive relief and profit damages, including triple damages if knowing violations
- shop – right doctrine protects employers for employee workplace inventions like Gatorade (UF) and Taxol (FSU)
- legal defense is "invalid patent"

B. Basics of Copyrights

- creative works of authorship – writings, music, films/videos, software
- exclusive right to ownership/usage governed by federal law (Copyright Act of 1976 - Sonny Bono Extension Act of 1998 – 20 years added to prior 50 years at urging of Walt Disney Corp.) No Electronic Theft Act of 1997 – eliminated requirement of financial gain, Digital Millenium Copyright Act of 1998 – unlawful to merely access /copy encrypted digital works)
- registration procedure (Form TX) filed with Register of Copyrights, Washington, D.C., simple, inexpensive ($30), fast – required to allow legal remedies – copyright protection exists moment of creation/publication
- registration application requires enclosure of copyrighted material
- registration logo – "marca registrada 2010", "copyright 2010, ©2010
- grants exclusive right of ownership for life of author plus 70 years (individual) or 95 years from first publication (corporate for hire)
- legal remedy is infringement – "cease and desist", injunctive relief for likely confusion, seizure and destruction of infringing matter, and profit damages, including up to $100,000 for willful infringement
- legal defense is "fair use" – media reporting, research, teaching, academics, legislative/judicial proceedings and parody/satire.

The parody defense is especially effective in denying unfair competition and/or copyright relief. Webster's defines parody as, "treating a serious subject in a nonsensical or humorous manner." Since one of the essential legal elements for a successful palming off or infringement claim is the likelihood of confusion with the protected item – the non-serious nature of social commentary and its 1st Amendment freedom of speech protection is the key to the defense.

Smaller companies routinely market takeoffs of the most popular items in the toy industry. Examples are a Bavarian bondage parody of Mattel's "Barbie" doll, and the board games "Ghetto-opoly", "Hiphopoly" and "Redneckopoly" that mimic Hasbro's best-selling "Monopoly" board game.

C. Basics of Trademarks

- protects distinctive corporate names, symbols logos, colors, packaging (trade dress), to identify product/service in which owner has goodwill
- exclusive right of use governed by federal law (Lanham Act of 1946, revised 1988 – protects against customer confusion) - also some state statutes
- filed with U.S. Patent & Trademark Office. Washington, D.C. and Secretary of State's Office in states of usage
- registration procedure is a bit complex, reasonable ($350), relatively fast
- registration logo – "Trademark", TM, ® (name of owner)
- grants unlimited time for exclusive right of use – 10 years, renewable
- legal remedy is infringement (registration required) –"cease and desist", injunctive relief for likely confusion, dilution action, seizure/destruction of infringing matter, profit damages, including triple damages for willful acts
- legal defense is (1) "generic usage" – public confuses popular product's distinctive name with its descriptive category – Kleenex, Aspirin, Zerox copies, Hershey bars, Coke cola drinks, Toll House chocolate chip cookies, Raisin Bran cereal, Rollerblade online skates; (2) "secondary meaning", when descriptive or geographic terms acquire consumer recognition due to a history of product use (Apple computer, Philadelphia cream cheese, Ferrari automobile)

Business Strategy: Companies will sometimes knowingly infringe a competitor's IPR, weighing the possibility/probability of litigation against immediate financial gains from copying a patented invention, pirating copyrighted material, or gaining immediate market penetration from consumer identification with a trademarked product. This becomes a managerial risk / reward decision, and explains in part why the penalty for knowing infringement includes as a deterrent the award of Triple Damages. (The Excedrin v. Tylenol dispute)

Reported court cases involving IPR disputes are illustrative - note how technology has expanded the category:

Patents:

(1) *Diamond v. Chakrabarty, 447 U.S. 303 (1980)(patent allowed for crude life form of bacterium, not found in nature (man-made organism), that would break down crude oil and help clean up oil spills)*

(2) *Lamb-Weston, Inc. v. McCain Foods, Ltd., 78 F.3d 540 (Fed. Cir. 1996)(patent application for making waffle-fries was denied as an obvious process)*

(3) *J.E.M. Ag Supply, Inc. v. Pioneer Hi-Bred Int'l, Inc., 534 U.S. 124 (2001) (patent allowed for sexually reproducing hybrid plants)*

(4) *Diamond v. Diehr, 450 U.S. 175 (1981)(computerized synthetic process for curing rubber based upon a known mathematical formula was ruled patentable)*

(5) *State Street Bank & Trust Co. v. Signature Financial Group, Inc., 149 F.3d 1368 (Fed. Cir. 1998)(computerized accounting system for managing mutual funds that determines mutual fund share prices through mathematical calculations was ruled patentable)*

(6) *Amazon.com, Inc. v. Barnesandnoble.com, Inc., 239 F.3d 1343 (Fed. Cir. 2001) (business model for a 1-click ordering system existed in "prior art" before patent filing by Amazon, so usage of it by competitor did not infringe and injunction would be denied)*

(7) *Pfaff v. Wells Electronics, Inc., 525 U.S. 55 (1998)(computer chip socket patent was not enforceable against competitor that copied it under "public use" exception, since application was filed over one year after inventor's sales contract)*

Copyrights:

(1) *Campbell v. Acuff-Rose Music, Inc., 510 U.S. 569 (1994)(Rap Band 2 Live Crew's parody of the Roy Orbison song "Pretty Woman", commercially released without copyright owner's consent, was not infringement under the "fair use"exception)*

(2) *Brown v. Twentieth Century Fox Film corp., 799 F.Supp. 166 (Distr. D.C.)(use of 27 seconds of James Brown's "Please, Please, Please" music cuts in motion picture "The Commitments was ruled a non-infringing "fair use")*

(3) *American Geophysical Union v. Texaco, Inc., 60 F.3d 913 (2nd Cir. 1995)(Texaco's copying of 8 entire scientific journal articles for benefit of its scientists was not "fair use", and its denial of licensing and subscription revenue was an infringement)*

(4) *New York Times Company, Inc. v. Tasini, 121 S.Ct. 2381 (2001)(authors hired as freelance writers whose newspaper and magazine articles were placed in electronic databases without their consent and then were made available to the public through subscriptions charged by electronic publishers were entitled to receive royalties)*

(5) *A&M Records, Inc. v. Napster, Inc., 239 F.3d 1004 (9th Cir. 2001)(Napster's free peer-to-peer music swapping technology provided through its Internet website to more than 50 million registrants was enjoined – down loaders were copyright infringers and Napster was a contributory/enabling infringer)*

(6) *Bright Tunes Music Corp. v. Harrisongs Music, Ltd., 420 F.Supp. 177 (Dist. N.Y. 1976)(Former Beatle George Harrison's company was successfully sued for copyright infringement due to alleged plagiarizing in his 1970 song, "My Sweet Lord" of plaintiff's 1962 song "He's So Fine".*

(7) *Basic Book, Inc., et. al. v. Kinko's Graphics Corporation, 758 F.Supp. 1522 (Dist.N.Y. 1991)(copyright infringement action relating to Kinko's creation and sale to students of "course packets", at the request of college professors,containing extensive excerpts from plaintiff's registered works – deemed not "fair use".)*

3. Trademarks:
(1) *Harley – Davidson, Inc. v. Grottanelli, 164 F.3d 987 (2nd Cir. 1999)(defendant's use of the generic acronym "hog" in his motorcycle repair business was not an infringement of plaintiff's trademark, but usage of the Harley bar and shield logo was prohibited)*

(2) *Fun-Damental, Too, Ltd. V. Gemmy Industries Corp., 111 F.3d 993 (2nd Cir. 1997)(trade dress infringement action was sustained for Gemmy's intentional copying in China of plaintiff's toy coin bank called the "Toilet Bank" which it called the "Currency Can", and which had identical packaging and color scheme)*

(3) *V Secret Catalogue, Inc. v. Moseley, d/b/a Victor's Little Secret, 259 F.3d 464 (6th Cir. 2001)(plaintiff won trademark dilution action for its 1981 trademark that was copied in defendant's strip mall adult toy/lingerie store opened in 1998, due to tarnishing of the Victoria's Secret name by associating it with lewd products)*

(4) *America Online, Inc. v. AT&T Corp., 243 F.3d 812 (4th Cir. 2001)(plaintiff lost its suit for infringement of its service marks "You've Got Mail" and "You Have Mail", due to the generic nature of these terms just describing what the service is rather than who is providing it)*

(5) *Miller Brewing Co. v. Falstaff Brewing Corp., 655 F.2d 5 (1st Cir. 1981)(plaintiff introduced "Lite" beer in the 1970's and spent millions promoting it. Defendant's "Lite" beer was introduced 10 years later. Plaintiff lost its lawsuit seeking to enjoin defendant's use of the term "Lite" due to the name's generic nature.*

(6) *Mead Data Central, Inc. v. Toyota Motor Sales, Inc., 875 F.2d 1026 (2nd Cir. 1989)(plaintiff's claim that 1972 trademark "Lexis" for computer-assisted legal research diluted defendant's 1987 "Lexus" luxury auto was denied)*

(7) *Sony Corp. of America v. Universal City Studios, Inc., 464 U.S. 417 (1984)(Universal unsuccessfully sought to enjoin Sony's sale of VCR's to the public as contributory copyright infringement of consumers copying its motion pictures shown on television)*

3. **THEFT OF TRADE SECRETS** – successful businesses often have commercially valuable information, such as formulas, manufacturing processes, digital codes, customer lists, and the like that they intentionally keep confidential, guarding it from the public in general and their competitors in particular.

If they wanted to patent the information, their dilemma was that filing of the patent application required disclosure of the unique invention and put its privacy in jeopardy. Rather than risking a competitor copying their invention and requiring them to file a costly and time-consuming lawsuit for patent infringement, many companies chose to rely upon the civil lawsuit relief granted by the Uniform Trade Secrets Act of 1979, amended 1985, which has now been adopted in most states.

Due to the increasing use of technology in business and the corresponding increase in industrial spying to gain access to a company's valuable trade secrets, Congress passed in 1996 the Economic Espionage Act. It adds a new deterrent to unlawful conduct by making it a federal crime to steal trade secrets. The punishment allows individual fines up to $500,000, organization fines up to $5 million and imprisonment of violators for up to 10 years.

The broad definition of a "trade secret" includes, "all forms and types of financial, business, scientific, technical, economic, or engineering information, including patterns, plans, compilations, program devices, formulas, designs, prototypes, methods, techniques, processes, procedures, programs, or codes, whether tangible or intangible, and whether or how stored, compiled, or memorialized physically, electronically, graphically, photographically, or in writing . . ."

Theft is defined to include, "(1) stealing, obtaining by fraud, or concealing such information; (2) without authorization copying, duplicating, sketching, drawing, photographing, downloading, uploading, photocopying, or mailing such information; (3) purchasing or possessing a trade secret with knowledge that it has been stolen."

Plaintiff's relief in a civil action for theft of trade secrets may include recovery of profits made by defendant and lost by plaintiff, punitive damages, and injunctive relief to prohibit the defendant from disclosing or using the trade secret.

In order to sustain his burden of proof in a civil action, plaintiff must show:

- plaintiff took reasonable measures to safeguard the information
- the information has economic value from not being made public
- defendant gains a competitive advantage from the information
- defendant obtained the information unlawfully

The defendant can win a trade secrets case by asserting the defense of "reverse engineering", which negates the *secret* and *theft* aspects of the tort by proof that the information was readily obtainable by taking apart plaintiff's product and examining it, or re-constructing the ingredients or components of the item in question through engineering, chemical or technological expertise.

Example: James is sales manager of ABC Computers. He regularly reviews customer lists and contacts them regarding existing projects and solicits future business. The lists are kept in a locked cabinet in his office, and he has the only key. One night, after hours, he removes and copies the lists, replaces them, resigns from the company 30 days later, opens a competing business, and solicits former customers. ABC sues for theft of trade secrets,

The lawsuit will succeed. All required elements of the tort are present.

A related case: *Mason v. Jack Daniel Distillery, Inc., 518 So.2d 130 (Ala. App. 1987),* involved a claim made by plaintiff for alleged misappropriation by defendant of his formula, or recipe, for a popular alcoholic beverage called "Lynchburg Lemonade" he had created and served at his restaurant and lounge as its exclusive specialty. Mason claimed he had met a sales rep of defendant *in 1982* who sampled the drink, and was told a part of its recipe based upon the assurance that, "the defendants would use him and his band in the advertising and promotion of the beverage," and compensate him accordingly.

The sales rep informed his superiors and one year later defendant developed a national promotion campaign for "Lynchburg Lemonade" without the knowledge or permission of plaintiff. He sued for theft of his trade secret and sought compensatory and punitive damages. The trial court jury returned only a nominal verdict for plaintiff of $1 and the judge refused to grant defendant's motion for directed verdict. Both parties appealed, and the case was reversed and remanded, allowing the possible award of larger damages to plaintiff.

Defendant's main contention was that Mason's recipe was not a trade secret because it could be easily duplicated by others. (The drink contained Jack Daniel's whiskey, Triple Sec, sweet and sour mix, and 7-Up.)

In rejecting this argument, the court said, "Mason's ability to combine these elements into a successful (beverage), like the creation of a recipe from common cooking ingredients, (may be) a trade secret entitled to protection. . . The fact that every ingredient is known to the industry is not controlling for the secret may consist of the method of combining them which produces a product superior to that of competitors."

Note: The lawsuit was subsequently settled with the defendant paying a large amount for a license to market "his" drink. It has become one of the most popular drinks at T.G.I. Friday's, and other national chain restaurants.

4. INTERFERENCE WITH AN EXPECTANCY

A. An Existing Commercial Contract

The law has long recognized the tort of intentional interference by the defendant with the advantageous contractual relationship the plaintiff has with another. The essence of the business tort is its interference with the commercial advantage that plaintiff intends to receive in the future from the existing contract.

When the defendant improperly induces the contracting party not to deal with the plaintiff, usually for its own financial advantage, the cause of action occurs.

Example: A&M University notifies its eraser and chalk vendors that it is soliciting sales bids for that concession for the next school year. Donald and Ralph are competing bidders. Donald's bid is the lowest and is accepted by the University. Ralph discusses the bidding with the school's bid manager and slanders Donald by falsely stating that he is being investigated by the FBI as a suspected terrorist. As a result of this conversation, the University cancels their contract with Donald and awards it to Ralph.

Donald's damages for the tort could include any out-of-pocket expenses he incurred in reliance upon the contract, loss of prospective profits from the contract, loss of future business from others due to his damaged reputation, and punitive damages for the malicious nature of Ralph's actions.

A related case: In *Texaco, Inc. v. Pennzoil, Co., 729 S.W.2d 768 (Tex. App. 1987)*, Pennzoil made a public tender offer to buy shares of Getty Oil at $100 per share. It then entered into a memorandum of agreement with the J. Paul Getty Museum to buy its 11.8% of Getty stock for a price of $110 per share, which was later increased to $115.

Both parties issued an identical press release announcing the transaction. Texaco then held private talks with the Getty people, made false statements about Pennzoil's finances, offered $125 per share, the Getty board then approved that sale and tried to cancel their Pennzoil agreement.

Pennzoil sued Texaco for tortuous interference with its contract. The trial jury award of compensatory damages of $7.53 billion and punitive damages of $3 billion was upheld on appeal. This was, at that time, the largest civil damage award in history.

Note: After the case was concluded, Texaco demanded that Pennzoil voluntarily reduce its award or Texaco would have to file for bankruptcy protection. When this demand was refused, Texaco actually filed for Chapter 11 reorganization as a negotiating tactic. At that time, it was the largest such filing in U.S. history. This had the legal effect of temporarily staying all pending legal actions and put in possible jeopardy the ability of Pennzoil to ultimately collect. It also sent world financial markets into a temporary tailspin due to the enormous financial implications.

The tactic ultimately proved successful when the parties sat down and worked out a settlement whereby Texaco agreed to pay the total sum of $3 billion and their bankruptcy filing was dismissed. If you were a member of the Pennzoil board, how would you have handled Texaco's threat of bankruptcy filing?

B. A Future Lifetime Gift

A number of states recognize a cause of action for tortious interference with an *inter vivos* gift. The plaintiff must prove (1) the reasonable expectancy exists due to donor having declared the intent to make a gift, (2) a reasonable certainty the gift would have been made but for the unlawful interference of the defendant, (3) the intentional tortious interference by defendant, and (4) money damages by the plaintiff.

The most notable is the Texas case involving the late Anna Nicole Smith, that some reporters called "the billionaire and the bimbo. The rage to riches story of the Playboy Playmate and reality T.V. personality is well-known. She was a former topless dancer who at 26 married the 89 year old eccentric Texas oil billionaire J. Howard Marshall. He died 13 months later, and she claimed one-half of his $1.6 billion estate based on his alleged oral promise if she would marry him.

Pierce Marshall v. Vickie Lynn Marshall (Anna Nicole Smith), 275 B.R. 5 (Dist. Ct. Cal. 2002) involved her successful claim of this tort committed by the son and financial advisor of her late husband to deny her the financial benefits of his lifetime gift promise of a catch-all trust. She was originally awarded compensatory damages of $44,292,767 (8% of the deceased's fortune) and an identical amount of punitive damages to punish him for his willful and malicious conduct. This was cut in half by a Federal Judge, and the U.S. Supreme Court affirmed her right to sue there.

The court opinion examines each of the required elements of the tort:
(1) "J. Howard made numerous promises to Vickie that she would receive half of what he owned. . . the amount that J. Howard intended to give her, was half of his 'new community.'

This term was defined by J. Howard as one-half of the growth of his assets during the time of their marriage."

(2) "Vickie has introduced evidence that shows a high degree of probability that J. Howard would have made a gift to Vickie. He directed two attorneys to prepare documents giving her a substantial gift as early as Fall 1992 . . . The evidence shows that through the very end of his life, Vickie was the most important person to J. Howard."

(3) "The evidence shows that Pierce and Hunter began undertaking estate planning transactions for J. Howard soon after they learned that he was seeking to make a substantial gift to her. All of these transactions were intended to drain J. Howard of his assets . . . Evidence of Pierce's tortuous conduct is legion. Acting in concert with Hunter, they backdated documents, altered documents, suborned falsified notary statements, presented documents to J. Howard under false pretenses, and committed perjury."

Case history: This decision was vacated and remanded back to the Texas probate court in 2004. Certiorari to the U.S. Supreme Court was granted in 2005, and in 2006 it affirmed her right to finalize her case in Federal Court. Though Pierce Marshall died in 2006 and Anna Nicole Smith died in 2007, the case continued in the name of her estate until a Federal Appellate Court denied recovery in 2010.

C. A Future Estate Inheritance

This tort has, until recently, received little attention, but that is now changing due to a number of scholarly articles about some recent cases, including one in Florida. Although the facts giving rise to these disputes are often identical to a traditional will contest, they are not the same. Damages may be recovered directly from the offending party rather than from an estate that may have minimal assets. And the plaintiff can sue while the maker of the inheriting will is still alive on the theory that the offender has interfered with the rights of the expectant heir at the moment of the improper interference.

The tort involves a claim that one estate beneficiary intentionally interfered with the free will of the deceased so that he or she made a will provision that wrongfully excludes or diminishes the amount of the claimant's inheritance. The claimant is not limited to compensatory damages, like the usual probate court proceedings, but can also seek punitive damages as well as payment of attorney's fees.

Typical offending acts are:
- preventing lifetime gifts that affect expected inheritances
- offering a forged or revoked will or codicil for probate
- illegally destroying a will or codicil
- interfering with the signing of a will or codicil

The required proofs of the tort by the plaintiff are the same as those for any interference with prospective economic advantage – existence, intentional interference, and damages.

A related case: In *Martin v. Martin, 687 So.2d 903 (Fla. App. 1997)*, the deceased's sons sued the widow, their stepmother, alleging she unlawfully interfered with their inheritance rights by "fraudulently and maliciously alienating their father from them, which caused him to reduce what they would inherit."

The sons were allowed to try to recover directly from the widow rather than through a will contest in the probate proceedings, because 95% of the estate's $8 million worth had passed outside the will into revocable trusts.

"Cases which allow the action of tortuous interference with a testamentary expectancy are predicated on the inadequacy of probate remedies . . . We thus reverse the order determining that the sons in the present case are barred from litigating their tortuous interference case in so far as it precludes them from challenging the trusts."

5. THEFT OF IDENTITY

The signature crime of the Internet era is identity theft, where offenders acquire one's personal information from a variety of websites, use it to make personal purchases charging the victim's account, or otherwise unlawfully impersonate the victim.

Yet law enforcement officials call it a "victimless" crime, because a person whose credit identity is stolen is not legally obligated to pay the bills incurred by the imposter. But the non-monetary damages can be substantial.

"A person's credit history can be virtually destroyed, significantly impairing the individual's ability to obtain credit loans, mortgages and employment. A bad credit report may even prevent someone from obtaining something as simple as a checking account. In addition, it may take a victimized consumer numerous months and significant personal expenses to contest all of the fraudulently obtained charges and to correct the credit reporting errors." *Wood & Schecter, Identity Theft, ABA Consumer Newsletter, Summer 2002.*

The number of Internet – related identity theft claims has more than tripled in the last year, according to statistics compiled by the Federal Trade Commission. Even though this represents less than 5% of the nationwide reports of ID theft, the growth is significant due to the numbers of consumers who are now shopping online.

Example: Steve's getting a great deal when he buys a digital camera for $1,000 on eBay from Verne, a long-time seller with over 200 favorable customer comments. But the person who Steve actually pays prior to delivery, is not Verne. Rather. There is a bogus seller who has done an "account takeover" in which he somehow guesses or unlawfully accesses Verne's password, and is therefore able to post a realistic, but fictitious, sales ad. Steve sends his payment to a designated overseas address, and never received the merchandise. He can't find the offender in cyberspace and sues eBay for his damages. Steve will probably lose his case. His claim is properly against the ID thief, rather than the owner of the Website where the transaction took place.

Note: The dramatic increase in cyber-fraud has caused eBay to recently start a posting on all its sites of safety tips for consumers, such as don't transact business offshore, don't negotiate privately, be careful when the deal looks too good, and verify the deal with a direct conversation by phone or email with the other party. eBay has also begun to post a stated limitation of its liability for damages to a maximum of $500 for most transactions.

But claimants are now seeking to even sue deep-pocket website owners, credit card companies and financial institutions on a tort theory of "Negligent Enablement of Imposter Fraud".

This may involve the improper release of confidential personal information that enables an identity theft to occur, such as "phisher" scams where e-mails with links to bogus website fish for personal data such as the consumer's credit card numbers and private codes. Such phony e-mails, often called "fraud alerts", warn that "your account will be closed unless you now verify your user name and password."

Enablement claims may also result from the granting of credit and/or issuance of a credit card to an imposter, and other negligent security procedures that result in an identity theft.

To date, few states have extended the negligence doctrine to create this new tort, but cases are being filed that test these legal waters, such as the following South Carolina case:

In *Huggins v. Citibank, 585 S.E.2d 275 (S.C. 2003),* plaintiff alleged that Citibank, Capital One and Premier Bankcard negligently issued credit cards to an unknown imposter who had applied, claiming he was plaintiff. The imposter made charges, they were unpaid, and the banks sought initially to recover from plaintiff, thinking he had made the charges.

Huggins claimed negligence by the banks in: (1) issuing the cards without any verification of the applicant's identity, (2) failing to adopt proper verification procedures, and (3) attempting to collect from him the unauthorized charges. While sympathetic to Huggins' predicament, the court ruled against him.

"We are greatly concerned about the rampant growth of identity theft and financial fraud in this country. Moreover, we are certain that some identity theft could be prevented if credit card issuers carefully scrutinized credit card applications. Nevertheless, we agree (with New York cases) and decline to recognize a legal duty of care between credit card issuers and those individuals whose identities may be stolen. The relationship, if any, between credit card issuers and potential victims of identity theft is far too attenuated to rise to the level of a duty between them"

6. SPOLIATION OF EVIDENCE

The recent Enron and Arthur Andersen Co. financial scandals have brought back to public attention this civil tort that involves destruction or disappearance of documents and related work product in anticipation of or during litigation.

Judges often enter "Show Cause" court orders for production of documents and other relevant evidence, which may lead to criminal sanctions against the violating offenders who are often the officers, directors or employees of corporate litigants and their attorneys and accountants. Civil fines and penalties may also be imposed, depending upon the answers to these questions:

- Was the conduct intentional? If so, to what degree?
- Was the innocent party prejudiced? If so, to what extent?
- Is alternative evidence available? If so, to what effect?

In the case of *Bondu v. Gurvich, 473 So.2d 1307 (Fla. App. 1985),* plaintiff was admitted to Cedars of Lebanon hospital for a triple bypass. During administration of anesthesia he suffered cardiac arrest and died. His wife sued the anesthesiologist and hospital for negligence, and "in Count IX, that the hospital intentionally interfered with Mrs. Bondu's right of action in that it 'purposely and intentionally lost and/or destroyed,' among others the anesthesiology records, again 'frustrating the plaintiff's ability to pursue certain proof which may be necessary to establish her case."

The trial court dismissed that Count on the ground that it didn't state a legally recognizable cause of action. On appeal, the ruling was reversed and the Florida court acknowledged the legal existence of such a claim:

"Courts before us have recognized the existence of causes of action for negligent failure to preserve evidence for civil litigation . . . and for intentional interference with prospective civil action by spoliation of evidence . . . against a defendant which, as here, stands to benefit by the fact that the prospect of successful litigation against it has disappeared along with the crucial evidence."

More and more states are recognizing this independent tort, but the majority still take the contrary position as stated in the dissenting opinion:

"In my view, such a rule (recognizing the tort) runs counter to the basic principle that there is no cognizable independent action for perjury, or for any improper conduct even by a witness, much less by a party, in an existing lawsuit. Were the rule otherwise, every case would be subject to constant retrials in the guise of independent actions."

7. WORKPLACE TORTS

The workplace injuries of an employee are usually determined by State workers compensation laws. But they vary in application. Some states preclude employees from bringing a tort cause of action for workplace injuries. But others, including Florida, allow separate tort civil lawsuits and jury trials for damages if they prove that the employer knew or should reasonably have known of the likelihood of injury. These cases may involve any or all of the intentional torts mentioned in this section.

Tort lawsuits by employees against employers also often allege improper hiring and firing, supervision, promoting, retaliation for whistle blowing, safety, sexual harassment. and discrimination.

Title VII of the Civil Rights Act of 1964 and related state/ local anti-discrimination statutes cap the amount of allowable damages. But civil tort cases are uncapped and often involve additional claims for punitive damages. Many statutes also require arbitration, while civil litigation has a greater probability of large damage awards.

8. SPECIAL NEGLIGENCE RULES

You will recall that negligence is an unintentional tort that arises when the defendant breaches his duty to maintain a certain standard of care, and as a direct result the plaintiff is injured. There are a number of special rules that assist a plaintiff's negligence claim by eliminating, lessening, or otherwise modifying certain proof requirements in all types of disputes:

A. *Res Ipsa* Loquitor –
This is a latin phrase meaning, "the thing speaks for itself." It applies to situations where the defendant is exclusively in control of the cause of plaintiff's injury, so that the injury would not ordinarily have occurred unless someone was negligent. The law then raises a presumption that the defendant is at fault and shifts to him the burden of proving otherwise. This helps the plaintiff, who otherwise would be unable to prove fault of a particular party.

Example: Beth is injured when her cruise on the Love Boat abruptly ends due to the ship running aground. The specific cause of the wreck is unknown and the possible defendants (boat manufacturer, navigational system manufacturer, corporate owner, captain, crew, engineer, maintenance chief and others) all deny liability. The doctrine furnished proof of legal liability.

B. *Innkeepers Law* –

Hotels, motels and bed & breakfast establishments that provide public lodging owe the highest duty of care to their guests to provide reasonably adequate security procedures for their health and safety.

This duty is greater than the customary negligence "standard or ordinary care." The public may legally assume these businesses will do what is necessary to properly protect them.

Example: Alice is a businesswoman who travels nationwide. She always stays at defendant's nationwide motel chain, relying upon the advertised level of service, experience and expertise. She is injured one evening as she goes down the hall for ice and soft drinks when an unknown person assaults her. Assuming she could not prove a specific breach of ordinary care, she is still legally protected due to the defendant's higher duty of care owed her.

C. *Social Host Alcohol Liability*-

The states have different laws regarding host liability for situations where a guest at their social function becomes intoxicated and injures a fellow guest or a stranger. Some jurisdictions absolve social hosts of liability, similar to the Dram Shop laws that protect bar owners and other commercial operators, unless the vendor serves a minor or an adult that they know is habitually intoxicated. Others allow claims against both commercial and social hosts, and put upon them the burden of monitoring the sobriety of their guests.

This area of the law is controversial. What do you recommend as a hard and fast rule to be applied nationwide, rather than on a case-by-case and state-by-state basis? Would you differentiate between commercial and social hosts?

Example: Tanya celebrates her college graduation by having a party at her home for her closest friends. There is an open bar where liquor is served. Vera drinks too much and loses control of her car as she drives away, injuring plaintiff who sues both Vera and Tanya in a pro-recovery state. Tanya's liability is based upon the law's perception that she made alcohol available and was in the best position to monitor whether her social guest was intoxicated.

D. *Landowner's Visitor Liability* –

Whether or not the owner of real estate is liable for injuries sustained by a visitor to the property depends upon the injured party's legal status:

- Trespassers have no legal right to enter the property. The owner owes them the lowest duty of care – to just not intentionally injure them such as with booby traps or setting spring guns with hidden trip wires.

- Licensees enter the property with the implied consent of the owner to perform necessary functions, such as meter reading, police and fire department safety matters, and sales visits unless there is a " no solicitors" sign prominently displayed. The owner owes them the duty of ordinary care, and is only liable for injuries caused by hazards "known" to the owner.

- Invitees are on the property with the express consent of the owner, such as guests at a social function or customers in a store. They are also owed a duty of due care, but the owner's liability is extended for hazards, the existence of which he "knows" or "should have known". The owner's lack of actual knowledge is not a defense in these cases.

E. *Good Samaritan Laws* -

All states have laws to encourage and protect emergency care givers. These laws absolve them from liability for all injuries suffered by the victim in the course of attempted rescue, unless due to gross negligence or intentional misconduct.

Some states also have Guest laws that protect a driver who picks up a hitchhiker from liability for passenger injuries caused by the driver's ordinary negligence. These laws were also based upon the "good deed" concept, but have been systematically repealed because hitchhiking is frowned upon in modern society. Drivers now pick up hitchhikers at their own risk.

Example: Maria and her friend Martha are walking on the beach when they hear cries for help from a swimmer caught in a rip current. They rescue the now unconscious person and administer CPR while they wait for fire rescue personnel. They succeed in reviving the victim but some of his ribs are broken by their treatment. He sues both of them for his damages. They are protected if certified in CPR, since at worst they may have been guilty of only ordinary negligence. But if they try to administer CPR without any formal training in it they commit gross negligence and lose the law's liability shield.

F. *Policeman's/Fireman's Rule* –

Law enforcement, fire or other emergency public employees injured while performing their duties may not bring a civil suit for damages against the person who "negligently" causes the situation to which they are responding. The rationale is that if potential victims faced liability, they would not call 911 or otherwise request assistance. However, if the cause of the problem is someone's intentional or illegal act, they are liable to the injured rescuer under a doctrine called, "danger invites rescue."

CASE RESEARCH CYBERCISES

The following recent appellate cases relate to the material in this section, illustrate the types of disputes that may occur, and demonstrate how they are judicially decided. Notice how the court opinions follow a predictable format – (1) the facts creating the dispute are summarized, (2) the rules of law that apply to the legal issues presented are set forth, based upon the prior cases or statutes of the state in which the lawsuit is decided, or the cases/laws of other states if this is a case of first impression, (3) the majority opinion applies the case facts to the applicable law in order to do their reasoning as to which party should win, and (4) the decision is rendered as affirming, reversing, or remanding for a new trial the decision of the lower trial court. For each one of the listed cases, do the following:

1. Locate the case by name or citation, using an Internet research site such as Lexis-Nexis, Westlaw, or any other site providing court case transcripts. (Print out a copy of the entire case, or highlight and print relevant excerpts)
2. Briefly summarize the dispute and the legal claims of both sides.
3. Who won at the trial court level? Who won/wins at the appellate level?
4. Who won if there was a third level of Supreme Court review?
5. What rules of law govern this dispute? Majority/minority views?
6. What reasoning was used in the majority/minority opinions?
7. Do you agree or disagree with the final decision? Explain why.
8. What business law time bomb(s) were involved? Discuss.
9. How could the time bomb(s) have been defused? Discuss.
10. Can you replay the case's facts to achieve a successful result for the loser?

Cases:
1. *Russell v. Kinney Contractors, Inc., 795 N.E.2d 340 (Ill. App. 2003)(employer's locking up union workers behind company gates gave then a cause of action for false imprisonment)*

2. *Sloan v. S.C. Dep't. of Public Safety, 2003 WL 21783232 (S.C. 2003)(state's sale of driver's license information and photographs to private firms was valid under state law and not invasion of privacy)*

3. *Doe v. TCI Cablevision, 2003 WL 21783708 (Mo. 2003)("Spawn" comic book which used without permission a villain named "Tony Twist", who is in real-life a well-known hockey player, resulted in jury verdict of $24.5 million for tort of right of publicity)*

4. *Wagner v. Miskin, No. 20020200 (N.D. 2003)(university professor expressly targeted for defamation on student's web site received a $3 million libel award)*

5. *Falwell v. Cohn, CV 6:02CV00040 (W.D. Va. 2003)(Rev. Jerry Falwell was denied defamation libel relief because web site used was directed toward a national audience, and had not expressly targeted Virginia Residents)*

6. *Krasnecky v. Meffen, 777 N.E.2d 1286 (Mass. App. 2002)(no recovery for emotional distress allowed where family lost seven "companion" sheep to neighbor's dogs)*

7. *Tiller v. McLure, 2003 WL 21026572 (Tex. 2003)(extremely rude and insensitive behavior made in a business context, with no personal or physical threats, could not support action for the tort of emotional distress)*

8. *Langeslag v. KYMN, Inc., 2003 WL 21665019 (Minn. 2003)(making false police reports, threatening litigation, and nasty arguments were not the "extreme and outrageous conduct" required for tort of emotional distress)*

9. *American Communications Network, Inc. v. Williams, 568 S.E.2d 683 (Va. 2002)(defamation judgment in favor of ex-company CEO criticized in private memo circulated by his board of directors was reversed as being justified true facts or a reasonable opinion)*

10. *Pegasus v. Reno Newspapers, Inc., 2002 WL 31487455 Nev. 2002) (defamation denied because restaurant that received negative food review was considered a public figure requiring proof of actual malice)*

11. *Mohr v. Grant, 68 P.3d 1159 (Wash. App. 2003)(defamation suit allowed for television story that contained true information but left out other important facts)*

12. *Pachowitz v. LeDoux, 2003 WL 21221823 (Wisc. App. 2003)(invasion of privacy suit allowed where medical technician revealed medical information about EMT patient)*

13. *Denver Publishing Company v. Bueno, 54 P.3d 893 (Colo. 2002)(state does not recognize tort of false light, in dispute where newspaper published long article calling plaintiff "Denver's Biggest Crime Family", since adequate legal protection exists in tort of defamation)*

14. *Netscape Communications v. Konrad, 295 F.3d 1315 (Fed. Cir. 2002)(public use of invention prior to patent filing by inventor showing how it worked rendered his patents invalid)*

15. *Scholastic, Inc. v. Stouffer, 2002 WL 31093616 (S.D. N.Y. 2002)(author of Harry Potter books did not infringe copyright or trademark claims of earlier author who produced a story booklet with creatures called "muggles", and received sanctions of $50,000 against plaintiff due to falsification of evidence)*

II. THE LAW OF AGENCY

"principal: a person who has controlling authority . . .
one who employs another to act for him
subject to his general control and instruction . . .
the person from whom an agent's authority derives"
"agent: one who acts for or in place of another by authority from him"
Webster's Ninth New Collegiate Dictionary, (1987).

Agency law is a great challenge to being able to successfully transact business in today's marketplace. Let's look at why agency is a potential legal time bomb:

1. Civil commercial disputes originate either from contract or tort claims.

2. Plaintiff must prove that the defendant's acts or omissions created a legal "liability" owed plaintiff, who as a direct result of suffered legal "damages."

3. If the third-party plaintiff sues the party with whom they had direct contract dealings or the party that committed the tort – there is *direct liability.*

4. If the plaintiff sues a party with whom they had no contract dealings or someone who did not commit the tort that damages them – there is *no liability.*

5. But under agency law's *indirect* or *vicarious liability* – the principal may be liable for the acts of the agent – as an exception to the general rule of non-liability for non-dealings.

6. In the typical contract case, the third party plaintiff sues the agent with whom they dealt, and the principal who allegedly gave the agent authority to act.

7. In the typical tort case, the third party plaintiff sues the agent who committed the tort, and the principal in whose scope of employment the act took place.

To say that this possibility of liability for the conduct of another is financially dangerous understates its importance. Think about it. In today's business marketplace, few if any transactions take place without the parties acting through their agents. Employees, corporate officers, business managers, associates, sales representatives, formal and informal designees? All are agents and the parties that hire, use or otherwise direct them are principals.

In this section we will analyze the ins and outs of agency law, locate its potential liability time bombs and find useful strategies to defuse them.

A. The Agency Relationship

Even though there are legally specific agency relationships, such as those created by written agreements and designated agency contracts, no special formalities are required.

Agencies can be created verbally, through custom and usage, prior dealings, and under a wide variety of interactions. Although agents are normally individual persons who act for another, an agent may also be a business association or entity such as a partnership or a corporation.

The main contractual requirement of agency is mutual consent, not the usually required exchange of legally sufficient consideration between the parties, thus allowing gratuitous agencies.

Any person having legal capacity may appoint an agent. The appointment of an agent by a minor or someone mentally impaired is voidable. But persons who lack legal capacity may serve as agents, since the contracts they make and the actions they take are not deemed to be their own but those of the principal.

The purpose of an agency relationship must be lawful. If not, it fails as void, illegal and unenforceable. This includes violation of a regulatory law, such as hiring unlicensed agents to perform legal or medical services, or hiring a hit man to eliminate business competition which violates public policy.

Some of the more familiar types of agency relationships are:

- Written powers of attorney, where one party designates another to act as his attorney-in-fact, such as voting proxies, joint banking/investment accounts, safe-deposit box entry cards, and special task designations.

- Employment relationships – all employees are agents.

- Common business agencies, such as professional/client; real estate broker/customer; travel agents; insurance agents; sports agents; etc.

- Court appointed guardians or other legal representatives.

- Situational agencies, where the facts of each dispute determine the legal relationship of the parties.

The first line of defense whenever a deep-pocket principal is sued vicariously for contracts made or torts committed by his agent is that the acting party "is not my agent, he/she/it is just an *independent contractor*." But the mere labeling of a party as having a particular legal status is not what governs.

The courts use a weighing test of various factors in each case to make the employee v. IC determination. The most important factor is usually the amount of control the employer/principal can exert.

The Agency Restatement (2nd) defines as independent contractor as: "A person who contracts with another to do something for him who is not controlled neither by the other nor subject to the other's right to control with respect to his physical conduct in the performance of the undertaking."

Here are some of the factors looked for in an agency dispute to determine if the independent contractor relationship exists, thus preventing imposition of vicarious liability on the non-acting party:

- Little or no supervision/control over the job
- Sets own work schedule
- No continuing working relationship
- Specific work to be done for a specific task
- High degree of skill or specialization required
- Personal tools and work implements used
- Payment by job rather than time basis
- Worker hires others to assist in completing the job
- Designated as IC in job contract, or other documents
- Independently licensed business for the job tasks

In *Jaeger v. Western Rivers Fly Fisher, 855 F.Supp. 1217 (Fed. Dist. 1994)*, Western was licensed as an "outfitter" by the U.S. Forest Service. Its business was arranging fishing expeditions down the Green River in Utah. Mike was licensed by the Forest Service as a fishing expeditions guide, but could not sponsor fishing trips on his own.

He worked for various outfitters, including Western, in guiding expeditions, and would display their insignia on the boat he was using as a routine procedure, as well as his vehicle used for transporting the party. His responsibilities to Western were to use his own boat for fishing trips, supply food and overnight needs, assist patrons in fly fishing, and transport them from the river back to their cars using his own vehicle. Western directly paid him a fixed amount per fishing trip he was guiding, with no tax deductions. Although it rarely occurred, he had the right to reject the offer of a guiding job.

A fishing expedition was arranged with Western where plaintiff was a member. His party paid Western their agreed price for the trip, planned the itinerary, rented them fishing rods, and arranged for Mike to be their guide. When he met the party he told them he worked for Western.

At the conclusion of the trip, while driving the party back to town, Mike lost control of his vehicle, plaintiff was injured, and sued Western and others for the tort of negligence. Western moved for summary judgment on the grounds that Mike was an independent contractor, and therefore they were not liable vicariously, as a matter of law.

The court denied their motion ruling that, "the court concludes a determination of the nature of Petragallo's (Mike) relationship with Western is a factual issue inappropriate for summary judgment."

The case involves factors on both sides of the Employee/IC equation. What do you think? What factors would you argue on behalf of Western's position on non-liability for Mike's negligence? Which ones would you argue on plaintiff's behalf?

B. Duties owed between Principal and Agent

The nature of an agency relationship requires the imposition of certain legally required obligations, beyond those that they may have chosen to specify in a formal contract. The nature and extent of these duties is important when claims arise directly between principal and agent in a two-party dispute. The duties are equally important in third party claims for vicarious contract or tort liability, where a losing principal will often cross-claim against his agent for breach of a duty that causes indirect liability for the principal . In either case, the cause of action is "breach of duty."

Duties of the Principal

- **Compensation** – the principal must pay the agreed amount, unless the agency is gratuitous and the agent serves without compensation, such as when your neighbor agrees to pick up your opera tickets at the local auditorium.

- **Reimbursement** – whether the agency is for hire or gratuitous, the principal is obligated to reimburse the agent for authorized expenditures, such as monies advanced for meals and lodging on an employee's business trip.

- **Indemnity** – this is the most important duty for an agent's protection, since it requires the principal to hold the agent harmless and make good any claims, costs or losses incurred during the authorized activities performed. The agent-employee that contracts directly with the third-party on behalf of the principal is often joined as a party in a breach of contract lawsuit. The principal has the duty to defend and pay all necessary costs and expenses including an adverse money judgment if the plaintiff wins.

- **Provide safe working conditions** – when the agent is an employee, the work area must be reasonably safe and the employer has a duty to be aware of potential hazards, correct them, or at the very least warn the employee of potential risks.

- **Disclose known dangers** – since the agent acts at the principal's request and pursuant to his directions, there must not only be full disclosure of potential problems in the work environment, but in all aspects of the agency, such as sending someone to collect rent from a tenant that has prior arrests for assaulting collection agents.

Duties of the Agent

- **Loyalty** – known as the fiduciary duty, this obligation of the agent arises out of the special relationship of trust and confidence between the parties. The agent owes the highest allegiance to the principal, acting only on his behalf and in his best interests, with no conflict of interest, self-dealing, theft of opportunity, or other failure to honor the priority of duty to the principal. Breach of this duty may allow a recovery of both actual and punitive damages, due to its willful and reckless nature, such as overstating an expense account or making private business deals.

- **Confidentiality** – though originally considered a part of the duty of loyalty, the high-tech nature of today's marketplace and its emphasis on trade secrets (such as customer lists, formulas, processes, and computer codes) triggers this duty. The agent may not use or disclose private information obtained in the course of employment for private gain or to harm the principal.

- **Obedience** – the agent must obey the principal's reasonable and lawful instructions and directions, including not exceeding the authority granted, such as being told that all payments must be made by cash or cashier's check and then accepting the customer's personal check which is later returned by the bank for insufficient funds.

- **Notification** – the agent must inform the principal of all relevant information. Since the law makes notice to the agent the same as notifying the principal, it is critical that the communication be completed, such as the insurance agent who receives a claim from the policyholder and then promptly notifies the carrier.

- **Accounting** – the agent must maintain accurate records of all money and property in his possession during the agency, properly use entrusted property, and promptly return unused funds and other assets. The principal has a legal right to demand an accounting from his agent at any time to assure compliance.

- **Diligence** – the agent must perform the required acts of the agency with proper skill and care as measured by the objective standard of what a "reasonable" agent in the same or similar circumstances would have done. But if the agent represents he has higher than average skills, he is held to the higher standard, such as a real estate broker who claims to be an expert in commercial property.

C. 3rd Party Contract Claims – Authority of Agent

In a typical indirect liability contract dispute, the agent contracts with the Plaintiff, a dispute arises about the agreement, and the plaintiff brings an action for breach of contract against both the agent with whom he dealt and the principal for whom the agent is acting.

The rules of law for recovery in these cases can be stated as:

- Principal is liable for the agent's "authorized" contracts
- Agent is not liable for his contracts because he is acting for principal
- Agent is liable if he exceeds his authority in making the contract
- Principal is liable for agent's unauthorized contracts if he ratifies them

The key to recovery by the plaintiff is whether or not the agent had some type of legal *authority* to act. There are four basic types of agent authority that can create vicarious liability for the principal:

1. **Express authority** – the principal spells out exactly what the agent can or cannot do, verbally or in writing.

   Example: sales manager is given a written list of what he can/ cannot do.

2. **Implied authority** – though certain duties are not expressed, the agent has incidental authority to do what is reasonable necessary to accomplish his usual and customary functions.

   Example: sales manager is not told anything about what he should do in event of a burst pipe and water leak, but he has implied authority to contract with a plumber for emergency repairs.

3. **Apparent authority** – the agent is specifically told not to do something, so he has neither express nor implied authority, but it reasonably appears to the customer that he was authorized to contract and the agreement is made. This type of authority if a legal fiction imposed for fairness purposes and is also known as "agency by estoppel." Viewed through the eyes of the customer, the principal has clothed the agent with the appearance of authority, and the customer's reasonable reliance upon that appearance legally prevents the principal from denying liability.

Example: Boss owns a computer store, instructs Sales Manager not to sell any ZRX printers because of a manufacturer's recall, and then goes out of town. Sales manager mistakenly sells one of the defective printers to customer, who then sues both Boss and Sales Manager for contract damages.

Note: Boss would lose due to apparent authority. Sales Manager would lose since he exceeded his stated authority and thus breached his warranty of authority. His failure to obey instructions would also make him liable to Boss for breach of the duty of obedience.

4. Ratification – if the agent has no authority whatsoever to make the contract the principal may still become liable by acting in support of its validity, such as accepting payment or making delivery under an improper contract.

Example: Using the same apparent authority example, no express or implied authority for the acts exists, and there would also not be any apparent authority if the printer purchased by the customer was obviously subject to recall because of a large "defective" label placed upon it. That fact would make unreasonable the customer's reliance on the agent's appearance of authority.

The high-tech era has also introduced us to the electronic agent in our common usage of automated teller machines. The ATM is the agent for the bank that owns and operates it for the benefit of the banking public. Another common electronic agency is online buying of merchandise from e-vendors. The convenience of easy access by ordering customers is sometimes offset by the fact that computer errors on the site must be borne by the vendor principal who holds out the electronic agent as having the apparent authority to complete transactions.

Example: Ted places an online order to buy a laptop computer. Because of a computer error, he is identified as a wholesale buyer entitled to a purchase discount. After Ted clicks acceptance of the order, the error is discovered and his discount is removed, raising the effective price he is paying. If Ted objects, the cost of the error must be borne by the seller. It was his electronic agent who caused the problem, and since the vendor-principal clothed the agent with apparent authority to act, Ted reasonably relied by his click-on acceptance, and the seller must honor the lower price.

D. 3rd Part Tort Claims – Vicarious Liability

In a typical vicarious liability tort dispute, the agent commits a tort upon the plaintiff who sues both the agent and his principal for money damages. The principal's liability is not for his own fault, but derived from the fault of another.

The rules of law for recovery in these cases can be stated as:

- Principal is vicariously liable for the agent's torts if they were committed within the "scope of employment." This is the doctrine of *respondeat superior.*
- Agent is always liable for the torts he commits.
- Scope of employment is governed by the unique facts of each case, and is measured differently depending upon whether there is an unintentional or intentional tort committed by the agent.

A. The most common unintentional tort is negligence, where the agent has a duty to maintain a particular standard of care, breaches that duty, and the plaintiff suffers damages as a direct result.

"Scope of employment" in cases of negligent torts is often decided through application of the following legal tests:

- Coming and going – torts committed on the way to or from the workplace are usually "outside" scope of employment and not recoverable from principal. But if principal asks agent to perform a work task or run an errand before or after regular hours and the tort then occurs, principal is liable.

- Lunch-hour – when the lunch hour is a part of the regular paid work day, torts committed to, from or at lunch are within the scope of employment. But if the agent must punch out for lunch or it is otherwise unpaid or not part of a regular days work, lunch torts of agent are not enforceable against principal.

- Frolic and detour – if the agent's tort occurs outside the usual geographical area of his duties, his material detour brings it outside the scope of employment. The same situation exists if he deviates from his usual work duties on a personal errand or frolic for his own benefit rather than his principal.

B. In cases of intentional torts, the scope of employment issue is decided based by either the "personal motivation test" or the "work-related test."

- Personal motivation test – we look at "why" the agent committed the tort. If it was the result of a personal argument that erupts during his workday, it is deemed outside the scope of employment even if it occurs during business hours on the work premises. A minority of states follow this test.

- Work-related test – we look at "where" the tort occurs. If the agent commits the tort during business hours on the work premises or at a corresponding work location, it is deemed within the scope of employment even if it occurs as a result of a personal argument. A majority of states follow this test, which reflects the popular sentiment that such losses should be borne by the deep-pocket employer whose interests were being served by his agent, and such added costs of doing business are usually passed on to the consumer anyway.

Example: Harry is an employee of Koka-Kola and his duties require stocking the shelves of the local A-1 supermarkets. Ralph is similarly employed by Bepsi-Cola.

While doing his job in one of the markets, Harry pushes the competing cola to the back of its shelf and moves his cola in front, so that his employer's company has a better display area. Unknown to Harry, Ralph is in the store at the same time, sees Harry's actions and confronts him. Their words escalate into a personal argument and Harry hits Ralph on the head with a bottle of Koka-Kola. Ralph sues both Harry and his employer for money damages resulting from the tort of battery.

If we apply the personal motivation test to the example, Harry's employer escapes vicarious liability for his tort as having occurred outside the scope of his employment, and is limited to recovering from Harry's available assets.

But if we apply the work-related test, Ralph can recover from both Harry and his employer, since the tort was committed during work hours at the designated workplace.

What do you think? Which test would you use in judging these intentional tort disputes? Argue their pros and cons.

E. Franchisor – Franchisee Apparent Agency

Franchising is one of the major ways of doing business worldwide. Many of our largest corporations are involved, such as McDonald's, Burger King, Subway, Taco Bell and Kentucky Fried Chicken in food service and Holiday Inn, Best Western and Howard Johnson's in tourist accommodations.

They provide investment opportunities in franchising their operations in various venues, while at the same time maintaining many company-owned locations.

As far as the public is concerned, it looks like all one standard operation and the large advertising budget benefits all locations. But in the typical arrangement, the company- Franchisor allows the investor-Franchisee to operate the identical restaurant, motel or other business by charging a sizable fee to license use of its distinctive manner and methods of operation, including trademarks and trade secrets.

Even though the franchisee's location is "independently owned and operated", in the absence of some type of conspicuous notice to that effect the public may reasonably believe that a particular location is owned by the financial deep-pocket franchisor. If this is the case and there is a contract or tort dispute that arises from the actions of the franchisee, the plaintiff often seeks recovery from the franchisor under a legal theory of Apparent Agency.

In *Miller v. McDonald's Corporation, 945 P.2d 1107 (Or. App. 1997)*, 3K Corp. owned and operated a McDonald's restaurant under a License Agreement which specified that 3K was not an agent of McDonald's for any purpose, but required them to operate it in a manner consistent with the 'McDonald's System'. This system included proprietary rights in "trademarks, designs and color schemes for restaurant buildings and signs, and specifications for certain food products as well as other business practices and policies."

Miller bit into a heart-shaped sapphire stone while eating a Big Mac sandwich at the 3K location, and sued for damages. She testified that, "she went to the Tigard McDonald's because she relied on defendant's reputation and because she wanted to obtain the same quality of service, standard of care in food preparation and general attention to detail that she had previously enjoyed at other McDonald's restaurants."

The trial court granted summary judgment to McDonald's on the ground that it didn't own or operate the restaurant, but on appeal that decision was reversed.

"The kind of actual agency relationship that would make defendant vicariously liable for 3K's negligence requires that defendant have the right to control the method by which 3K performed its obligations under the Agreement. . . . we believe that a jury could find that defendant retained sufficient control over 3K's daily operations that an actual agency relationship existed. The Agreement did not simply set standards that 3K had to meet. Rather, it required 3K to use the precise methods that defendant established, both in the Agreement and in the detailed manuals that the Agreement incorporated."

"Everything about the appearance and operation of the Tigard McDonald's identified it with defendant and with the common image for all McDonald's restaurants that defendant has worked to create through national advertising, common signs and uniforms, common menus, common appearance, and common standards."

Then the court noted some guidelines for a franchiser to try to protect itself from the appearance of ownership through the use of an "independently owned and operated" sign. "The possible existence of a sign identifying 3K as the operator does not alter the conclusion that there is an issue of apparent agency for the jury. There are issues of fact of whether that sign was sufficiently visible to the public, in light of plaintiff's apparent failure to see it, and of whether one sign by itself is sufficient to remove the impression that defendant created through all of the other indicia of its control that it, and 3K under the requirements that defendant imposed, presented to the public."

In *Orlando Executive Park, Inc. v. P.D.R., 402 So.2d 442 (Fla. App. 1981)*, the franchise involved was one of the Howard Johnson Company's (HJ) motor lodges in Orlando, Florida operated by OEP. P.D.R. checked in to the location in the evening, pursuant to her previous reservation, parked her car in the motor lodge parking lot, and proceeded with her suitcase to her ground floor room located directly behind the registration office. She went back to her car for some papers, and as she proceeded down an interior dark, secluded stairwell toward her room she was brutally beaten and robbed by an unknown assailant. She sued both OEP and HJ for her damages.

The jury found both OEP and HJ liable for $750,000 compensatory damages. Evidence showed there had been past criminal activity on the premises but guests were not warned. In addition, OEP had actively discouraged criminal investigations by local law enforcement. The jury also found HJ liable under the doctrine of apparent agency, noting that the registration form did not inform guests that the hotel was an HJ franchise.

"There was sufficient evidence for the jury to reasonably conclude that HJ represented to the traveling public that it could expect a particular level of service at a Howard Johnson Motor Lodge. The uniformity of signs, design, and color schemes easily leads the public to believe that each motor lodge is under common ownership or conforms to common standards, and the jury could find they are intended to do so."

Discuss: What company-wide risk management procedures would you implement as a franchisor of one of the major food, beverage, restaurant or lodging chains to protect your company from apparent agency?

F. Direct Tort Liability of Principal

The principal may still be held legally responsible for his agent's tort committed outside the scope of employment if he directs the agent to do it, such as telling the employee to punch a complaining customer. This creates direct liability due to the principal's own actions, which are an extension of the tort.

The principal may also be held liable for negligent hiring or supervision of employees that result in a tort being committed, such as failing to do a proper background check on a convicted pedophile who is hired as a teacher of young children and then commits an offense against one of the students.

The principal may even be held liable for the acts of an independent contractor if the work being done is inherently dangerous, such as demolition of a building, where the contractor uses too much dynamite and causes injury to the plaintiff.

G. Criminal Liability of Principal

Normally only the perpetrator of the crime can be charged because of the required legal element of criminal intent. Thus responsibility for an agent's crime cannot be imputed to his principal, unless the principal is a co-actor or co-conspirator who directed, planned or participated in the crime.

However some state laws remove the "intent" requirement for certain offenses determined to not require any finding of fault on the part of the principal, such as the owner of a liquor store being arrested, along with his guilty employee, for unlawful sale of alcoholic beverages to a minor or a nightclub owner in which illegal drugs are sold by employees.

H. Termination of the Agency

The agency relationship, as we have seen, can create significant liability problems for both principal and agent in breach of duty disputes and third party indirect contract and vicarious tort claims. So it is important to know when the relationship legally ends. There are various situations in which the agency is terminated:

- Operation of law – death or insanity of principal or agent, bankruptcy of principal, and declaration of war between principal's and agent's country.
- Impossibility of performance – subsequent illegality of the transaction, destruction of its subject matter or suspension of regulatory licensing.
- Fulfillment of the stated purpose of the agency.
- Completion of the stated time period for the agency.
- Mutual agreement of the parties to end the agency.

What if the principal fires the agent or the agent resigns, and there are strained feelings between the parties who have mutually agreed to terminate the agency? If the former agent chooses to make financially unfavorable contracts with former or new customers as a revenge move, how can the principal protect himself from indirect liability due to the still existing apparent authority of the agent?

This problem of "how to unplug apparent authority" led to legal assists:

1. Existing customers – give direct notice of agency termination by regular mail, e-mail, hand-delivered notice, or verbal notice in the presence of witnesses.

2. New customers – give constructive notice by publishing advice of agency termination in a local newspaper of general circulation. Note: it is not necessary that the notice actually be read by the customer, so the burden is on the customer to verify the agent's authority *before* contracting.

CASE RESEARCH CYBERCISES

The following recent appellate cases relate to the material in this section, illustrate the types of disputes that may occur, and demonstrate how they are judicially decided. Notice how the court opinions follow a predictable format – (1) the facts creating the dispute are summarized, (2) the rules of law that apply to the legal issues presented are set forth, based upon the prior cases or statutes of the state in which the lawsuit is decided, or the cases/laws of other states if this is a case of first impression, (3) the majority opinion applies the case facts to the applicable law in order to do their reasoning as to which party should win, and (4) the decision is rendered as affirming, reversing, or remanding for a new trial the decision of the lower trial court. For each one of the listed cases, do the following:

1. Locate the case by name or citation, using an Internet research site such as Lexis-Nexis, Westlaw, or any other site providing court case transcripts. (Print out a copy of the entire case, or highlight and print relevant excerpts)
2. Briefly summarize the dispute and the legal claims of both sides.
3. Who won at the trial court level? Who won/wins at the appellate level?
4. Who won if there was a third level of Supreme Court review?
5. What rules of law govern this dispute? Majority/minority views?
6. What reasoning was used in the majority/minority opinions?
7. Do you agree or disagree with the final decision? Explain why.
8. What business law time bomb(s) were involved? Discuss.
9. How could the time bomb(s) have been defused? Discuss.
10. Try to replay the case's facts to achieve a successful result for the loser.

Cases:
1. *Clackamas Gastroenterology Assoc., P.C. v. Wells, 2003 WL 1906297 (U.S. 2003)(four physician-shareholders who owned medical clinic and were its board of directors were ruled not to be employees, for the purpose of determining whether the ADA requirements of "15 or more employees" applied)*

2. *Meyer v. Halley, 2003 WL 141310 (U.S. 2003)(when a principal is sued for his agent's alleged racial discrimination in violation of the Fair Housing Act, the traditional rule of vicarious liability applies)*

3. *Hannington v. Trustees of the Univ. of Penna., 809 A.2d 406 (Super. Ct. Pa. 2002) (student's suit for breach of contract regarding how much he owed in tuition and fees settled by his attorney and later rejected by client created apparent authority that was binding on client)*

4. *Olin v. George E. Logue, Inc., 2000 WL 1610619 (M.D.Pa. 2000)(landowner not liable for injuries suffered by independent contractor surveyor who fell into an excavation pit on his property and was injured, because of lack of significant control over the work)*

<u>NOTES</u>

III.   FORMS OF DOING BUSINESS

"Corporations have neither bodies to be punished,
nor souls to be condemned,
they therefore do as they like."
Edward, 1st Baron Thurlow (1731-1806)

OVERVIEW

No matter how skillful we are in anticipating legal time bombs that may create potential business liability, how lucky we are in avoiding them, how successful we are in defusing problems or restructuring problematic transactions, we won't be able to totally eliminate them.

There may be a "direct liability" contract or tort claim arising from our own conduct. There may be an "indirect" or "vicarious" liability third party contract or tort claim arising under the laws of agency from the conduct of our agent.

In either case, we may face a claim that ripens into a lawsuit, with the potential for entry of an adverse money judgment of large amount against us personally, and our personal assets may be totally at risk.

Example: David has worked hard all his life and accumulated financial net worth of $1 million. He has always dreamed of going into the restaurant business. He opens a restaurant serving Sushi and Italian cuisine with a capital investment of $50,000 for each. When his employee injures Alice during a pizza delivery and Mary becomes seriously ill from bad seafood, they both sue David and recover a total money judgment of $1 million.

David's assets may be totally wiped out by this lawsuit. Or his liability may have effectively been limited to only what was invested in the business, so that the bulk of his net worth is preserved. It all depends upon the legal form in which he is conducting the business at the time of the incident for which liability is claimed.

That is why the legal form in which we choose to conduct our business is equally as important as the financial aspects of a particular commercial transaction.

Often the parties formally designate a legal form for their business transaction. Equally as often, even if they designate a particular form, the legal elements of each form of doing business when viewed through the specific facts showing the manner and method of how they did business will govern. And quite frequently there is no conscious thought at all given to the question of, "what form of business am I engaged in?" until a claim is made by someone who alleges liability for a civil wrong and seeks a recovery of money damages.

Let's examine the basic characteristics, advantages, and disadvantages of the six major forms of doing business, which are Sole Proprietorship, General Partnership, Limited Partnership, Limited Liability Partnership, Limited Liability Company and the Corporation.

A. Sole Proprietorship (SP)

- Most common method of doing business – automatic inception
- Isolated owner transactions and continuing business activities
- Formation - no legal formalities other than fictitious name registration and occupational licensing, inexpensive, fast
- No separate legal entity
- One person owns the business – agency rules applicable
- Total control of all management decisions in owner
- Full profits and losses to owner
- No continuity - duration limited to lifetime of owner
- Raising capital – limited by owner's assets and loan credit
- Transferability – sale of business assets / liabilities
- Dissolution – liquidate assets, pay debts, surplus to owner
- Taxation – profit/loss pass through to owner
- Liability – unlimited personal liability of owner for all debts
- Governing law - Cases
- Forms – trade name/fictitious name publication

B. General Partnership (GP)

- Association of two or more persons doing business for profit – traditional business and professional associations
- Expanded operations beyond one person ownership
- Partners can be individuals, other partnerships or corporations
- Formation – no legal formalities, other than trade name and licensing, often by default due to the actions of the parties, inexpensive, fast
- Separate legal entity – can do business, hold title in partnership name
- Tests of formation: sharing of control, profits, property
- Control and management shared by the partners
- Profits shared equally, no matter what is capital contribution, unless otherwise specified
- Partnership interest is share of profits / surplus – not separate assets
- No continuity – duration limited to any partner's lifetime
- Raising capital – limited by assets and loan credit of the partners
- Transferability – sale of business assets / liabilities
- Dissolution – death, bankruptcy, illegality, judicial order - liquidate assets, pay outside creditors, repay partner's loans, return capital contributions, distribute surplus as profits
- Taxation – profits/losses passed through to each partner

- Agency - partners are principals/agents/owe fiduciary duties to each other
- Liability – partnership assets first, then personal assets of all individual partners
- Special rules – (1) partnership by estoppel, (2) liability of outgoing partners, (3) liability of incoming partners
- Governing law – UPA, Cases
- Forms – General Partnership Agreement

C. Limited Partnerships (LP)

- Formation – must be written, registered in state of operation, lawyer services preferable, may be expensive, not as fast as GP
- Name – must have Ltd., Limited, LP as suffix
- Statutory requirements – available in all states
- Requires at least one general partner/one limited partner
- Separate legal entity can buy/sell property, borrow funds
- Expanded operations beyond one person ownership
- Speculative/high risk ventures/real estate syndications
- General partner may be individual / partnership / corporation
- Limited partner may be individual / partnership / corporation
- General partner has full control / management / unlimited liability
- Limited partner's liability usually limited to capital invested
- Profits shared – same as capital contributed, unless written otherwise
- Profit priority – limited partners usually paid first
- Continuity – must always have one general partner, but limited partners may be substituted
- Raising capital – expanded by adding limited partner investors
- Transferability – sale of business assets / liabilities
- Dissolution – death, bankruptcy, illegality, judicial order – pay outside creditors, repay partner's loans/advances, return capital contributions; distribute surplus as profits
- Taxation – profits/losses passed through to each partner
- Agency – only general partners are principals/agents/fiduciaries
- Liability – partnership assets first, then assets of general partner(s)
- Special rules – potential limited partner individual liability – (1)defective formation, (2) surname rule, (3) control/management rule, (4) safe harbor exceptions
- Governing law – ULPA, RULPA, Cases
- Forms – Limited Partnership Agreement/Certificate

D. Limited Liability Partnership (LLP)/Company (LLC)

- Formation – must be written, registered in state of operation, lawyer services preferable, may be expensive, not as fast as GP
- Name - must have LLP or LLC as suffix
- Statutory requirements - not available in all states
- One "member" ownership or multiple "members" allowed
- Separate legal entity can buy/sell property, borrow funds
- Perpetual existence – dissolution allowed per state statute
- Expanded operations beyond one person ownership
- LLP – business professionals / LLC – non-profession business
- Full management and control allowed by all members
- No formalities of meetings, minutes, written resolutions required
- Profits / losses shared equally, unless otherwise specified
- Raising capital – sell participation "interests" to investors, but may be difficult to borrow funds due to lender unfamiliarity
- Transferability – sale of business assets/liabilities
- Taxation – profits/losses passed through to each "member", avoids double taxation of "C" Corporations
- Agency – "members" are principals/agents/fiduciaries
- Liability – "members" not personally liable beyond capital contribution investment
- Special rules – IRS reg. for partnership taxation (single layer)
- Governing law – Statutes, Cases
- Forms – Articles of Organization for LLP / LLC

E. Corporation (Corp.)

- Formation – must be written, registered in state of operation, lawyer services preferable, may be expensive, not as fast as GP
- Name – commercial business requires Corp., Co., Company, Inc., Incorporated as suffix, professional business requires P.A., P.C.
- Statutory requirements – available in all states
- One stockholder-owner or multiples allowed
- Separate legal entity – can buy/sell property , borrow funds
- Perpetual existence – dissolution allowed by state statute
- Management – officers and directors
- Operation – stockholder-owners elect directors who set policy and appoint officers for day-day management who then hire employees
- Compensation - employees and officers are salaried, directors receive incentives/bonuses, stockholders receive dividends if declared by directors and stock price appreciation
- Raising capital – greatly expanded, lender familiarity, sell shares

- Transferability – free sale of shares, business assets / liabilities
- Taxation – (C) Corp. double taxation / (S) Corp single taxation
- Agency – officers are principals/agents/fiduciaries, sometimes directors, never stockholders
- Liability – stockholders not personally liable beyond investment
- Special rules – potential personal liability – (1) Subscriber's pre-incorporation contracts, (2) Promoter's pre-incorporation contracts, (3) Stockholders "Piercing the Corporate Veil", (4) Officers and/or Directors violating "Business Judgment Rule" or "Corporate Opportunity Rule".
- Governing law – Statutes, Cases
- Forms – Articles of Incorporation

A. Sole Proprietorship

The sole proprietorship is the most common and is usually the first form of business organization one uses in the commercial marketplace. Often this occurs without a conscious choice of business form. You decide to go into business and, like the famous Nike logo, you "just do it." Any kind of business activity can be conducted in this form – buying or selling goods or services – a one-time venture or a continuing commercial activity – so long as you and only you are the party conducting the business.

> Example: Harvey sees an advertisement that reads, "be your own boss – set your own hours – keep all your profits – sell delicious Wiener Dogs from your own cart." He buys the starter kit from the manufacturer/distributor and then sets up his Wiener Dog food stand on Main Street, U.S.A.

This is a typical private entrepreneurship. Harvey will probably want to operate under a trade name such as "Wiener Dog #1." There are usually just two legal formalities required:

(1) a "fictitious name registration" published in a local paper of general circulation for the legally prescribed time, signed by Harvey with his full name and address d/b/a (doing business as) Wiener Dog #1, so that the public knows who and where is the owner in the event of a problem, and

(2) an "occupational license" required by the city where the food stand will be operated, which raises revenue ($100 - $300) for the municipality.

Failure to satisfy the two requirements will not invalidate the owner's contract dealings with third parties, but may render him subject to fines for non-compliance.

Advantages: The sole proprietor has unlimited control of his enterprise. He makes all business decisions, keeps all profits, operates the business any way he chooses, answers to no one, and there is only one layer of taxation.

Disadvantages: The owner must absorb all losses from his personal assets, having unlimited personal liability for claims that may arise. His ability to raise capital and finance expansion is limited to his personal assets and funds he borrows from family, friend or commercial lenders. There is also a lack of continuity because his death, bankruptcy or legal incompetency terminates the business.

B. General Partnership

The general partnership is probably the oldest form of conducting business, having its roots in ancient times. It is part of the natural progression from simple to more complex business forms as a commercial enterprise expands. It is created by agreement of the parties.

It is also the standard form of how professionals have conducted business, such as lawyers, doctors, accountants, architects and engineers. They are members of their "firm". Young associates work hard and hope to "make partner," although more and more professions are shifting to a limited liability form of doing business such as the L.L.P. or the Professional Corporation so that they can be insulated from potential unlimited liability for business debts.

Example: Harvey's food stand business is going very well. He now operates three Wiener Dog locations and wants to expand further, but has exhausted his credit line. He needs outside capital as well as manpower and sales expertise. He brings in Trent as a partner for their business they now call Wiener World.

The standard definition of a general partnership is, "an association of two or more persons, doing business as co-owners, for profit." The persons may be individuals or other legal entities such as partnerships and corporations.

When two parties seem to be doing some type of business together and a contract or tort dispute arises, the injured third party plaintiff invariably claims that a partnership exists because of favorable liability rules. They specify that recovery for claims shall come from (1) the available partnership assets, that include the capital contributions of the partners, and then if not fully paid, (2) the personal assets of the individual partners.

If the creditor recovers a disproportionate amount from the individual assets of a partner, that partner may require contribution toward his excess payment from the other partners.

1. Does a general partnership exist?
The Uniform Partnership Act (UPA) was created in 1914 by a group of legal scholars as part of a National Conference to establish nationwide consistency and predictability in the formation, operation and dissolution of general partnerships.

It has been revised and updated as the Revised Uniform Partnership Act (RUPA), and currently both uniform laws are in effect in all states except Louisiana. They provide the basis of partnership law, unless the agreement of the parties provides otherwise.

The parties are best served by reducing their verbal partnership agreement to written form, so that all important aspects of the business relationship are specified. If any items are not covered, UPA provisions will serve to fill the gaps.

Some basic items covered by a typical general partnership agreement include:

- Trade name and business address of the business
- Names and addresses of all general partners
- Purpose and duration of the business
- Division of profits/losses between partners
- Capital contributions of partners
- Wages or other compensation, if any, to be paid partners
- Required management duties of partners
- Authority granted partners to bind the business
- Buy-sell procedures for changes in partner affiliation
- Procedures for dissolution, liquidation or continuation of the business
- Various other operating agreements or restrictions

In a verbal general partnership, the possibility of faulty memory and fabricated testimony can be the determining factors in the event of a dispute, and thwart the original intentions of the parties.

Also, since a general partnership need not be in writing or formally registered with the state of operation, many such legal associations arise by default due to the actions of the parties, whether they intended the legal form or not. The issue becomes important because an individual "partner" incurs unlimited personal liability if partnership assets are insufficient to satisfy creditor claims.

The legal test for existence of a general partnership, which differs from a joint venture in the fact that it is a continuing business enterprise, is determined on a case by case basis. It looks at the three sharing factors of control, profits and ownership.

If parties are sharing control or management of their business enterprise and they are sharing profits/losses, there *is* a legal presumption that their association is a general partnership. If a party is sharing profits of a business enterprise, there *may* be a GP if the control and management aspect also exists. But profit sharing alone may not be enough to create potential GP liability, such as these situations:

- Percentage rent leases where landlord shares in tenant's profits
- Lender-creditor relationships with repayment from profits
- Employment contracts where wages are paid from profit shares
- Independent profit participations such as broker's commissions

2. What is partnership property?

Since the first level of claimant recovery is general partnership assets, disputes often arise as to what constitutes "partnership property?"

Example: In the Wiener World partnership, Harvey individually owns a truck used in the business. When adverse publicity about the health hazards of eating hot dogs causes an abrupt drop in revenues, a trade creditor sues the partnership and the individuals, seeking recovery from partnership assets, including the truck. Harvey claims it is his individual property and not reachable by the creditor.

The cases that involve such disputes use a weighing test of factors to determine whether or not a particular asset should be treated as partnership property. While no one factor is conclusive, they are compared in each factual situation in order to decide the question. The factors include the following:

- In whose name is the asset titled?
- Who paid for it?
- How is it used in the partnership business?
- Is it listed on the partnership books?
- Who pays for expenses such as taxes and repairs?
- Who receives rent or other income it produces?

3. What are a partner's rights in partnership assets?

The partners themselves also have rights in the partnership property. The question is what are those rights? Can one of the partners sell or mortgage separate partnership assets? Can the creditor of an individual partner seize partnership assets to satisfy an individual judgment? The answer to both is no.

Partners do not own individual assets of the partnership. Rather, they share an undivided interest that relates to the profitability of the business. During its operations they have the right to share profits equally, unless a different percentage interest is agreed. When the partnership dissolves, they have the right to receive their profit share of any surplus that exists, after assets are liquidated and (1) outside creditors are paid, (2) partners loans, if any, are paid, and (3) capital contributions are returned. If only partial payments are available, they are divided proportionately.

4. What is the scope of partner authority?

General partners have the rights that are specified in their written partnership agreement. But since a written agreement is not a pre-requisite for the existence of a general partnership, they also have certain basic rights conferred by statute and common law which include the following:

- Interest in the partnership which is their right to share profits and duty to share losses in their agreed percentages, or equally if not agreed.

- Interest in dissolution which is the right to return of partner loans, return of capital contributions, and payment of their profit participation share of surplus.

- Absolute right to be reimbursed for personally paying partnership expenses.

- Limited right to receive compensation for their services if specifically allowed by their agreement.

- Equal participation in everyday management, unless otherwise limited.

- Right to require unanimity in choosing other partners.

- Right to contractually bind the partnership for normal business matters.

- Right to inspect partnership books and records

- Right to an accounting of partnership financial transactions

Majority decision usually applies among partners, unless unanimous approval is specifically required. If there are an even number of partners, a deadlock in approval will prevent partnership action.

Notice the danger of a general partnership with an even number of members. A deadlock often results, unless there is a written agreement that provides a procedure to resolve such a problem. What would you recommend?

Individual partners, by virtue of being co-managers of the enterprise, have implied authority to perform such acts that are reasonably necessary to carry out the business purposes. This includes making contracts to buy and sell goods or needed services in the ordinary course of business, borrowing money for business purposes, indorsing and depositing checks payable to the partnership, hiring and firing employees, and otherwise performing usual and customary duties.

There are certain transactions that individual partners are legally prohibited from entering into because of their impact on the partnership business, unless there is unanimous approval.

Outside third parties who are parties to such transactions do so at their own risk, since the law assumes they are aware of such limitiations on implied or apparent authority.

The UPA/ RUPA requires unanimous consent for:

- Sale of a majority of partnership assets, including business goodwill
- Confession of judgment against the partnership
- Submission of partnership disputes to arbitration
- Assignment of partnership property for benefit of a creditor
- Agreeing to pay the personal debt of a partner
- Serving as surety or guarantor for the debt of another

5. What duties do the partners owe each other?

The partners in a general partnership are agents and principals for each other. Therefore agency rules apply both as to breach of duty disputes between themselves, and third party claims for contract or tort liability. The major duties owed by the partners to their partnership and each other are loyalty, diligence, obedience, notification, accounting and indemnification for payments on creditor claims that exceed their partner share of ownership.

6. What is the creditor liability of partners?

Partners have joint liability for the contract debts of the partnership, meaning that all are at risk. They also have joint and several liability for tort claims, meaning that they are potentially liable regardless of whether or not they committed the tort. If partnership assets are insufficient to pay a claim, the excess amount may be recovered from the assets of any or all of the partners. (Hint: A corporation, which is a limited liability entity, can legally be a general partner, thus defusing the potential personal liability time bomb that awaits individual partners.)

A. Outgoing Partner Liability

Outgoing partners remain liable for partnership debts or claims incurred while they were partners, unless a novation agreement is reached with the creditor who releases the partner and agrees to substitute the liability of someone else such as one of the remaining partners.

The novation is usually in express form, set forth in a written document signed by the outgoing partner, the incoming partner, and the creditor. It may also be implied from the surrounding facts and circumstances, such as where the creditor is aware of the old partner's withdrawal and does not object while continuing to extend credit to the partnership.

B. Incoming Partner Liability

Incoming partners become liable for partnership debts or claims that arise after their entry. They are not liable for prior debts or claims unless they specifically agree to pay them, such as under a guarantee agreement.

7.   What is partnership by estoppel?

Estoppel is the contract doctrine that pervades our legal system by creating legally fictional relationships in the interest of fairness between the parties. If someone (1)makes a promise, under circumstances where (2) they know or should know you may rely upon it, (3)you do reasonably rely, and (4)change your position in detrimental reliance upon the promise – then the promisor is estopped (legally prevented) from denying the enforceability of their promise.

The law of contracts has its estoppel equivalent in "quasi contract", where contract liability is imposed on a non-contracting defendant who was unjustly enriched because of contract benefits mistakenly conferred by the plaintiff.

The agency law equivalent occurs in the doctrine of "apparent authority", where the principal-defendant clothes his agent with the appearance of being authorized to contract and the third party plaintiff reasonably relies to what looks to him to be an authorized act by the agent.

And the partnership by estoppel concept follows the same legal guidelines. Let's see how a dispute arises in this partnership context:

Example: A and B are partners doing business as Southern Antiques. They need to borrow more money from Shore Bank for expansion but their application is denied. They then invite a wealthy local businessman, C, to join the partnership. He refuses because he is wary of potential unlimited personal liability, but would like to help so he says, "Why not tell the bank I'm your partner – they know me- that may cause them to give you your loan."

A and B tell the bank that C is their partner and the bank approves their loan, the business then fails, A and B declare bankruptcy, and the bank sues C for repayment. He denies liability on the grounds he was not really a partner.

Partnership by estoppel requires (1) a holding out by the alleged partner who he knows or should know he is being represented to the creditor as a partner, (2) reasonable reliance by the creditor, who (3)changes his position in detrimental reliance, and (4)creditor suffers monetary loss.

At first glance, it would appear that C is a partner by estoppel and liable for the debt due the bank. But what about element (2)? Did the bank reasonably rely? Would you approve a loan just because someone told you that a wealthy person was their partner? The law requires the creditor to act with due diligence. It could easily have called C to verify, but didn't, so it loses the dispute.

8. How is the partnership dissolved?
Under UPA, section 29, "Dissolution is the change in the relation of the partners caused by any partner ceasing to be associated in the carrying on of the business."

The ending of the partnership business may be a natural result of the partnership's purpose being accomplished or the end of a specified time frame, such as the purchase and re-sale of a limited number of Super Bowl tickets and the event has concluded. It may be due to subsequent illegality, such as the passage of a law prohibiting sale of imported cars by a business whose purpose was exactly that activity.

It also may result from a general partner's death, bankruptcy, withdrawal, expulsion or any other change in business status. It may also be based upon mutual agreement of the parties to end operations or a judicial decree to the same effect.

Dissolution is the first stage of the termination process. While the business may continue for a period of time, its purpose is now shifted from an active, forward-looking view to a defensive posture where the purpose is essentially to liquidate assets and convert them to cash so that the winding-up process can be completed. New contracts can be made, but they are primarily for this "conversion to cash" process. What contracts would you enter into for this purpose?

Once dissolution occurs, there should be a prompt end to the actual, implied or apparent authority of any general partner to bind the other parties under agency rules. This is accomplished by giving actual notice of intended dissolution to existing customers and constructive notice by publication to all others. They are presumed aware of the dissolution and cannot legally bind the partners for post-dissolution notice contracts, regardless of whether or not they ever saw or read the notices. But a failure to give proper notice allows creditors to enforce new contracts made by partner - agents, even if they had no express or implied authority, due to the estoppel doctrine of apparent authority.

After the asset liquidation process is completed, the order of priority in distributing available cash is the following, with partial payments being divided in the same proportion as profit participations:
1. Non-partner creditors (outside creditors)
2. Partner's loans (inside creditors)
3. Partner's capital contributions
4. Surplus profits

9. How is the partnership taxed?

There is only one layer of taxation. All profits and losses are passed through the entity, under the "conduit theory", and are accountable only by the partners in their individual income tax returns (Form 1040) or if they are corporate partners (Form 1041). The general partnership's calendar year or fiscal year return reflects the pass-through by Schedule K-1 that is distributed to each partner.

C. Limited Partnership

1. Formation Requirements

Limited partnerships are also creatures of state statutory law, designed to utilize the business advantages of a general partnership and at the same time eliminate its main advantage of potential unlimited partner liability for creditor claims.

The purpose of a limited partnership is usually a speculative venture requiring the infusion of large amounts of investor capital. Oil and gas ventures, movie and theatre production, and heavy equipment leases are traditional types of limited partnerships. Most prevalent are real estate syndications, where the general partners locate the investment property, put together the limited partnership, sell participations to raise the needed funds, and manage the investment for the benefit of all parties.

The risk-reward aspects of these deals dictates that limited partners are usually repaid first as to their capital contributions and large share of profits, before any distributions of capital or profit are made to general partners.
In other words, the investment is front-loaded to attract the limited partner investors, and the general partners are rewarded on the back-end.

The Uniform Limited Partnership Act (ULPA) was created in 1916 to guide in the formation, operation and dissolution of limited partnerships and formed the basis for most state laws.

It was modernized in the 1970's as the Revised Uniform Limited Partnership Act (RULPA), and that is the basis of current state laws in all states except Louisiana. Like the UPA, the Uniform Acts provide "default rules" if the agreement between the parties does not specify otherwise.

Example: A and B are partners doing business as Southern Antiques. They need additional capital and ask Mr. Moneybags to join them as an equal partner. He respectfully declines saying, "No thanks, I'm afraid of total liability exposure for claims that exceed partnership assets, but I wouldn't mind investing as a limited partner." A, B and C then file articles of limited partnership in their state.

Formation requires a written document that complies with state law. There cannot be a verbal formation, such as is allowed in a general partnership. The writing requirement is to protect the business public, since they are subject to possible limited liability and should not have to bear the risk of a purely verbal formation.

Once the required articles of limited partnership, containing all required information, are filed and formally accepted by the state, with required filing fees fully paid, a certificate of limited partnership is issued bearing a date/time stamp and an official filing number. At that point in time the legal entity is formally effective.

The state authorities will also verify that the chosen partnership name is available and also that it ends, as required by law with the proper suffix designation that tells the public there is a partner with limited liability – "Limited","Ltd.", or "Limited Partnership."

There must be at least one general partner who contributes capital and is in charge of all management and control and at least one limited partner, who also contributes capital but is only an investor, and therefore does not participate in day to day management. If there was such a participation by a limited partner, it would give the appearance of being a general partner to a creditor that extended credit in good faith, and would cause the limited partner to be estopped to deny personal liability. The general partner has unlimited personal liability for partnership debts that exceed its assets, but the limited partner's liability is *limited*, as a general rule, only to monies invested.

The general partner also owes to his limited partners the same fiduciary duties that were discussed previously in the Agency section as being due from an agent to his principal, but is not a guarantor of the success of the business.

The general partner of a limited partnership is usually an L.L.C. or a Corporation, so that successful creditor claims can only reach business assets, and the individual assets of the owner - investors of the general partner are shielded from liability. The limited partner is usually an individual, due to the statutory limited liability granted. However, as we shall see in the next section that highlights situations creating potential unlimited liability for individual limited partners, a skillful investor would also be well advised to create his or her own corporate liability shield, rather than hope for a favorable court ruling when a dispute occurs.

3.   Liability of limited partners

The basic organizational premise of the form is that the investors do not risk more than the amount of their invested capital. This is why limited partners assume that they can invest in their individual name and still be protected. They would not otherwise take the investment risk.

However there are certain situations that create exceptions to the limited liability rule that may put parties who think they are limited partners in financial jeopardy:

A. Defective Formation – a typical dispute involves Sam who assumes he is a limited partner because he has signed all the organizational papers, contributed his capital investment, and been given a certificate that proclaims him to be a limited partner. In most states the mere filing of the application to become a limited partnership is not the effective event. Formal state approval is required.

Q: But what if the proposed limited partnership entity is never officially accepted by the state? A: The association is in actuality a general partnership and *all* partners have potential unlimited liability.

Strategy: Prospective investors can avoid the time bomb by simply withholding the payment of their initial investment until they receive a certified copy of the approved filing or other confirmation of filed status from the office of the secretary of state. This is a simple protective strategy, but often investors don't appreciate the legal consequences of a third-party liability claim that arises during the time period after signing of the organizational agreement but before formal document approval.

B. Surname Rule - general partnership liability for third-party claims exists if the last name of a limited partner is included as a part of the business name, unless it is also the last name of an existing general partner or unless the business was conducted using that name before the limited party joined. The legal rationale for this rule is that the public generally assumes a named partner is involved in day-day management as a general partner.

Strategy: Prospective investors can avoid the time bomb by simply refusing to allow the use of their surname unless one of the two exceptions to liability clearly exists. Again, problems such as these usually occur due to the investor's ignorance of the liability danger, rather than any intention to mislead the public.

C. Participation in Control/Management – potential general partnership unlimited liability also exists if the investor crosses the invisible legal line of involvement in management of the business that normally separates his limited liability from the absolute liability of the general partner.

A limited partner is not an agent of the business enterprise and has no authority to bind it by his acts or non-acts. He is granted limited liability in exchange for giving up the right to be involved in the day-day management of his investment. If the limited partner participates in business operations to the extent that a third party creditor reasonably assumes he is a general partner, the limited liability status is lost. The limited partner is then *estopped to deny unlimited liability.*

How much control can the limited party exercise before he forfeits his protected status? The investor certainly has the right to inquire from time to time about how the business is doing. He can receive, review and comment upon the usual accounting financial statements. He can attend business meetings as a spectator, and receive regular correspondence updates as business progresses.

But the uncertainty of exactly "when" the management/control threshold is crossed led to the creation of "safe harbor" rules under Section 303 of the RULPA that specify certain additional permissible activities that do not forfeit limited liability:

"(a) Being a contractor for or an agent or employee of the limited partnership or of a general partner;

(b) Being an officer, director, or shareholder of a corporate general partner;

(c) Consulting with and advising a general partner with respect to the business of the limited partnership.

Strategy: Notice that such "permissible activities" would otherwise clearly be prohibited participation in management/control. Therefore, third-party claimants routinely join all limited partners as lawsuit defendants and shift to them the burden of establishing safe harbor. The best way to legally establish the safe harbor is to have a written agreement specifying permissible activities, obtained from the general partner when the limited partner pays his initial investment.

Note: Some states, including Florida, have amended LP laws to include safe harbor. However the best strategy remains a written confirming letter.

3.   Sharing of profits and losses

Unlike the rules for general partnerships, sharing of profits and losses is in the same proportion as the capital contributions of the partners. This may be changed however, by a specific provision in the limited partnership agreement.

4.   Dissolution procedures

They are essentially the same as for a General Partnership, except the distribution of assets following liquidation and conversion to cash is: (1) outside creditors, (2) partner's unpaid distributions, (3) partner's loans, (4) capital contributions and (5) surplus.

5.   Taxation requirements

The rules are the same as a General Partnership pass-through of profits and losses to the principals via K-1 forms for individual or corporate income tax returns.

D. Limited Liability Partnership (LLP)/ Company (LLC)

1. Formation Requirements

There was originally nowhere near the uniformity for these types of unincorporated business associations that exists for the general or limited partnership. The first L.L.C. statute was enacted by Wyoming in 1977, followed by Florida in 1982, languished in the 1980's, but expanded greatly in the early 1990's so that by 1998 every state had such a law.

Many states originally taxed LLP's as a corporation, and prohibited single-member LLC's, hampering their growth. Later in the late 1990's those requirements were amended to allow partnership tax status and one person formation, thus clearing the way to more frequent usage.

In 1994 the concept of LLP's came into existence through amendment to the RUPA, and was then reflected in the various state laws. The LLP is formed for conducting a profession, while the LLC is used for all other types of business activities. And the name designation must also include a suffix such as, "L.L.P", "L.L.C." or "a limited liability entity" to place the public on notice that creditor claims may be limited only to the business assets.

Law firms were originally prohibited from organizing on a limited liability basis, but most states now allow it. In view of the personal liability exposure of the traditional general partnership and the litigious nature of our society, the LLP is in the process of becoming the dominant organizational form for the practice of law in larger firms that cannot qualify as subchapter S corporations.

The LLP statutes were initially drafted to shield innocent partners from vicarious liability for negligent malpractice committed by other partners, and were then expanded to shield contract liability for partnership obligations. In every state however, LLP partners are fully liable for their own malpractice and the wrongful acts of their employees and others whom they supervise and control.

These forms of doing business share the common purpose of gaining most advantages of a limited liability association that only exposes the amount of one's actual investment to business risk and preserves personal assets. They are hybrids containing aspects of all other forms of business association.

Similar to the limited partnership, there must be a formal written filing of business articles of organization and approval by the state of intended operation, including designation of a main business office and an agent to receive service of process. Once approved, the entity is legally formed. If there is defective formation, the legal relationship is a general partnership. There is also an "operating agreement" customarily entered into that regulates how the business is to be conducted.

They are separate legal entities, like corporations, that can sue or be sued, buy and sell property, enter into contracts, and incur civil and criminal liability. They are created under formal written "operating agreements" and their owners are called "members." The ownership interests are represented by "certificates of interest", similar to the capital stock shares of a corporation.

2. Other Partnerships Compared

- Unlike the general or limited partnership, *all* members and managers enjoy limited liability, risking only the amount of their invested capital. There is a full liability shield for innocent partners for both contract and tort obligations incurred by other partners.

- Unlike the limited partnership, there is no requirement for a general partner who has unlimited personal liability for business debts.

- Unlike the limited partnership, *all* members may fully participate in everyday management and control of their business. If "member-managed", all members have binding agency authority, and equal votes. If "manager-managed", only the designated parties can bind the association.

- One-layer taxation is the same as in general or limited partnerships.

- There is no separate ownership of assets as in general partnerships.

- Profits and losses are allocated equally, unless there is a separate provision in the operating agreement.

- A member's financial interest may be assigned, but the assignee does not receive any rights of membership unless and until being admitted by the remaining members.

- The basic agency fiduciary duties apply to all members.

3. Advantages / Disadvantages

The LLC and LLP business forms provide the limited liability advantages of the Corporate form, without many of its disadvantages such as the formality of regularly scheduled annual and special meetings, preparation of written minutes or resolutions to memorialize important business decisions, and the filing of annual reports in the state of incorporation as well as the payment of annual capital stock taxes. In addition, the one layer of pass-through taxation is far preferable to the double taxation of the standard "C" corporation.

On the other hand, these forms lack many of the long-standing advantages of corporate existence including familiarity and customary usage by the business and lending community, the long line of legal precedents available to resolve disputes, the ability to provide limited liability for one person businesses or professions, ease of borrowing through the issuance and sale of debt instruments, ease of raising capital through the issuance and sale of equities, and relative ease of formation from a cost and time standpoint in today's marketplace. The problem of double taxation is also avoided through the usage of the "S" corporation, so long as there are no more than 100 U.S. citizen shareholders, only one class of stock, and the corporation derives no more than 25% from passive income. Finally, if the business wants to "go public" by selling ownership interests, only the corporate form is allowed.

4. Future Usage

When LLC's and LLP's were granted federal tax flow-through partnership treatment in 1988 by IRS Revenue Ruling 88-76, their usage expanded greatly. Today their usage continues to expand, especially in situations where a business association cannot meet the requirements of corporate subchapter-S status, and as fraud and finance business scandals remind professionals of their liability vulnerability under their traditional general partnerships.

The newest innovation is the LLLP. Its key advantage is that even general partners in an LP incur no personal liability in their business involvements. Many real estate LP's have been converted to LLLP's to accomplish this liability shield.

The collapse of the saving and loan banks in the late 1980's resulted in enormous money judgments against some of the country's leading general partnership form accounting and law firms due to negligence in rendering professional opinions that overstated earnings, understated liabilities and covered up the industry's precarious financial situation.

This caused renewed focus on the unlimited personal liability dilemma of the traditional law firm general partnership, and the need for limited liability.

"For decades, becoming a partner in a law or accounting firm was almost better than getting tenure at a university. The promotion guaranteed job security, prestige and a large, steady income."

"But these days, with the bankruptcy of many firms and increasing Government litigation against law and accounting firms and their partners, some people are finding that making partner is no longer the magic moment it once was. Offered a partnership, some people are thinking twice – and some are even saying no thanks, deciding that the prospect of a higher salary and the improved status do not offset the greater exposure to lawsuits and the firm's financial problems."
The New Letdown: Making Partner, New York Times, April 1, 1992

D. The Corporation

The corporate form of doing business derives from English Law as far back as the 16th century. It is by far the dominant financial form, representing almost 90% of the total of annual gross business revenues in the United States. Almost 5 million corporations are currently registered to do business in the various states, with assets exceeding 4 trillion dollars. In addition, more than 50% of us own stock in domestic corporations, through direct individual ownership, jointly with others, indirectly through banks, insurance companies and other institutions, and as part of our retirement or pension plans.

The great majority of corporations are small and closely owned by from one to 5 stockholders. These "close corporations" involve many "Mom & Pop" businesses, where the shareholders actively participate in the day-day management.

There is usually no ready market for buying or selling their shares, internal operations are conducted with little or no formality, and typically the shareholders are also officers and directors.

On the other hand, the Fortune 1,000 list of the largest corporations in the world, most of whose securities are publicly traded, control the vast majority of the world's wealth and resources. The managerial decisions of these entities have global implications, and control is often concentrated in a relatively small group of directors and officers. The fiscal and legal accountability of these large corporations has been brought center stage in the last few years by the scandalous conduct of a few, which has had a ripple-effect on the entire business marketplace. This, in turn, has led to sweeping governmental reforms to try to remedy past misconduct and prevent future abuses.

The corporation is a perpetual legal entity that has the legal power to buy and sell property, sue and be sued, and conduct business all in its own name. It can raise capital by selling shares of equity ownership or borrowing money under debt obligations. It exists separate and distinct from its stockholder, directors, officers and employees, so long as it is properly formed and maintained.

Let's look at the basic corporate structure. Visualize and draw an inverted pyramid with four horizontal layers. Assume the pyramid is a large ship. The wide base of support is the stockholders who own the ship. They elect the directors who set corporate policy, deciding where it will travel. Directors appoint the officers who carry out their policy on a day-day basis, running the ship. The officers hire the employees to carry out their orders and fulfill the many tasks involved in keeping the ship properly running.

The stockholders technically own the corporation, but not its separate assets, nor are they personally liable for its liabilities. This is the major advantage of the corporate form – liability of the stockholders is limited to their investment.

They do not, as a general rule, have personal liability for contract or tort obligations of the corporation. This corporate veil protects them, whether they self-incorporate or are one of many shareholders, and the liability shield protects them whether they are involved in a commercial business or a profession.

However, as we shall see, in the special rules at the end of this section, if legal grounds exist for a third party creditor to "pierce the corporate veil," a shareholder's liability shield is lost. We will also examine some special rules that illustrate how, although corporate officers and directors are also usually protected by the limited liability shield, they may face unlimited personal liability for certain actions.

But first, let's look at basic aspects of the corporate form of doing business.

1. Formation Requirements

Corporations are artificial legal persons created by state statute, governed by the statutory laws or corporate codes of the state in which they incorporate, which is where they maintain their home office and conduct their primary business. Most state laws are based in whole or part upon the Model Business Corporation Act (MBCA) created by the American Bar Association in 1946 to provide uniformity and legal predictability for corporate activities. The Act was revised and updated in 1984 (RMBCA), and certain portions were amended thereafter.

Delaware has for many years been the state of incorporation and headquarters for many of America's largest companies due to the following:
- laws very favorable to management
- numerous case precedent to predict the outcome of business disputes
- easy, fast and relatively inexpensive incorporation
- moderate annual fees and taxes
- no minimum capital requirements
- shares may be issued for cash, goods, property or services
- one-person corporations allowed
- shareholder's meetings may be held outside the state
- directors need not reside within the state
- corporate articles may insulate directors from personal liability

Most other states, including Florida, have now created equally comprehensive governing statutes, and attract an equal number of new corporations. They also allow professional corporations, with anywhere from one to many incorporators/stockholder natural persons or other entities..

The incorporators/stockholders file proposed articles of incorporation with the secretary of state's office with payment of required filing fees.

The articles require information as to the names and addresses of incorporators and directors, corporate purpose, initial issuance of shares, and address of the corporate registered office and identity of its registered agent for service of process.

If a corporation is "doing business" in a foreign state, it can be sued there. It is also often required to qualify in that state and pay a registration fee. It similarly cannot sue in a foreign state without qualifying and paying the required charges. Disputes often arise regarding what is "doing business?" Most states have adopted the *minimum contacts* test, which covers almost any business activity in the state, such as selling, buying, advertising, maintaining an office, hiring and firing personnel, or other activities. Those states however allow an exception to this test of jurisdiction called the *isolated transaction rule*. It provides that a single transaction or isolated business event that essentially completes within 30 days is not considered to be "doing business."

If the filing is correct as to name availability, the required suffix designation of Co., Corp., Corporation, Inc., or Incorporated, and other statutory compliance with the furnishing of information the form of the articles, a certificate of incorporation is issued. It is usually date and time stamped so that the exact moment of legal formation is known. If however formation is defective, the association is treated as a general partnership for liability claim purposes, and third party contract or tort claims may be pursued against the non-corporate assets of the supposed shareholders.

Note: In most states, including Florida, corporation formation is not effective until the corporate papers are filed *and accepted by the secretary of state.* Until formal registration, the corporate filing is a mere offer to create the entity. But under the RMCA, some states deem the formation to occur as soon as the articles of incorporation are *filed.*

2. Types of Corporations:
   - Domestic – in its state of incorporation
   - Foreign – in every other state
   - Alien – incorporated in a foreign country
   - Close – its shares are owned privately
   - Public – its shares are publicly traded
   - Nonprofit – for charitable, educational, scientific purposes, where earnings are expensed "above the line", including salaries, and there are no "below the line" net profits
   - Municipal – established for governmental purposes
   - Professional – to conduct the business of licensed professionals
   - Parent/Subsidiary – the parent holds a majority or more of the capital stock shares, and thus owns the subsidiary

3. Taxation:

All corporations are presumed to "C" by IRS for income tax purposes unless they promptly and properly file an election to be taxed as an "S" corporation. The differences between the two are significant. Since a corporation is a separate legal entity, it normally pays taxes on the net income earned in its calendar or fiscal year at required corporate rates. If it has surplus funds left over, and the board of directors declares a dividend, that money is distributed to the stockholders who pay taxes on the earned income according to their individual tax rates. Thus the "C" corporation has the disadvantage of double taxation.

If however the corporation elects to be treated as an "S" Corporation by filing form 2553 with IRS, it is taxed like a partnership in that it pays no taxes at the entity level and the profits/losses pass-through its corporate income tax return (1041) via form K-1 to its shareholder's to be included in their personal income tax return (1040). Thus there is only a single layer of taxation.

Subchapter "S" requirements are:
- Maximum 100 shareholders
- Only U.S. citizen shareholders
- Only domestic corporations
- No partnership or corporate shareholders
- Only one class of stock
- No more than 25% passive investment income
- Must file election within 75 days of formation

4. Financing Corporate Business

Every corporation needs to raise money in order to finance existing operations, expansion, unexpected outlays, new opportunites, research and development, and many other business needs.

When the entity if formed, the incorporators provide initial capital, the stockholders buy their shares at stated value, borrowing is arranged through banks and other credit lines, and those finds go into the corporate treasury for commencing operations.

But there are continuous needs for additional capital beyond revenues from operations which are used to pay current expenses including salaries, pay debt service, plowed back into the business for growth, or paid out in stockholder dividends.

The two main sources of new corporate financing from the public are (1) sale of debt securities and (2) sale of equity securities. Debt securities have a repayment priority over equity securities.

(1) The sale of debt securities by the corporation to individuals, institutions, banks or governmental agencies establishes a debtor-creditor relationship. The company is borrowing money from the lender-purchaser who buys the debt instrument.

The borrower-issuer agrees to repay the principal at a named maturity date, with periodic or lumped interest payments at a stated percentage rate, and the parties are bound by such other contractual terms as are stated in the loan agreement. The three basic types of debt securities are:

- **Bonds** – long term (20-30+ years) secured debt. Interest rates offered are lower than if unsecured. In event of default, the owner may foreclose on the stated collateral security.

- **Debentures** – long term (20-30+ years) unsecured debt. Interest rates offered are higher to attract investment capital. In event of default, the owner must look to the general credit of the borrower-issuer.

- **Promissory Notes** – short term (maximum 5 years) unsecured debt. Interest rates track current market conditions. Although companies may issue short term secured notes when they are unable to sell unsecured obligations, the usual note financing is an unsecured bridge loan to satisfy a current need. In event of default, the financial condition of the issuer determines repayment.

Purchase decision by investors in debt securities usually relate to the degree of security they will have and the interest yield they will receive. Sometimes the investing public is offered additional debt instrument features (sweeteners) to induce purchase. These can include the following:

- **Convertible Bonds** – exchangeable at a certain time and conversion formula for other securities, usually common stock.

- **Revenue Bonds** – repayment is earmarked from a specific source, such as Turnpike Revenue Bonds used to finance its construction.

- **Callable Bonds** – subject to early redemption by the issuer at a stated premium over face value. Bonds are usually called, or refinanced, when market interest rates fall below the bond's coupon/yield rate.

(2) The sale of equity securities by the corporation, either privately as a close Corporation or by "going public", is the usual way the business is financed. While issuance of debt securities creates a debtor-creditor relationship, issuance of equity securities grants ownership rights to the purchaser. The equity holder participates in the company's management, earnings/dividends paid, price appreciation or depreciation, and distribution of any residue on corporate dissolution. The two basic types of equity securities are:

- Preferred Stock – has contractual dividend rights superior to common stock. "Fixed" preferred has a stated rate of return stated as a percentage of the initial offering price.

  "Cumulative" preferred requires priority payment of any dividend arrearages, such as for omitted or reduced dividend, before any common stock dividends may be declared.

  "Redeemable" preferred works the same way as callable bonds, providing the company an opportunity to buy back the shares at a stated price if market interest rates fall below the share's fixed rate.

  "Convertible" preferred has the same conversion into common stock feature of its bonds counterpart.

  "Participating" preferred allows sharing in corporate profits beyond the fixed preferred dividend rate. There is also usually a "liquidation preference" where preferred shareholders receive a set dollar amount on dissolution before any payments to common stock shareholders. As we can see, preferred stock is a hybrid, sharing features of both debt and equity.

- Common Stock – represents one's ownership interest in the corporation. It usually has none of the preferences or special investment features that highlight bonds and preferred stock. It has no stated rate of return or maturity date. Debt security creditors and preferred stockholders have a payment priority over common shares.

  Common stock usually has "par value" shares which are sold at a price set by the articles of incorporation or by resolution of the stockholders or directors. Proceeds from initial sale of shares are the "stated capital" or "paid-in capital" of the company. Shares purchased for a price in excess of stated par value create "capital surplus." Shares can also be issued by the company on a "no-par value" basis, which provides management more flexibility in creating capital surplus.

5. Shareholder's Equity

The two main ways a corporate stockholder profits from that ownership during the operating life of the company is the receipt of dividends and price appreciation of share value.

Price appreciation in a close corporation is hard to determine since there is no readily available indicator of daily market prices. That is why the terms of the corporate articles, the by-laws which are the internal rules and regulations of the company, and any buy-sell or similar valuation procedure agreements are critical.

But in public companies that are listed on trading exchanges the valuation process is simple. Just compare the per share acquisition cost with current per share price and we know at a glance if we have paper profit or loss.

One of the great misconceptions of the investing public is the erroneous belief that a profitable corporation must pay dividends. In actuality, there is no such legal requirement. Dividends are declared and paid at the discretion of the Board of Directors at a regularly scheduled annual or special meeting.

This was not always the case however. Before the rise of the corporate form of doing business and its implementation through the various state statutes, shareholders of a profitable company had a legal right to compel payment of dividends.

In the famous case of *Dodge v. Ford Motor Co., 170 N.W. 668 (Mich. 1919)*, Henry Ford who was President, Chairman of the Board, and majority shareholder told minority shareholders John and Horace Dodge that special cash dividends paid in past years would now be reinvested for expansion of the company, increased hiring of workers, and reduction of automobile prices so that more customers could buy Ford cars. The Dodge brothers sued to compel declaration of the dividend.

At the time of defendant's demand, Ford had concluded its most successful business year with an expected profit of $60 million. (Remember this is 1919) Surplus was almost $112 million, net cash available was almost $34 million, and assets exceeded $132 million. They contended that Henry Ford intended to operate the company as a semi-charitable organization rather than as a business, when he said:

> "My ambition is to employ still more men, to spread the benefits of this industrial system to the greatest possible numbers, to help them build up their lives and their homes. To do this, we are putting the greatest share of our profits back in the business."

The court ruled that the withholding of the special dividend was an arbitrary and improper action by the Board, and required declaration and payment of a dividend of over $19 million.

> "His testimony creates the impression, also, that he thinks the Ford Motor Company has made too much money; has had too large profits, and that although large profits might still be earned, a sharing of them with the public, by reducing the price of the output of the company, ought to be undertaken. . . . A business corporation is organized and carried on primarily for the profit of the stockholders. The powers of the directors are to be employed to that end."

Note: An interesting sidelight to this case was the fact that after its conclusion, the Dodge brothers were so angry with Henry Ford that they sold their shares and then started their own automobile company to compete with Ford – General Motors!

74

The normal corporate dividend is a cash payment per share for each shareholder as of the "record date", which is when the dividend is declared by the Board. Distribution of the dividend follows a short time thereafter on the "payment date." Stockholders on the record date will still receive their dividends even if they sell their shares before the payment date. If a dividend is declared by the Board but for some reason not paid, shareholders have a right to legally compel payment.

Stock dividends may also be paid in proportion to a shareholder's existing stock ownership. This is often done in addition to regular annual cash dividends, as a year-end bonus or special distribution when the company experiences unusually large profits, sells assets for large gains or otherwise has experienced a financial windfall.

There are however legal parameters governing how and when directors can exercise their dividend discretion. In most states, including Florida, payment of dividends can only be made from earned surplus, rather than capital surplus, so the company's capital structure is not compromised.

At the time of dividend declaration and payment the corporation must not be "insolvent," meaning that if the company cannot pay its debts as they come due, or its liabilities exceed its assets – the dividend is illegal. Directors who vote in favor of declaration may be personally liable to repay the illegal dividends to their company, as well as stockholders receiving illegal dividends who knew or should have known of the insolvency.

6. Rights/Duties of Shareholders

In addition to the receipt of dividends, if declared by the Board, stockholders have a number of basic rights relating to their ownership interest. These rights are essentially the same whether the amount of stock ownership is small or large, and include the following:

- Receive financial information – the annual financial reports including, balance sheets, profit & loss statements, and other reports filed with IRS and state agencies, including changes in shareholder ownership are sent to shareholders at the time of the annual report of operations, or are otherwise available on request.

- Inspect company books and records – shareholders are entitled to know what is taking place in their company, through the management of the directors and officers. They have the right to request inspection of corporate books and records for a "proper purpose" at a reasonable time and place. To avoid harassment by recent/minimal ownership shareholders, some states have adopted provisions of the Model Act that require inspecting shareholders to have owned 5% or more of outstanding shares for at least 6 months.

Inspection is usually requested for corporate articles of incorporation, minutes of meetings, committee resolutions, business ledgers, bylaws and other internal rules and regulations, shareholder lists, stock issuance/transfer registers, and related documents regarding employee and executive compensation, and other financial incentives that may affect cash flow and earnings projections.

The "proper purpose" doctrine walks the line between the shareholder's need to know and management's duty to disclose. Many disputes involve a request for lists of shareholder names and addresses. Seeking the information to sell it to a competitor is clearly improper.

But the current trend is toward a more open policy allowing reasonable inspection requests, especially in view of the "Enron" era's numerous corporate financial scandals involving improper management, cooked books, spoliated records, and related corporate misfeasance, malfeasance and nonfeasance.

The trend was suggested by the Delaware case of *Compaq Computer Corp. v. Horton, 631 A.2d 1 (Del. 1993)*. Horton owned 112 shares and requested inspection of his company's stock ledger to communicate with other shareholder's regarding his pending fraud claims against the company and to determine whether they wanted to join that litigation.

Compaq refused, claiming improper purpose. Horton sued and won the right to the information as being a "proper purpose" related to his interest as a stockholder-owner, "for the purpose of communicating with fellow shareholders, not only about pending litigation, but to solicit their interest in joining it."

"If anything, the corporation and its stockholders, as well as public policy, will best be served by exposure of the fraud, if that is the case, and restoration of the stock to a value set by a properly informed market."

Note: The case is especially important since its decision in favor of the suing shareholder was a significant departure from Delaware's traditional management bias, and reflects a more even-handed approach to disputes between ownership and management.

- Sue the corporation or third parties on its behalf – shareholder lawsuits are either (1) direct or (2) derivative.

(1) A direct action involves a claim made by a shareholder against his own corporation, and winning proceeds belong directly to the plaintiff. Examples of direct actions are individual and class action lawsuits to compel payment of declared dividends, to require inspection of books and records, and to enforce voting rights.

(2) A derivative action is brought "on behalf of" the corporation, because the board has refused to file the requested suit on their own.

All monetary proceeds belong to the corporation. The Model Act suggests the complaining shareholder must make written demand for action which is ignored for 90 days by the board. Examples of derivative actions are suits against parties who have defaulted in their indebtedness to the company for loans that have come due, or unpaid account balances for goods sold or services rendered, and the board has failed to take action to collect.

The "demand rule" as stated in the Model Act is the generally required procedure. However, there is also a "futility exception" which allows filing a derivative action without making formal demand if it appears reasonably obvious from the surrounding facts and circumstances it would be unsuccessful.

The distinction between direct and derivative stockholder lawsuits was examined in the case of *Richardson v. Arizona Fuels Corp., 614 P.2d 636 (Utah 1980)*, where plaintiff and others were stockholders of Major Oil Co. and brought a class action against its officers and directors for misappropriation of its assets, requesting they disgorge their unlawful profits and return them to the corporation. The court refused to certify the case as a class action, saying:

> "A derivative action must necessarily be based on a claim for relief which is owned by the stockholder's corporation. Indeed, a prerequisite for filing a derivative action is the failure of the corporation to initiate the action in its own name. . . A class action, on the other hand, is predicated on ownership of the claim for relief sued upon in the representation of the class and all other class members in their capacity as individuals."

- Transfer their shares by sale, gift, or as collateral for a loan – since one's stock ownership is a valuable intangible interest in property that has a certain calculable value; it represents an asset that may be treated by its owner as any other property. Share certificates are originally issued for stated consideration as part of paid in capital. Issuance is made on the internal stock register, or electronically in large corporations, and any transfer is by endorsement of the certificate or a separate stock power.

"Authorized shares" are the total allowed stock capitalization reflected in the articles of incorporation, and may be increased from time to time by amending the articles. "Issued shares" are those that are sold by the corporation as reflected in its stock register. "Outstanding shares" are the shares still in outside ownership. "Treasury shares" are those that the corporation repurchases from its shareholders, usually as an investment in times of lower stock prices when the company deems its shares to be undervalued. It then either retires, reissues in new sales, or pays to stockholders as special, year-end, or bonus dividends.

- Attend corporate meetings – (1) Annual meetings are held to elect a board of Directors for the next year, and to authorize regular and recurring corporate business matters.

The initial annual meeting will in addition provide for opening of bank accounts, initial lines of credit, basic capital purchases, salary structures, and ratification of promoter's pre-incorporation contracts. (2) Special meetings may be called at any time for non-recurring, important or emergency matters by the board of directors, by holders of at least 10% of shares, or designated corporate officers such as its President.

• Vote their shares – shareholders vote in person or by written proxy. To have a valid stockholder's meeting a "quorum" must be present, which is usually a majority of outstanding shares; although the Model Act permits one-third of the shares entitled to vote. Voting is usually on a one share/one vote basis, with a majority vote usually required to approve proposed action. However, the articles of incorporation may require a supermajority for such important corporate business as the approval of corporate mergers or sale of substantial assets.

Most states now allow "cumulative voting", changes the usual straight voting to permit shareholders to multiply the number of their per share votes by the number of directors to be elected.

This enables minority shareholders, acting in unison, to accumulate or split their votes of a larger block of shares for a particular director or two and possibly achieve some board representation for the particular points of view. In the absence of cumulative voting, the majority owners of at least 50.1% of outstanding shares would be able to control all agenda items.

• Agency laws – stockholders are neither agents or fiduciaries of the corporation. Their acts are usually not binding on each other or the corporation, because of their separation from management/operational decisions made by officers and directors.

7. Rights/Duties of Directors

Although directors are elected by the shareholder - owners and presumably will implement corporate policy in accordance with their wishes, the actuality of many corporations is that the directors really run the show. They appoint their management team of officers who carry out their direction on a day to day basis, and through the officers the employment team is put into place. Some other director basics are the following:

• Agency duties - directors are technically not agents of the corporation's stockholders or the corporation, because they are not involved in daily management, but they occupy a special fiduciary relationship of highest trust and confidence. This relationship carries the same agency-type duties owed to the corporation and its stockholder-owners as bind officer-agents.

The most important duties owed by directors are Loyalty, which prohibits conflicts of interest and self-dealing, and Diligence, which requires both obedience to their responsibilities as set forth in the corporate documents and a level of performance with reasonable exercise of care and skill.

- Financial duties – directors influence the finances of their company in many ways which include, (1) setting the selling price of new shares, (2) determining the value of non-cash share purchases, (3) issuing new equity securities, (4) borrowing money in the form of notes, bonds and debentures, (5) leasing, selling and exchanging assets in the ordinary course of business, (6) setting salary compensation of their appointed officers as well as, where allowed, providing non– salary compensation packages for themselves that usually include annual retainers, meeting attendance fees, and year end bonuses, (7) creating management committees, and probably of most importance to their stockholders, (8) declaring and paying dividends.

- Election – directors are elected by the stockholder-owners at their annual meetings and may themselves fill interim vacancies due to resignations, illness or death of a sitting director. Directors meetings are held annually or at special times as specified in the corporate bylaws. A majority of the board usually creates a quorum so that a valid meeting will take place.

Voting is usually one director-one vote and majority vote prevails. The day-day management team of officers is appointed by directors as one of the regular orders of business at their meetings, as well as other important issues of corporate finance, operations and administration.

Directors are normally elected for annual terms but they may also be elected to serve staggered terms so that not all are to be elected each year, thus allowing more control over the corporation by the majority shareholders. The number of initial directors is specified in the articles of incorporation, and is one or more, but always a odd numbered amount such as 3-5-7-9, so that there will be no voting deadlocks.

The Board usually consists of inside and outside directors. Inside directors, often described as "active", are also corporate officers and are involved in daily operations. Outside directors often serve as an honorarium and are not part of internal management, being often referred to as "passive".

8. Rights/Duties of Officers

Officers are appointed as the company management team by the directors, and are in charge of carrying out the directorial policies on a daily basis, including the hiring of necessary employees, professionals and other functionaries. Directors have the authority to appoint and remove officers, similar to how the officers have the legal right to hire and fire employees.

In consideration for this high degree of daily responsibility they are paid salaries by the corporation and since they act on its behalf they are its legal agents. All the agency rules we have previously discussed in Section II, especially Loyalty, apply to their contracts and torts, including the potentials of vicarious liability.

9. Dissolution/Termination

Although the corporate entity can have perpetual life, it may nevertheless be terminated voluntarily by its directors or stockholder-owners, and involuntarily as the result of an administrative order by the state or pursuant to a court in a judicial proceeding for that purpose.

(1) Voluntary – Directors/Stockholders: sometimes the corporation has been validly formed, but plans change, no corporate stock is issued, and no corporate action is taken. We just have the legal shell of the entity and nothing else. Although these inactive companies may be kept "on the shelf" for future use, annual payment of capital stock taxes to the state of incorporation, filing of state corporate tax returns, or other ongoing procedures may dictate against continuation. A majority vote of the incorporators or initial directors in these cases will dissolve the corporation.

If however, the corporate existence has moved beyond its initial phases into actual operations and dissolution is desired at a later date, such as when a particular piece of property or business has been sold, the board of directors recommends it to the stockholders and they must approve it by majority vote of outstanding shares at a valid meeting.

(2) Involuntary – State: each incorporating state has procedural requirements for the validly formed corporation to maintain its legal existence, the violation of which will cause dissolution. This is a situation where the corporation may cure the default within a stated time period (60 days under the Model Act), and then be reinstated. If not reinstated, a formal certificate of dissolution is issued by the state.

The Model Act mentions the following grounds for "administrative" dissolution: (a) time duration stated in the articles of incorporation has expired, (b) required annual corporate report was not filed, (c) required annual franchise fees or capital stock taxes were not paid, (d) the required registered corporate office and/or registered agent for service of process was not maintained or updated as to current changes.

(3) Involuntary – Court: there may be disagreements or deadlocks in the operation of close corporations, where a conflict develops between management (directors/officers) and ownership (stockholders). The parties may seek judicial intervention to resolve the problems, or if not solvable, a court order of dissolution.

The legal effect of dissolution, whether voluntary or involuntary, is similar to partnership dissolution. The entity continues in existence for the limited purpose of winding up its business affairs. This is carried out by its directors, officers and employees. The assets are liquidated by collecting debts due the company, converting illiquid into cash assets, sale of hard assets, and distributing the proceeds in the following priority:

- expenses of winding up and liquidation
- outside creditors
- preferred stockholders
- common stockholders

Articles of dissolution are filed with the state of incorporation, and it issues a Formal "certificate of dissolution" which legally evidences the end of corporate existence.

**10. Special situations causing unlimited personal liability
The main advantage of the corporate form of doing business is the liability shield known as "the corporate veil." Stockholders of a corporation are not, as a general rule, personally liable for corporate debts.

Their liability exposure is limited only to the amounts of capital they invest in acquiring their stock ownership interests. Their other personal assets are not normally at risk.

In addition, the business strategy of creating a corporate entity to insulate us from unlimited personal liability is not frowned upon by the law. Far from it, the law encourages us to use the corporate form to act behind a corporate shell, even to self-incorporate, and thus achieve maximum liability protection for all our business involvements and investments. We can and should follow all these strategies:

- Self-incorporate to act as a sole proprietorship.
- Use the corporate form to act as a general partner.
- Use the corporate form to act as a limited partner.
- Form separate corporations for each business/investment.
- Practice a profession using the corporate form.
- Elect "S" tax status, when allowed, for each corporate formation.
- If "S" tax status is unavailable, use the LLC or LLP form.

We will not have to be concerned about the possibility of unlimited personal liability, as long as we "do it correctly." But what if we don't? The result can be financially devastating because we face unlimited personal liability, just like being an individual general partner.

Officers and directors of a corporation are also usually protected by the same liability shield.

They may be involved in disputes with each other, with their shareholder-owners, or with third part creditors for alleged breaches of fiduciary duties, but only in the context of potential corporate – not individual – liability. However there are some exceptional situations where the breach of duty, especially duty of loyalty and duty of skill, care and diligence, may result in unlimited personal liability for damages suffered.

Let's look at the various types of unlimited personal liability situations:

A. Pre-incorporation Liability

1. Promoter's pre-incorporation contracts:
A "promoter" is one of the original incorporators who takes charge of one or more of its preliminary organizational requirements before the entity is legally formed. Customary activities include putting together the investment group, arranging financing and initial capitalization, negotiating leases and employment contracts, and entering into formal contracts in anticipation of legal creation of the corporation.

The most often cited case illustrating promoter liability for pre-incorporation contracts is *Coopers & Lybrand v. Fox, 758 P.2d 683 (Colo. App. 1988)*. In that case Fox requested a tax opinion from plaintiff, a national accounting firm. He advised them he was acting on behalf of a named corporation that was in the process of being formed, and plaintiff agreed to perform the work.

The corporation was formed, the work was completed, and it was billed over $10,000 by plaintiff for services rendered. When the bill was unpaid, plaintiff sued Fox for collection. He claimed no personal liability. The trial court ruled for him, but the decision was reversed in plaintiff's favor on appeal.

"One cannot act as the agent of a nonexistent principal. On the contrary, the uncontroverted facts place Fox squarely within the definition of a promoter. A promoter is one who, alone or with others, undertakes to form a corporation and to procure for it the rights, instrumentalities, and capital to enable it to conduct business.

"As a general rule, promoters are personally liable for the contracts they make, though made on behalf of a corporation to be formed.

"The well-recognized exception to the general rule of promoter liability is that if the contracting party knows the corporation is not in existence but nevertheless agrees to look solely to the corporation and not to the promoter for payment, then the promoter incurs no personal liability. Release of the promoter depends on the intent of the parties. As the proponent of an alleged agreement to release the promoter from liability, the promoter has the burden of proving the release agreement."

Pre-incorporation contracts usually fall within one of these three types:

- For undisclosed principal – contract is signed in promoter's own name. Example: (signed) "Pete Promoter"

- For partially disclosed principal – contract is signed on behalf of an unnamed future entity. Example: (signed) "Pete Promoter, for a Florida Corp. to be formed."

- For fully disclosed principal – future principal is fully identified. Example: (signed) "Pete Promoter, for ABC, Inc., a Florida Corp. to be formed."

Under modern law, the promoter usually has personal liability in all three of these examples, as suggested by the *Coopers & Lybrand* case. If the corporation is never legally formed he is the only party available for liability. Upon corporate formation, he is still liable and the corporation is not, until it assumes liability by adopting/ratifying the promoter's pre-incorporation contract at the first organizational meeting of shareholder-owners. At that point, both the promoter and the corporation are liable.

The promoter can be legally relieved of personal liability: (1) if the original contract specifies that he is signing "not individually", or clearly states, "the undersigned is a corporate promoter, signing on behalf of a corporation to be formed and, as such, has no personal liability," or (2) a Novation occurs.

A novation is a three party contract (promoter /corporation/ creditor); where the third party creditor agrees to substitute the liability of the newly formed corporation for the promoter and, in turn, release him from liability. But the timing of the promoter's request to the creditor for a novation is crucial.

Let's strategize: Assume the pre-incorporation contract was a lease of commercial space for the corporate offices. If the promoter waited to request a novation until after he signed the lease, the entity was formed, and it ratified his contract – no creditor in his right mind would agree to release one of the two legally responsible parties without a substantial cash payment for privilege.

The maximum bargaining leverage of the promoter is when he is originally negotiating his pre-incorporation contract. He could require, as a deal-maker or deal-breaker, that the lease have an *automatic novation clause* that stated, "Upon legal formation of ABC, Inc. and its adoption of this lease, it shall be substituted as the sole lessee and Pete Promoter shall be released from liability."

2. Subscriber's pre-incorporation subscriptions:
A subscriber is a party who offers to buy shares in a corporation to be formed, per a subscription agreement.

Most states view the offer to purchase shares as a condition precedent – it can be revoked at any time by the subscriber before corporate formation, which then satisfies the condition, the offer is legally accepted, and the subscription agreement becomes a binding contract.

Other states, including Florida, take the minority view which considers the pre-incorporation subscription to be an irrevocable offer from the moment it is made, and its acceptance automatically upon corporate formation.

The Model Act takes a middle-ground, viewing the pre-incorporation subscription offer as irrevocable for six months, so that corporate formation must be finalized within that time, or the offer is considered revoked by lapse of time.

B. Defective Incorporation Liability

1. **Non-Filing Defective Formation** – if the corporation is not legally formed due to the failure to properly file articles of incorporation with the required state office at a time, the business association is really a general partnership. If a creditor's contract or tort claim exceeds business assets, all the parties involved have joint and several unlimited personal liability. The mere fact that they may call themselves a corporation and believe they were acting as one is immaterial in most states.

2. **De Facto Formation** – a good-faith attempt has been made to form the corporation and the incorporators believe the entity is formed, but the filing is incomplete in some aspect such as the required fee payment is missing, the check is unsigned, or the articles themselves lack signatures.

While some states will allow this incomplete formation to preserve the liability shield that protects its shareholders, others take a strict view and will not. They say either the corporation is fully formed or it isn't – no "almost formed" excuses are allowed.

"The corporate existence begins when the articles of incorporation are filed with the secretary of state accompanied by payment of the incorporation and filing fees. The filing creates an irrefutable presumption that the corporation is and has been incorporated in this state." *Warthan v. Midwest Consolidated Insurance Agencies, Inc.,450 N.W.2d 145 (Minn. App. 1990).*

3. **Corporation by Estoppel** - some courts feel the imposition of unlimited liability is too harsh and allow the legal concept of "corporation by estoppel", which prevents *the creditor* from questioning corporate existence if there was a holding out or representation of it being a corporation that the creditor relied upon, and he dealt with the business as if it was a corporation in his activities that created the debt or claim in question.

4. Administrative Dissolution – if a properly formed corporation fails to pay its annual capital stock taxes and/or file required annual reports, dissolution of corporate status may be declared by the state of incorporation. It remains in effect, and the association loses its corporate status unless it "reinstates" by filing the lacking administrative items within a specified time.

While it is technically dissolved, the stockholder's limited liability shield may be lost depending on state law – some continuing limited liability until a stated future date, and others ending it upon declaring the dissolution and then allowing it to be re-established when the corporation is reinstated.

C. Stockholder Unlimited Personal Liability

1. Piercing the Corporate Veil – once the corporation is properly formed by the state of incorporation issuing its date/time stamped Certificate, the limited liability shield that protects stockholders is in place. There is a legal presumption that the liability of corporate shareholders is limited only to their capital investment.

But this presumption may be rebutted under certain circumstances which are determined on a case-by-case basis by creditors who try to go behind this liability shield and "pierce the corporate veil" to reach a stockholder's personal assets to satisfy an outstanding claim that remains unpaid by the corporation. These are the typical factors that creditors attempt to prove to allow courts to ignore the corporate form and some leading cases that illustrate them:

- **Alter-ego theory** – there is a lack of separation between the entity and the individual stockholders. Example: commingled funds, personal expenses paid from corporate funds, no separate corporate bank account, no honoring of the corporate veil.

- **Lack of formalities** – there are few, if any, implementations of corporate procedures. Example: corporate stock not issued, no meetings held, no written minutes or resolutions, no corporate books/records maintained.

- **Thin capitalization** – the amount of initial or paid-in capital is inadequate to reasonably establish a proper financial basis for commencing business. Example: stockholders contribute minimal capital, the entity incurs a disproportionately large debt that exceeds its assets, and the stockholders claim insulation from personal liability.

- **Watered stock** – purchase price of shares is not fully paid for by their stockholder-buyers or are issued for less than fair market value. The deficiency of value is the "water", and the shareholder-owners are personally liable for that difference. Example: required $500 par value shares are issued for cash, property or services valued at $100.

- Improper dividends – shareholders who "knowingly" receive dividends whose payment causes corporate insolvency or were declared at a time of insolvency are legally required to return them to the corporation. Example: the company accountant has audited its books, knows its liabilities exceed its assets, but accepts payment of a dividend declared after the Board received his adverse financial report.

- Defrauding creditors or minority shareholders – controlling stockholders sometimes close down or abandon a company that has incurred large creditor balances.

- Looting the corporation - when the fraud victims are creditors and a "freeze-out" when minority shareholders are being oppressed. Example: the majority shareholders drain net income by paying themselves unreasonably high salaries or bonuses, sell assets for full value to false buyers, sell assets for discounted value to themselves, pay themselves high rent for leased premises, illegally refuse to declare dividends, fail to pay properly declared dividends, unlawfully refuse access to corporate books and records, or embark upon a "dirty tricks" campaign to force out dissident stockholders.

  "The variety of shams is infinite, but many fit this case's pattern: a closely held corporation owes unwanted obligations; it siphons off corporate revenues, sells off much of the corporate assets, or does other acts to hinder the on-going business and its ability to pay off its debts; a new business then starts up that is basically a continuation of the old business with many of the same shareholders, officers, and directors." *Castleberry v. Branscum, 721 S.W.2d 270 (Tex. 1986).*

- Parent/subsidiary corporation disputes - large, deep-pocket corporations often form subsidiaries for which they owns all or controlling stock ownership, to be involved in various business transactions. Normally, claims against the subsidiary are limited to its corporate assets. But if the same criteria to "pierce the corporate veil" listed above are present in both companies, courts may allow the liability shield of the parent to be pierced. The main factor is whether or not the parent so *dominates* the subsidiary that it has lost its separate corporate existence. Example: ABC Co. owns all stock of XYZ Co., the officers/directors/employees are the same, assets are the same, and the parent operates its business on the subsidiary's premises.

E. Officer/Director Unlimited Liability

The corporate stockholders rely upon their elected directors and the appointed officers to properly operate their company. Therefore, highest fiduciary duties of trust and confidence are owed to the stockholders by their officers and directors.

Officers and directors are normally shielded from personal liability as they discharge their duties, are insured's under O&D liability insurance policies purchased for their benefit by the company, and are protected by their company's duty of indemnification to hold them harmless for litigation or other claims expenses assessed against them. But they may incur personal liability in the following situations:

1. Improper Dividends – if the board declares a stockholder dividend when the corporation is financially insolvent, or its payment causes insolvency, the dividend is illegal and the directors who voted in its favor will be personally required to repay it to the corporate treasury.

2. Business Judgment Rule – Officers and directors owe a fiduciary duty of diligence, to exercise reasonable care and skill in their business decisions. But they are not guarantors that their business decisions will result in financial success. So long as they use "due diligence" by properly researching and evaluating the pro's and con's, and solicit and reasonably rely upon opinions of professionals and experts, they are protected even if their decisions result in corporate losses.

The "business judgment rule" *protects* officers and directors. They are not liable for honest, good faith mistakes of business judgment. Under the "objective standard", they need only act as a reasonable person would have under the same or similar circumstances. Even if their conduct amounts to ordinary negligence, so long as some prudent people might have made the same decision, they are still not personally liable for its adverse results.

However, if decisions are made under circumstances that constitute bad faith or "gross negligence", or "willful and wanton misconduct", such as situations where no reasonably informed and rational person would make such a decision, personal liability may result. This is determined case-by-case. Florida law defines bad faith as:

"Acting (i) in reckless disregard of a known or obvious risk
'so great as to make it highly probable that harm would follow;'
(ii) in bad faith or with malicious intent; (iii) in wanton and
willful disregard of human rights, safety or property."

In the famous case of *Smith v. Van Gorkum, 488 A.2d 858 (Del. 1985),* defendant was a large stockholder, chief executive officer, and chairman of the board of Trans Union, a public company. He was nearing retirement age of 65 and was desirous of "cashing out" his investment. He privately approached Abe Pritzker, a well-known corporate buy-out specialist, to discuss possible sale of Trans Union. The company's stock was being publicly traded at $38 per share when Defendant proposed a purchase price of $55 per share, which was agreed to by Pritzger.

Defendant hurriedly called a special meeting of the Trans Union board to approve the sale one week later. He explained the transaction in a brief presentation, the proposed merger agreement was not furnished to the board, no valuation study of the value of company shares was prepared, and the board approved the sale and voted not to seek any other offers.

Plaintiff and other minority shareholders sued defendant and his other directors for damages alleging violation of the business judgment rule. The trial court ruled for defendants, but that decision was reversed on appeal, and the cased was remanded to determine the fair market value of the company's shares.

"Under Delaware law, the business judgment rule is the offspring of the fundamental principle . . . that the business and affairs of a Delaware corporation are managed by or under its board of directors.
In carrying out their managerial roles, directors are charged with an unyielding fiduciary duty to the corporation and its shareholders.

"The rule itself 'is a presumption that in making a business decision, the directors of a corporation acted on an informed basis, in good faith and in the honest belief that the action taken was in the best interests of the company.' Thus, the party attacking a board decision as uninformed must rebut the presumption that its business judgment was an informed one.

"The determination of whether a business judgment is an informed one turns on whether the directors have informed themselves prior to making a business decision, of all material information available to them. Under the business judgment rule, there is no protection for directors who have made an unintelligent or unadvised judgment.

"The directors (1) did not adequately inform themselves as to Van Gorkum's role in forcing the sale of the company and in establishing the per share purchase price; (2) they were uninformed as to the intrinsic value of the company; and (3) given these circumstances, at a minimum, they were *grossly negligent (emphasis added)* in approving the sale of the company upon two hours' consideration without prior notice, and without the exigency of a crisis or emergency."

3. The Corporate Opportunity Rule – Officers and directors owe a fiduciary duty of loyalty, which required primary allegiance to his corporation, and prohibits conflicts of interest, self-dealing, private profits from business matters, and any other theft of corporate benefits.

The "corporate opportunity rule" *prohibits* officers and directors from diverting to themselves, usurping or otherwise misappropriating a possible business opportunity without offering it first to their corporation. The rationale for personal liability is that the fiduciary is stealing the opportunity from his own company. These are the usual proofs required to sustain a breach of the rule:

- The opportunity came to the officer/director as a direct result of their corporate business status,
- The opportunity was related to the corporation's line of business,
- The opportunity was not presented to the corporation for consideration,
- The corporation had the financial ability to act upon it if it had been offered,
- The officer/director took the opportunity for personal investment.

In *Klinicki v. Lundgren, 695 P.2d 906 (Ore. 1985),* the parties were laid-ff airline pilots who decided to start their own charter airline company called Berlinair. They met with the BFR group to negotiate a lucrative air transport contract. Later, when defendant learned that BFR was going to go forward with the deal, he formed his own separate company called ABC and negotiated on its behalf rather than Berlinair. When the contract eventually went to ABC, plaintiff brought a derivative suit against it and defendant for breach of fiduciary duties and usurping a corporate opportunity.

The trial court and appellate court ruled for plaintiff. Defendant appealed, unsuccessfully claiming that Berlinair was not financially able to undertake the BFR contract, and therefore there was no violation of the corporate opportunity rule.

"There is no dispute that the corporate opportunity doctrine precludes corporate fiduciaries from diverting to themselves business opportunities in which the corporation has an expectancy, property interest or right, or which in fairness should otherwise belong to the corporation. The doctrine follows from a corporate fiduciary's duty of undivided loyalty to the corporation.

"(1) The director or principal senior executive must promptly offer the opportunity and disclose all material facts known regarding the opportunity to the disinterested directors, . . .
(2) The director or principal senior executive may take advantage of the corporate opportunity only after full disclosure and only if the opportunity is rejected by a majority of the disinterested directors, . . .
(3) Where a director or principal senior executive of a close corporation appropriates a corporate opportunity without first fully disclosing the opportunity and offering it to the corporation, absent ratification, that director or principal senior executive holds the opportunity in trust for the corporation."

4. Liability Limitation Statutes – the trend of some state laws is to limit the liability of "outside" or "passive" directors", described as those who are not company executives with active management roles, for mistakes of business judgment. Delaware was the leader in this effort to attract and retain well-known directors to serve on corporate boards as honorariums, and many other states have followed suit, as well as the Revised Model Business Corporation Act (RMBCA).

Without these statutes, the threat of litigation and the prohibitive cost of providing liability insurance to protect them would otherwise cause them to refuse new appointments or resign from existing boards. They typically apply only to outside –passive directors, relieve them from liability for ordinary negligence, but do not protect grossly negligent or intentional actionable conduct. And in some states corporations are allowed in their articles of incorporation to expressly prohibit officer/director liability or specify a dollar limitation.

Discuss: Are you for or against such laws? The proponents argue that the laws are required to attract qualified persons to serve on corporate boards. The opponents argue that these limitations arbitrarily protect the wealthy and that all persons, regardless of income levels, should have to answer for their negligent acts.

    5. Criminal liability of officers and directors

Historically, while officers or directors have always been liable for crimes they personally commit, or those they authorized - their corporations were not legally capable of committing crimes because the required "criminal intent" was lacking if the defendant was an entity rather than a person.

However, the current trend is to hold the corporation itself accountable for criminal conduct of its officers, directors and authorized agents in the commission of crimes or the failure to prevent them, to the extent of imposing criminal fines and penalties. This has arisen as a result of such corporate abuses as the 1980's Savings & Loan Association failures, the Exxon Valdez oil spill, the Love Canal toxic contamination, the Dalkon Shield IUD damages, the Ford Pinto coverup and, of course the Enron bankruptcy.

CASE RESEARCH CYBERCISES

The following recent appellate cases relate to the material in this section, illustrate the types of disputes that may occur, and demonstrate how they are judicially decided. Notice how the court opinions follow a predictable format – (1) the facts creating the dispute are summarized, (2) the rules of law that apply to the legal issues presented are set forth, based upon the prior cases or statutes of the state in which the lawsuit is decided, or the cases/laws of other states if this is a case of first impression, (3) the majority opinion applies the case facts to the applicable law in order to do their reasoning as to which party should win, and (4) the decision is rendered as affirming, reversing, or remanding for a new trial the decision of the lower trial court. For each one of the listed cases, do the following:

1. Locate the case by name or citation, using an Internet research site like Lexis-Nexis, Westlaw, or any other site providing court case transcripts. (Print out a copy of the entire case, or highlight and print relevant excerpts)
2. Briefly summarize the dispute and the legal claims of both sides.
3. Who won at the trial court level? Who won/wins at the appellate level?
4. Who won if there was a third level of Supreme Court review?
5. What rules of law govern this dispute? Majority/minority views?
6. What reasoning was used in the majority/minority opinions?
7. Do you agree or disagree with the final decision? Explain why.
8. What business law time bomb(s) were involved? Discuss.
9. How could the time bomb(s) have been defused? Discuss.
10. Try to replay the case's facts to achieve a successful result for the loser.

Cases:
1. *Miner v. Fashion Enterprises, Inc., 2003 WL 21659093 (Ill. App. 2003)(creditor could pierce corporate veil to hold its parent liable for an unpaid debt because corporation has thin capitalization and violated alter-ego rules)*

2. *8182 Maryland Associates, LP v. Sheehan, 2000 WL 253649 (Mo. 2000)(general partners who signed an office lease are jointly and severally liable for breach of lease, including partners who quit before breach occurred)*

3. *C&J Builders and Remodelers, LLC v. Geisenheimer, 733 A.2d 193 (Conn. 1999)(when sole proprietorship converts into LLC, all prior obligations are transferred from original organization to successor)*

4. *MM Companies v. Liquid Audio, Inc., 2003 WL 58969 (Del. 2003)(board of directors ruled to have improperly impeded rights of shareholders by voting to expand from 5 to 7 directors, called board-packing)*

NOTES

IV. SECURITIES REGULATION

"A man stopped J.P. Morgan as he was leaving his Wall Street office,
and asked him for a tip on what the market was going to do.
'It will fluctuate,' said Morgan, walking away briskly."
Little, Brown Book of Anecdotes

"Here is the key to investing success.
There is plenty for the bulls, and plenty for the bears,
But never enough for the hogs."
Bernard Baruch

The more successfully a corporation operates as a closely held private company, the more reasons exist for it to want to "go public" by offering its securities for sale to the investment public. The basic advantages are:

- Cashing out – the original ownership stock shares of the founding shareholders that have a nominal cost basis are usually part of the sales offering to the public at a greatly increased value

- Raising substantial additional capital to finance company expansion

- Profit appreciation from rising stock prices after issuance

- Availability of employee and executive incentives through stock options

- Increased credit worthiness and overall business stature as a public company

- Merger and acquisition flexibility through exchanges of listed shares

There are also some basic disadvantages:

- Required compliance with federal and state securities laws including necessary disclosures/compliance and civil/criminal sanctions for violations

- Expenses of going public

- Increased regulations requiring corporate compliance

- Loss of privacy of internal finances and general operations

- Accountability to new shareholder-owners

- Diminished management control

The advantages usually outweigh the disadvantages, and once the company decides to go public it becomes subject to a wide variety of securities laws. We will examine them in numbered summary fashion after an initial discussion of the stock market crash of 1929 that was a significant cause of their creation.

THE 1929 STOCK MARKET CRASH

The October 24, 1929 stock market crash (Black Thursday) and the subsequent collapse of the U.S. and global economy that became "The Great Depression" triggered creation of the first federal laws regulating the securities markets. Their purpose was to protect investors from the widespread fraudulent business practices in the issuance and trading of securities that were one of the primary causes of the crash and resultant worldwide economic downturn.

Here is a summary of the events, courtesy in part from the informative website www.1929stockmarketcrash.com.

In the "roaring 1920's" the rapid increase in industrialization that started just before the turn of the century was fueling a huge economic boom. Both wages and consumer spending dramatically increased, and stock prices as well began to rise as billions of dollars were invested by millions of people who began speculating on the upward movement of stock values by buying large numbers of shares on margin. Many persons invested their life savings, mortgaged their homes, and cashed in safer investments in treasury bonds and savings accounts to get on the bandwagon of stock speculation as prices continued to rise. Financial institutions, anxious to increase their profits, also began speculating in their investments as well.

This large amount of unsecured margin debt created a potentially unstable market, since downturns in prices could trigger margin calls that would cause further sell pressures to raise the necessary cash to cover the borrowed funds. But the investing public, seeing stock prices continuously rising, ignored warnings from economic analysts as the buying craze continued throughout the decade almost without interruption.

The causes of the Crash were many related reasons, but they can be broadly categorized as:

- Rampant speculation fueled by unrestrained credit
- Manipulative trading activity practices by broker-dealers
- False and misleading statements by securities issuers
- Lack of periodic disclosure requirements for listed companies
- Massive insider trading

1. THE SECURITIES ACT OF 1933

The first federal securities law was The Securities Act of 1933, regulating the interstate *issuance* of "securities", and their sale and distribution to the investing public. This includes selling new shares of stock to the public in a "primary offering" as well as having existing shareholders sell some of their shares to the public in a "secondary offering." A company's first public offering is called an IPO, and while it usually involves stocks it can also be corporate bonds, debentures, notes or other commercial paper.

Unless the public offering qualifies as (1) an exempt security or (2) an exempt transaction, it must be fully described in a registration statement and accompanying summary prospectus filed with and approved by the SEC, the federal regulatory body having jurisdiction over securities laws.

Whether or not an offering is a "security" and subject to the provisions of the Act of 1933, or can be sold to investors without registration is determined by whether or not the facts satisfy the four-pronged test of *SEC v. W.J. Howey Co., 328 U.S. 293 (1946)*. In that case, the defendants operated an orange grove and wanted to expand their business. They sought the needed capital by selling rows of orange trees to out-of-state investors. They also sold a private service contract giving themselves complete authority over cultivation, harvesting and marketing of the oranges, because the investors obviously could not cultivate the groves themselves. Investors would receive their share of net profits out of the pool of oranges produced by the entire grove.

The court ruled that the Act of 1933 was created to provide "broad protection to investors" and ruled that the investment contract in question was in fact a "security", since it passed the test of :

1. an investment of money
2. in a common enterprise
3. with the expectation of profits
4. to come solely from the efforts of others

The Securities Act of 1933 is also known as the "Truth in Securities Act." Its two-fold purpose is (1) to provide investors with the material information they need to make an informed decision concerning securities offered for public sale, and (2) to prohibit misrepresentation, deceit, and any other fraudulent acts or practices in the general sale of securities, even if they are exempt from registration. The Act's emphasis is on "full disclosure", so that the registration of a security with the SEC simply means that the required information was furnished. Approved registration by the SEC has nothing to do with the investment merits of the security.

Registration of a security is not required if it falls within one of the following eight categories of an "exempt security" because the need for investor protection is minimal and is outweighed by the issuer's financial needs:

1. municipal bonds issued by governmental federal, state and local units
2. short-term commercial paper that matures in less than nine months
3. securities of non-profit issuers, such as qualified charities, religious institutions, colleges and universities
4. securities of banks and other regulated financial institutions
5. securities issued by common carriers regulated by the ICC
6. insurance policies and annuity contracts issued by licensed insurers
7. stock splits and stock dividends
8. securities issued in corporate bankruptcy reorganizations

Similarly, certain "exempt transactions" do not require the filing of a registration statement, even though they are still subject to the antifraud provisions of the Act of 1933 requiring investors to be provided with necessary information such as periodic business reports, financial statements, corporate notices , and related disclosures. The exempt transactions are:

1. Resale of securities by a non-issuer owner

2. Intrastate offerings (but as a practical matter this exemption doesn't exist because most all states have their own securities regulations, called "Blue Sky Laws", which impose similar restrictions as the federal laws)

3. Small offerings under Rule 504 allowing sale of $1 million of securities during a 12-month period to an unlimited number of specified investors

4. Regulation A offerings of up to $5 million in any 12-month period to an unlimited number of purchasers, so long as a short-form offering circular is filed with the SEC.

5. Section 4(6) limited offers of up to $5 million made only to accredited investors.

6. Private placements under Rule 506 allowing sale of an unlimited amount of securities to a maximum of 35 "nonaccredited" investors who must receive material information about the offering, and an unlimited number of "accredited" investors (corporate insiders, institutional investors, corporate buyers with assets exceeding $5 million, and natural persons with net worth of at least $1 million or annual income of $200,000 or more).

7. Regulation D offers under Rule 505 by non-investment company issuers of up to $5 million in any 12-month period to an unlimited number of accredited investors, and a maximum of 35 nonaccredited investors who must receive material information about the offering.

8. Restricted securities obtained by small offerings or private placement that, under Rule 144, must be held for one year before being re-sold, except for institutional investors owning at least $100 million in securities

If registration is required, the main criteria is "full disclosure" of various categories of information in the registration statement and the summary prospectus that will enable a prospective investor to make an informed decision whether or not to buy the security. These areas of required disclosure include:

- the type of securities being offered
- the registrant's existing or proposed business, and industry competition
- the management of the registrant, including names, addresses, compensation, stock options and/or other financial benefits, and other financial involvements with the registrant
- any relevant government regulation
- any threatened or pending litigation, or other potential adverse claims
- how the proceeds of the offering will be used
- certified financial statements

The securities are customarily sold and distributed to the public by investment bankers known as underwriters who receive a lucrative percentage of the proceeds for their services in publicly selling and distributing the sales offerings for their corporate customers. They also assist in evaluating a proposed public offering, its market timing, its pricing, and all related functions to hopefully result in a successful public offering. The customary types of underwritings are:

1. Firm commitment – the most common and best type for an issuer. The underwriter buys the securities from the issuer for a fixed price for its own account and then resells to the public, assuming the risk of successfully completing the public offering at their own set price.

2. Best Efforts – less risky for the underwriter because it does not require purchase of the offering in advance of the public sale. Rather, the underwriter acts as a broker, attempting to sell the shares of a commission basis payable if and when sold, or on an all-or-nothing basis. Small or not well-known issuers who wish to go public may be forced to use this type of underwriting. At the same time, strong companied may use this form because they have a known market and the commission is less that in a firm commitment.

3.   **Stand-by** – the underwriter agrees to buy for its own account the unsold portion of an offering. It is often used in "rights" sales to existing stockholders, giving them the opportunity to acquire more shares.

4.   **Competitive bid** – in securities offerings by public utilities, common carriers or governmental units the underwriting agreement is sometimes awarded to the lowest bidder in a sealed bid auction.

Section 5 of the Act of 1933 limits the activities of the issuer and underwriter during the registration process, dividing them into the following three periods of time:

(a)   **Prefiling period** – begins when the issuer first decides to go public and ends when the registration statement is filed. During this time no one may make any offer to buy or sell the security, including trying to pre-condition the market and stimulate demand through advertising or public relations media.

(b)   **Waiting period** – begins when the registration statement is filed and ends when the filing is deemed effective. "The "effective" date is automatically 20 days after the filing, unless extended or otherwise questioned by the SEC. During this period no sales may be completed, but the market may be prepared for the offering. Oral offers to sell may be made on a non-binding basis and prospective customers may sign indications of purchase interest so long as they also receive a preliminary prospectus. This document is a summary of the registration statement information, and is called a "red herring" because of distinctive red lettering on its border, and pricing blank, that cautions the reader that the securities have not yet been approved for sale. Tombstone ads may also be published in financial print media announcing the pending offering.

(c)   **Posteffective period** – begins when the registration statement becomes effective and continues until all the securities offered are sold or withdrawn from sale. During this period sales are finalized and each purchaser receives a final prospectus that includes pricing information, called a "statutory prospectus."

Liability for violations of the Act of 1933 falls under a number of its sections:

•   Section 12(a)(1) imposes express civil liability for the sale of an unregistered security that is required to be registered, the sale of a registered security without delivery of a prospectus, or any other violation of the prefiling period, waiting period and posteffective period requirements.

•   Section 8 allows the SEC to issue "stop orders" suspending the effectiveness of a registration at any time is it is determined there were materially misleading statements or omissions.

- Section 24 makes "willful violation" of any provision of the Act or of SEC rules a criminal offense, including those who knowingly "aid and abet" such violations. Offenses are punishable by fines and/or imprisonment.

- Section 12(a)(2) and Section 11 provide for direct actions against violators of the Act by private parties who have been financially injured. Section 12 targets underwriters and others who violate Section 5 of the Act. Section 11 imposes liability on parties who intentionally commit fraud or those who negligently failed to discover it. It has a broad application to all signers of the registration statement, as well as the issuer, officers, directors, underwriters and professional experts rendering opinions and reports - whether or not they personally knew of fraudulent misstatements or omissions.

  Actions must be brought within 1 year of discovery of the violation and 3 years of the first time the security was offered to the public.

  There is a liability escape clause called the "due diligence" defense, available to all potentially liable parties except the issuer, if they can prove that after their reasonable investigation efforts they reasonable believed that there were no material misstatements or omissions at the time the registration statement became effective.

2. THE SECURITIES EXCHANGE ACT OF 1934

The Act of 1934 created the Securities Exchange Commission (SEC) to enforce securities laws. It differs primarily from the Act of 1933 in its time focus. The Act of 1933 regulates the original issuance of securities while the Act of 1934 regulates the subsequent trading in already issued securities.

The Act of 1934 is similar to the Act of 1933 in its disclosure and continuous reporting requirements. Periodic information reports must be filed with the SEC by issuers (1) with assets of more than $5 million and at least 500 shareholders, (2) whose stock is traded on a national exchange, or (3) who have made a registered offering under the Act of 1933. These filings include annual reports (Form 10-K), quarterly reports (Form 10-Q), monthly reports of important financial events (Form 8-K), and monthly reports of statutory insider transactions (Forms 3,4,5).

All publicly held companies are required to register on a one-time basis with the SEC, differing from the Act of 1933's registration requirement for only the securities involved in a particular offering. This includes disclosure of information as detailed as that which appears in an Act of 1933 registration statement concerning the company, its business, its financial structure, its officers-directors-10% or more shareholders, its financial statements for the prior three years, and any bonus-stock option-profit sharing plans.

Disclosure requirements also apply in the following three situations:

1. acquisition of 5% or more of registered securities
2. a tender offer for 5% or more of registered securities
3. an offeror's offer to repurchase its own shares

Broker-dealers are also required to register with the SEC and comply with its rules. They are regulated to ensure basic competency, financial solvency, and maintenance of accurate books and records. They are also required to join a stock exchange self-regulatory organization (SRO) that has quasi-governmental authority, responsibility for policing its members, and enforcement authority.

The most well-known and frequently litigated portions of the Act of 1934 are its antifraud liability provisions and its prohibitions on insider trading. They allow prosecution for civil and criminal remedies by the Justice Department and also have been judicially interpreted to allow injured parties to directly sue violators.

Section 10(b) makes it unlawful "to use or employ, in connection with the purchase or sale of any security … any manipulative or deceptive device or contrivance" in violation of SEC rules. Pursuant to this section, the SEC adopted Rule 10b-5, which states as follows:

"It shall be unlawful for any person, directly or indirectly, by use of any means or instrumentality of interstate commerce, or of the mails or of any facility of any national securities exchange,
(a) To employ any device, scheme, or artifice to defraud.
(b) To make any untrue statement of a material fact or to omit to state a material fact necessary in order to make the statements made, in light of the circumstances under which they were made, not misleading, or
(c) To engage in any act, practice, or course of business which operates or would operate as a fraud or deceit upon any person, in connection with the purchase or sale of any security."

Thus Rule 10b-5 is broad enough to apply to all transfers of securities, whether by reporting companies or not, and whether made on a stock exchange, in the over-the-counter market, in a private sale or by virtue of a corporate merger – in which there has been a proven intentional violation.

Probably the most important regulations of the Act of 1934 are those related to "insider trading", which can be defined under Section 10(b) and Rule 10b-5 as the profitable buying or selling of securities of a company by specified classes of persons based upon access to material nonpublic information.

The class of prohibited insiders is very broad, including (1) officers, directors, employees and agents of the company, (2) underwriters, lawyers, accountants, consultants, (3) and others who owe fiduciary duties to the company not to take advantage of these opportunities, such as direct tippees and remote misappropriators.

In the *Matter of Cady, Roberts & Co., 40 S.E.C. 907 (1961)*, a director of Curtiss-Wright Co. called his broker during a recess of a board meeting to inform him that the board had just cut the company's upcoming dividend. The broker executed several sell orders on behalf of company clients before news of the dividend cut became public and the price of the stock dropped. The SEC found the broker in violation of Rule 10b-5 and imposed a fine. It also adopted the "disclose or abstain" rule of insider trading:

" Thus, *anyone* in possession of inside information must either disclose it to the investing public, or if he is disabled from disclosing it in order to protect a corporate confidence, or he chooses not to do so, must abstain from trading in or recommending the securities concerned while such inside information remains undisclosed."

The "disclose or abstain" rule applies to the following four classes of prohibited insiders:
- Corporate insiders – officers, directors and employees

- Temporary insiders – those who acquire inside information from a company source while performing services for it.

- Tippees – those who acquire inside information from an insider who does not unlawfully trade but gives them the opportunity to do so. Both are liable for the illegal profits obtained.

- Misappropriators – those who steal non-public in formation in violation of a fiduciary duty and then trade on it.

Violations under Rule 10b-5 have a broad application to trading in the stock of all companies, not just those registered under the Act of 1934. Also injured investors may bring suit in their own name without having to make demand upon the affected corporation to sue, and if they sustain their burden of proof any damages recovered go directly to them.

Section 16 is also an important component of the antifraud protection of the Act of 1934. Section 16(a) defines a "statutory insider" of a company as any person who is an executive officer, director or a 10% or more shareholder, and these persons are required to file timely reports with the SEC disclosing their ownership and trading in company securities. Section 16(b) prohibits statutory insiders from retaining any profits made from trading equity securities within a six-month period.

These "short-swing profits" are repayable to the issuing company in a direct lawsuit it brings, or by virtue of a derivative lawsuit brought by its shareholder(s).

The Williams Act, passed in 1968 as an amendment to the 1934 Act, regulated for the first time tender offers made by corporate raiders / sharks directly to corporate shareholders in hostile takeover attempts to gain control of their public companies when their Board is not in favor of the proposed takeover. It establishes specific disclosure requirements and antifraud provisions for the protection of shareholder – offerees, including:

- Fair price rule – increases in prices paid for tendered shares must be offered to all prior tendering shareholders
- Pro rata rule – if too many shares are tendered, they still must be purchased on a proportional basis

3.   THE TRUST INDENTURE ACT OF 1939

By 1939, investors in bonds, debentures and other similar corporate debt instruments that defaulted were prevented from suing to recover their funds by the terms of private trust indenture documents that governed their rights but allowed an investing bank to act as their trustee and often protect itself at their expense.

The Act protects against such conflicts of interest by requiring certain disclosures of information by the issuer of the debt instruments and setting minimum financial requirements for qualifying trustees. It was updated by The Trust Indenture Reform Act of 1990.

4.   THE INVESTMENT COMPANY ACT OF 1940

The Act regulates the organization of companies, including mutual funds, that engage primarily in investing, reinvesting, and trading in securities, and whose securities are offered to the investing public. The regulation is designed to minimize conflicts of interest that arise in these complex operations.

The Act requires these companies to (a) register with the SEC, (b) disclose their financial condition and investment policies, (c) give shareholders approval power over management contracts, and (d) avoid conflicts of interest by prohibiting transactions between the companies and their officers, directors or affiliates.

5.   THE INVESTMENT ADVISERS ACT OF 1940

An investment adviser is generally someone who, for compensation, advises others about the feasibility of investing in, purchasing, or selling securities but do not execute transactions on behalf of their clients like broker-dealers.

They are required to register with the SEC, and conform to rules created for the purpose of protecting investors, including record-keeping, advertising, proxy voting, custody of client assets and content of advisory contracts. In 1996, Congress amended the Act to provide that only advisers having at least $25 million of assets under management must register.

6.   THE SECURITIES INVESTOR PROTECTION ACT OF 1970

To protect customers of insolvent broker-dealers, Congress amended the Act of 1934 to create the Securities Investor Protection Corporation (SIPC) that protects in the same way that the Federal Deposit Insurance Corporation (FDIC) protects depositors in failed banks to the extent of $100,000 per account. By collecting fees from its member companies it creates a compensation fund that protects investors to a limit of $500,000 per account and a maximum of $100,000 for cash claims in each account. The SIPC also has standby authority to borrow needed funds from commercial banks and the U.S. Treasury.

7.   THE RICO ACT OF 1970

The Racketeer Influenced and Corrupt Organization Act provides both civil and criminal penalties against defendants who engage in "racketeering activity" in order to operate or gain control of "business enterprises." Since securities fraud falls within the definition of a racketeering activity, the government often brings a criminal action and private persons often bring civil actions that allow recovery of treble damages, attorney's fees and costs once a criminal conviction has been obtained. Criminal penalties include fine, imprisonment and forfeiture of any property acquired in connection with a violation of the Act.

Interestingly enough, Congress's original goal was to attack organized crime, but the Act has no definition of what that is or a requirement that a defendant's conduct be linked to organized crime. So the Act has evolved as an effective remedy against illegitimate business activities rather than a criminal tool against organized crime. Over 90% of civil RICO cases rely upon mail fraud, wire fraud or securities fraud.

8.   THE INSIDER TRADING SANCTIONS ACT OF 1984

A number of well-documented instances of insider trading in the "roaring 1980's" where the civil penalties imposed under the Act of 1934 were less than the unlawful profits obtained enabled the SEC to secure passage of this Act. It increased the penalties for illegal inside trading.

The maximum criminal fine penalty for each violation was increased from $10,000 to $100,000 for market manipulation, securities fraud and other violations including those of commodity laws.

Civil fines were increased from $10,000 per violation to a maximum of three times the profit gained or loss avoided from illicit traders and tippers. Fines are paid into the U.S. Treasury.

The Act is broadly worded in that it doesn't define "material inside information" or expressly limit its prohibitions to corporate insiders. Anyone who helps another person violate the insider trading rules is potentially liable.

9.   THE INSIDER TRADING AND SECURITIES FRAUD ENFORCEMENT ACT OF 1988

The increased penalties of the Insider Trading Sanctions Act of 1984 were strengthened even more by authorizing the SEC to pay a bounty of up to 10% of the civil penalty imposed to reward whistleblowers who alert authorities to the wrongful insider trading. These bounties are paid out of the penalty fines recovered, rather than from the U.S. Treasury. The Act also allowed penalties to be imposed on "controlling persons". They were not covered under the earlier Act.

10.   THE INTERNATIONAL SECURITIES ENFORCEMENT ACT OF 1990

The Act authorizes the SEC to cooperate with foreign securities authorities by providing financial records to them of suspected securities law violators, and to sanction securities professionals in the U.S. who violate foreign securities laws. The effect of the Act is to remove the geographical boundaries that could have previously protected suspected violators.

11.   THE SECURITIES ENFORCEMENT REMEDIES AND PENNY STOCK REFORM ACT OF 1990

The Act greatly increased the disclosures that must be made in penny stock transactions. Broker-dealers are required to disclose the spread between the bid and asked price, the depth and liquidity of the market for the stock, and how they are to be compensated for the transaction. Other disclosure requirements include risk, broker's duties and the legal remedies available to customers. The Act also greatly limited "blank check" offerings of penny stocks, where stock is issued by a development company with no specific business plan.
The SEC is also given power to issue cease-and-desist orders and to impose administrative civil penalties up to $600,000.

12.   THE PRIVATE SECURITIES LITIGATION REFORM ACT OF 1995

The Act amended the Acts of 1933 and 1934 to stop abusive litigation in which trial lawyers would file "nuisance" lawsuits to extract settlements from issuers and others. Prior to passage of the Act plaintiff's lawyer could file marginal case and demand production of millions of documents, greatly increasing the cost of defense. This would often result in a monetary settlement by the defendant(s).

To stop this form of judicial extortion and prevent legal "fishing expeditions", the Act requires (1) detailed pleadings by plaintiff identifying specific actionable conduct, and (2) an automatic stay of discovery until a judge rules on whether or not the lawsuit alleges sufficient legal grounds to state a proper cause of action.

The Act granted authority to the SEC to bring civil actions for specified violations of the Act of 1934 against "aiders and abetters", who knowingly provide substantial assistance to someone who violates the law.

The Act also provided protection for companies that include statements about future business plans and financial projections in SEC filings, by giving them "safe harbor" if those statements are accompanied by a cautionary warning identifying certain risk factors that may cause different actual results.

13.   THE NAT'L SECURITIES MARKETS IMPROVEMENT ACT OF 1996

The Act made major changes to the dual system of federal/state regulation of securities, while preserving state anti-fraud authority. The SEC remained the regulator of national activities, while the role of the states over local activities was preserved, including the right of state regulators to prosecute fraud.

Section 18 of the Act of 1933 was amended to provide that no state law requiring registration of securities shall apply to a "covered security," which includes securities traded on a national exchange, mutual funds and offers/sales of certain exempt securities. Differing state laws affecting broker-dealers were also preempted to assure uniformity of regulation.

14.   SECURITIES LITIGATION UNIFORM STANDARDS ACT OF 1998

The Act sets national standards for securities class action lawsuits involving nationally traded securities, and had the effect of bringing all such actions within the jurisdiction of federal courts and federal securities law.
The reason for the Act was that after enactment of the Private Securities Litigation Reform Act of 1995, trial lawyers began filing their frivolous lawsuits in state courts to avoid the stricter federal law. That loophole was closed by this law.

15.   THE SARBANES-OXLEY ACT OF 2002

This law is ranked with the Acts of 1933 and 1934 in its legal significance. It was finally enacted, after years of attempts, after the failure of Enron Corporation and other large publicly owned companies revealed massive accounting fraud and lack of accounting oversight. The law is also known as The Public Company Accounting Reform and Investor Protection Act.

The SEC describes the law as mandating a number of reforms to public companies to enhance corporate accountability and financial reforms, and combat corporate accounting fraud. It impacts the entire accounting profession in its business involvements doing auditing work for a publicly traded company.

The Act also created a new Public Company Accounting Oversight Board to be appointed by and overseen by the SEC regulating the activities of the auditing profession, with investigative and disciplinary authority, including foreign accounting firms that prepare or furnish an audit report involving U.S. registrants.

The Act provides tough penalties for those who destroy records, commit accounting fraud, or fail to report it:

- Failure to maintain workpapers – it is now a felony with penalties up to 10 years to willfully fail to maintain "all audit or review workpapers" for at least five years.

- Document destruction – it is now a felony with penalties up to 20 years to destroy documents in a federal or bankruptcy investigation.

- Securities fraud – criminal penalties have been increased to 25 years.

- Fraud discovery – the statute of limitations is extended to 2 years from the date of discovery, and 5 years after the act. Previous times were 1 year from discovery and 3 years after the act.

- Other provisions – protect corporate whistleblowers, ban personal loans to executives, and prohibit insider trading during blackout periods.

Issuers of public stock and their auditors must now follow new rules and procedures in connection with the financial reporting and auditing process that include:

- Second partner review and approval of every public company audit report

- Management assessment and reporting about internal control structures for financial reporting

- CEO signing of main financial statements

CASE RESEARCH CYBERCISES

The following recent appellate cases relate to the material in this section, illustrate the types of disputes that may occur, and demonstrate how they are judicially decided. Notice how the court opinions follow a predictable format – (1) the facts creating the dispute are summarized, (2) the rules of law that apply to the legal issues presented are set forth, based upon the prior cases or statutes of the state in which the lawsuit is decided, or the cases/laws of other states if this is a case of first impression, (3) the majority opinion applies the case facts to the applicable law in order to do their reasoning as to which party should win, and (4) the decision is rendered as affirming, reversing, or remanding for a new trial the decision of the lower trial court. For each one of the listed cases, do the following:

1. Locate the case by name or citation, using an Internet research site like Lexis-Nexis, Westlaw, or any other site providing court case transcripts. (Print out a copy of the entire case, or highlight and print relevant excerpts)
2. Briefly summarize the dispute and the legal claims of both sides.
3. Who won at the trial court level? Who won/wins at the appellate level?
4. Who won if there was a third level of Supreme Court review?
5. What rules of law govern this dispute? Majority/minority views?
6. What reasoning was used in the majority/minority opinions?
7. Do you agree or disagree with the final decision? Explain why.
8. What business law time bomb(s) were involved? Discuss.
9. How could the time bomb(s) have been defused? Discuss.
10. Try to replay the case's facts to achieve a successful result for the loser.

Leading Cases concerning the Acts of 1933 and 1934:
1. *Reves v. Ernst & Young, 494 U.S. 56 (1990)(promissory notes issued by a farmers co-op advertised to the public as investments were ruled to be securities whose sale violated the antifraud provisions of the Act of 1934)*

2. *Escott v. BarChris Construction Corp., 283 F. Supp. 643 (S.D.N.Y. 1968) (defendants did not qualify for the "due diligence" defense to Section 11 civil liability under the Act of 1933 that avoids liability for material misstatements or omissions of fact)*

3. *SEC v. Texas Gulf Sulphur Co., 401 F.2d 833 (2nd Cir. 1968)(defendants violated insider trading restrictions of Section 10(b) and Rule 10b-5 of the Act of 1934, and the SEC first applied the "disclose or abstain" rule)*

4. *Winston v. Federal Express Corporation, 853 F.2d 455 (6th Cir. 1988)(defendant was an officer of the corp. who bought and sold shares for a profit within six months, violating Section 16(b) of the Act of 1934)*

5.   *Herman & MacLean v. Huddleston, 459 U.S. 375 (1983)(a private right to sue for securities fraud exists under Section 10(b) of the Act of 1934)*

6.   *SEC v. Lund, 570 F.Supp. 1397 (C.D. Cal. 1978)(temporary insider liability under Rule 10b-5)*

7.   *SEC v. Cherif, 933 F.2d 403 (7th Cir. 1991)(misappropriation liability under Rule 10b-5)*

8.   *SEC v. Dirks, 463 U.S. 646 (1983)(tipper-tippee liability under Rule 10b-5)*

9.   *Paramount Communications, Inc. v. Time, Inc., 571 A.2d 1140 (Del. 1990)(incumbent management can 'just say no' to a tender offer so long as it shows it is acting in the long-term interests of its shareholders)*

NOTES

V. BANKRUPTCY

John Joyce was renowned as a heavy drinker and frequently in debt.
After his death, when his son, Irish writer James Joyce, was asked
What his father had been, he replied,
"He was a bankrupt."
Little, Brown, Book of Anecdotes

One would hope that we would be so successful in managing the legal factor that our business enterprise would not be threatened financially. But sometimes, no matter how skillful we are, how advanced our degree of anticipatory thinking, how precise our usage of preventive law concepts – "stuff" sometimes happens that requires us to consider utilizing the financial protection provided by our bankruptcy laws.

Go no further than the local true stories of South Beach restaurant and hotel business ventures that had grand openings set for the week of September 11, 2001, a time when the "snow bird" tourists usually began their annual pilgrimage to sunny Miami. After the Twin Towers terrorist attacks of that date, business worldwide collapsed for a period of time, and many seemingly profitable ventures failed.

1. The legal basis of our Bankruptcy laws

As we know, many our laws are based upon English law. In the England of the 17th and 18th century, when a person was unable to pay his debts he became the legal servant of his creditor until he repaid the obligation through his wages, or was sent to debtor's prison. This view of the legal relationship between debtors and creditors was extremely harsh.

This was one of the many reasons that the founders of this country fled their native England, seeking the various freedoms they expressed in the Constitution, Bill of Rights and related enactments that are our legal foundation.

Our law of bankruptcy derives from the U.S. Constitution, Article I, Section 8, which grants to Congress the authority to establish "uniform laws on the subject of bankruptcy throughout the United States."

Thus, our bankruptcy law is exclusively federal in its creation and implementation. There are federal bankruptcy courts in each federal district trial court jurisdiction, and the rules of law are statutes created under Title 11 of the U.S. Code, known collectively as The Bankruptcy Code of 1978, as revised by the Bankruptcy Reform Act of 1994.

The Bankruptcy Reform Bill of 2001 amended a number of the prior sections, and was passed by the U.S. Senate and House in March of 2001.

109

While awaiting conference committee resolution of differences between two versions of the bill, it was sidetracked by various events including the September 11th terrorist attacks, the Enron collapse of early 2002, numerous abortion and gay marriage issues that caused political conflict between House and Senate in late 2002. It was re-worked and passed again by the House in early 2004, and then after extensive debate it was passed by the Senate and signed into law on April 20, 2005 as the "Bankruptcy Abuse Prevention and Consumer Protection Act" of 2005, with a 6-month window to become effective October 20. 2005.

The full title reflected the inherent Bankruptcy conflict between debtors and their creditors. Credit card companies, major supporters of the new Act, said reform of the bankruptcy process allowing debtors to be discharged from paying valid debts was long overdue. Opponents argued the credit card companies caused their own problems by flooding the market with new accounts and encouraging customers to run large balances. Opponents also complained the basic "fresh start" premise of Bankruptcy was been compromised by making it too difficult for truly needy debtors to be relieved from their financial burdens.

The basic thrust of the new Act was to make it much more difficult for debtors to qualify for Chapter 7 debt discharges, and require Chapter 13 payment plans instead. It modified certain aspects of Chapters 7 and 13, while essentially keeping Chapter 11 Corporate Reorganization intact. (The changes of the new Act will be discussed after we first examine the main features of Chapters 7, 13 and 11.)

2. The purpose of Bankruptcy laws

The theoretical purpose of our bankruptcy laws is to try to balance the rights of both debtors and creditors. Honest debtors who have reached a point of financial no return may seek bankruptcy protection from creditors seizing their property.

This is provided in the form of an automatic stay of pending creditor proceedings in Chapters 7 and 11, debt discharge in Chapter 7, restructured debt reorganization in Chapter 11, and mandated creditor repay plans in Chapter 13.

In exchange debtors are required to make full disclosure of their financial condition and turning their non-exempt assets over to the court for sale to pay their creditors. The debtor is given a 2nd chance or fresh start in life by relieving them of the previous legal obligations or restructuring their debt. Creditors are repaid from the sales proceeds of the debtor's available assets or are repaid in modified form.

In actuality, our bankruptcy laws rarely please creditors. Bona-fide debts may be legally cancelled if a debtor is discharged in bankruptcy in Chapter 7. Debtors are allowed to keep exempt property. They also may be allowed to stay in active business while their creditors are restrained from doing anything to enforce valid debts in Chapter 11.

Pending legal actions in state courts may be stayed by the debtor's mere act of filing for bankruptcy, and all further proceedings halted unless the federal bankruptcy judge grants permission. The threat of filing for bankruptcy is often used as a bargaining tactic to re-negotiate bad business deals or re-structure previously agreed contractual obligations.

And in our financially permissive society, new credit is often extended to parties who have a history of one or more bankruptcies. The concept of a debtor working multiple jobs for as long as it took to pay off his debts in full has been seriously eroded by our liberal bankruptcy laws.

The basic three categories of bankruptcy protection for insolvent debtors are summarized below and remain in place under the new law except as amended:

(1) Chapter 7 liquidation is used primarily by individuals whose non-exempt assets are turned over to the bankruptcy trustee to be sold and used to pay listed creditors. Unpaid balances remaining due are cancelled.

(2) Chapter 11 reorganization allows companies with financial problems to operate while they try to come up with a mutually agreeable plan to restructure existing creditor debt and then emerge from bankruptcy. If unsuccessful, the proceedings are converted to a Chapter 7 liquidation. Creditor actions are stayed during the pendency of both Chapters 7 and 11.

(3) Chapter 13 consumer debt adjustment allows persons with financial problems to work out creditor repayment plans.

Chapter 7 – Liquidation

1. Basics
- The most common bankruptcy filing – available to individuals, partnerships and corporations. (Note: Only individual filings may result in debt discharge. Entities must liquidate under state law prior to completion of proceedings.)

- Voluntary petition – filed by debtor individually, jointly with spouse, or as entity, with attached schedules of assets, liabilities, income and expenses. (**Note: assets acquired by the debtor after filing are not part of the bankruptcy estate, except for inheritances, gifts, lottery winnings, divorce settlements, and life insurance proceeds received within 180 days after filing.)

- Involuntary petition – filed by 3 creditors if debtor has more than 12, or one creditor, if under 12, who is owed at least $11,625.

- If debtor is unable to pay debts as they come due, proceedings will proceed.

- Filing creates automatic stay of all legal proceedings until released by order of the bankruptcy court (filing new actions or enforcing old ones), freezes all creditors in existing priority positions, and shifts jurisdiction to federal bankruptcy court by its entry of "Order of Relief." (See *Jennings Enterprises, Inc. v. Carte, 481 S.E.2d 541 (Ga.App. 1997)(State judgment and lien foreclosure sale of Mercedes autos after bankruptcy stay order was void.)*

    However, actions to enforce domestic obligations for alimony and child support are not stayed by a bankruptcy filing.

- Court appoints Bankruptcy Trustee, creditors confirm it at first meeting, and Trustee becomes legal owner of all debtors' non-exempt property. Trustee's duties may include:

    o Employ needed professionals – lawyers, accountants, appraisers
    o Verify accuracy of petition and attached schedules
    o Document debtor's assets and liabilities
    o Separate debtor's exempt property
    o Attend/conduct 1st meeting of creditors
    o Communicate with debtor's
    o Verify accuracy of claims creditor submitted
    o File or defend necessary lawsuits
    o Make periodic reports to creditors and court
    o Sell assets, compromise claims, create a cash payment fund
    o Distribute cash proceeds per claim priorities
    o Sign off on debtor's discharge

- 1st meeting of creditors is held within 30 days of filing – debtor testifies and verifies accuracy of finances, answers creditor's questions – conducted by Trustee - Judge does not attend – creditors must file proof of claims within 6 months to participate in distribution of proceeds. Secured creditors are not affected by bankruptcy, but file claims as a recommended procedure.

    Priority of unsecured claims are in the following order:
- Costs/expenses of administration - fees due trustee and professionals
- Administrative claims arising after filing but before trustee appointment, commonly known as "gap creditors."
- Administrative claims during trustee's administration
- Claims for wages, salaries, commissions earned within 90 days before filing, but limited to $4,650 per person
- Claims for retirement plan contributions within 180 days of filing, but limited to $4,650 per person
- Claims for deposits made by consumer creditors up to $2,100 each
- Alimony and domestic support obligations

- Income and property taxes due governmental units
- All other unsecured creditors
- Balance, if any, returned to debtor

2. Debtor's Exemptions

The purpose of the Bankruptcy Laws is not to ruin a debtor, because recovery to financial health is good news for all parties. Thus certain property deemed essential for the debtor's well being is allowed to be retained.

Exemption categories may also be expanded by separate state laws. Married couple filings may double the exemptions. Pre-2005 exempt categories were:

- Real estate homestead exemption up to $17,450 (**Florida allows unlimited amount for ½ acre within city limits, or 160 acres rural) (Texas allows 1 acre urban and 200 acres rural)

- $850 "wild card" plus up to $8,075 of unused residence exemption

- Motor vehicle equity up to $2,775 (**Florida allows $1,000)
- Total household goods/personal property up to $9,300

- Personal jewelry up to $1,150

- Any other property up to $800 (**Florida allows $1,000)

- Professional books, implements up to $1,500

- Life insurance contracts up to $9,300 cash value (**Florida allows annuity contracts, disability and illness benefits)

- Government benefits and pensions, including social security, veteran's benefits, unemployment compensation and public assistance

- Retirement benefits, if exempt under state law – (See *In re Witwer, 148 Bankr. 930 (1992)(California doctor's retirement plan worth $1.8 million was exempt from his bankrupt estate)* – now all retirement benefits are exempt per *Rousey v. Jacomay, 125 Sup.Ct. 1561 (2005).*

- Death and disability benefits

- Alimony and child support payments

- Personal injury claim awards up to $17,425

- 75% of earned but unpaid wages (**Florida allows 100%)

- Crime victim reparations, personal injury and wrongful death awards, and life insurance proceeds needed for support

- Pension, profit-sharing and stock bonus plans if needed for support

3. **Debtor's Non-Dischargeable Debts**

Contrary to popular belief, not all debts of the bankrupt may be cancelled. Certain types of obligations survive bankruptcy based upon public policy considerations, and may be enforced by creditors after bankruptcy proceedings are concluded. These are the categories:

- Alimony, child support, and other financial family obligations

- Tax debts accrued within 3 years of filing, including loans to pay taxes

- Fines/penalties for law violations, including traffic tickets, and customs duties

- Claims for willful/malicious injury to person/property (See *Kawaauhau v. Geiger, 118 S.Ct. 974 (1998)(medical malpractice judgment of $355,000 against bankrupt doctor was dischargeable)*

- Claims for fraud or abuse of fiduciary relationships

- Purchase of luxury goods over $1,150 within 60 days of filing

- Credit card or cash advances over $1,150 to consumer-debtor within 60 days of filing

- Debts arising from driving a "motor vehicle" while intoxicated (See *In re Greenway, 71 F.3d 1177 (5th Cir. 1996)(money judgment against debtor for negligently operating a motorboat while drunk was dischargeable in his bankruptcy)* Note: The 2001 Revised Code added the word "vessel", eliminating this loophole.

- Creditor debts not listed in filed schedules

- Student loans, unless repayment causes "undue hardship" on the debtor and the debtor's dependents

The student loan category is interesting. Prior to October 7, 1998, they were legally dischargeable if in pay status for 7 years. Many students whose education was financed in whole or part by these loans abused the privilege and successfully wiped out the debts by discharge in Chapter 7 proceedings.

This caused intense media and congressional focus, resulting in passage of Section 523(a)(8) of the Bankruptcy Code, which denied discharge "for an educational loan made, insured, or guaranteed by a governmental unit" unless it "will impose an undue hardship on the debtor and the debtor's dependents." The drafters of the Code failed to define "undue hardship", so the courts did in this famous test case.

In *Brunner v. New York State Higher Education Services Corp., 831 F.2d 395 (2nd Cir 1987)*, the court set forth the three-part test for "undue hardship":

"(1) that the debtor cannot maintain, based on current income and expenses, a 'minimal' standard of living for herself and her dependents if forced to repay the loans; (2) that additional circumstances exist indicating that this state of affairs is likely to persist for a significant portion of the repayment period for student loans; and (3) that the debtor has made good faith efforts to repay the loans."

Bankruptcy judges require specific hearings for student loan hardship discharges, and strict proof is required.

In re *Hanson, 397 F.3d 482 (7th Cir. 2005)* was an unsuccessful attempt to be discharged from a student loan for Hanson's college education. He had borrowed from 1980 to 1987 and defaulted in 1989. A judgment of $31,500 was entered against him. He filed for Chapter 13, with a 60-month payment plan for part of the debt. After completing the payments, he was discharged from the balance due. (Note: Chapter 13 also allows hardship discharges.)

"Unless Hanson can show undue hardship at a hearing specifically to address the student loan, he is liable for the remainder of the debt. The 60-month repayment period was not intended to eliminate the debt, only provide a time for Hanson to deal with the problem. The Bankruptcy Code is explicit about such matters and the debt cannot be extinguished without a specific hearing on that matter, which was not done."

Other court decisions further clarified the test to require the debtor seeking discharge to also prove his financial prospects are so "hopeless" that he won't be able to make payments in the foreseeable future – and the debtor's entire loan payment history is to be examined as a part of the overall analysis.

4. Debtor's Discharge
After the assets of the bankrupt estate are distributed by the Trustee in accordance with required payment priorities and filed claims are satisfied to the extent monies are available, the remaining unpaid amounts due creditors are cancelled by virtue of "Order of Discharge" entered by the court.

A bankrupt who convinces new creditors to extend credit could theoretically make a career of incurring debt and then escaping payment by filing in bankruptcy every year. But this was anticipated by the drafters of the Code in making a discharge available under current law only once every six years. (Note: The Act of 2005 limits refiling to once every eight years.)

Certain debt's, which do not fall within the "non-dischargeable" category, may nevertheless be essentially treated that way if successfully challenged by a creditor or other party in interest. If discharge of a debt is denied, the legal obligation to pay survives the bankruptcy

This broad category covers various acts of deception by the debtor, which fall within a broad definition of "fraud." This includes financial misrepresentations, concealment of assets, removal of assets from court jurisdiction, falsification of records, and related breaches of trust including a failure to comply with required procedures in the bankruptcy proceedings.

5. Debtor's Avoidable Transfers
Debtors sometimes try to hide potential assets from an impending Bankruptcy by transferring them out of their name to a "straw person", or pay selected bills of "friendly" creditors, or sell existing assets for less than fair value. These types of actions, called "voidable transfers" or "preferences", are a fraud upon creditors and are specifically prohibited by the Code.

Upon demand of the Trustee, the Bankruptcy court may declare them null and void so that they may be recovered and disposed of as a part of the bankrupt estate.

A. Preferential Transfers

The Bankruptcy Code has a six-pronged test for what is a prohibited "preferential transfer": (1) a transfer of an interest of the debtor in property, including cash, kind or the granting of a secured lien interest; (2) made to or for the benefit of a creditor; (3) made for or on account of a pre-existing debt; (4) made while debtor is insolvent; (5) made on or within 90 days prior to the bankruptcy filing; and (6) that allows the transferee to receive more than it would in the chapter 7 proceedings.

There is a rebuttable presumption of insolvency in favor of the Trustee for any transfers made within the 90-day period. If the debtor wishes to uphold a prohibited preferential transfer transfers it must either disprove application of the six-pronged test, or that either of the following statutory defenses applies:

1. The subsequent new value defense – protects the recipient creditor to the extent that new value was given to the debtor. The three requirements are: (1) a preference payment is received by the creditor; (2) for which the creditor advances additional unsecured credit or new delivery of goods to the debtor; and (3) which amount is unpaid in whole or part at the date of bankruptcy filing.

2. The ordinary course of business defense – protects the recipient creditor if the transfer made within the prohibited time period is in the usual and customary course of business, based upon a review of the following five factors to determine if irregularities have occurred: (1) prior dealings between the parties; (2) amount of payments; (3) timing of payments; (4) circumstances surrounding the payments; and (5) whether or not the payments are ordinary, customary and usual in the industry.

B. Fraudulent Transfers

The Trustee may avoid the following transfers made to a creditor or made for the purpose of benefiting a creditor within one year of Bankruptcy filing: (Note: the new Act extended the time from one year to 2 years.

1. Insider Transactions – transfers made or liens created at a time of proven debtor insolvency, to "insiders", which includes relatives, partners, officers and/or directors of the debtor.

2. Fraudulent Transactions – transfers made or liens created at a time of proven insolvency, including transfers for less than equivalent exchange value, made with the intent to hinder, delay or defraud creditors.

But take note that the mere fact that a debtor sells assets or borrows money using assets as security within a few days of filing bankruptcy does not otherwise invalidate such transactions – so long as they are not preferential or fraudulent. Many legitimate transactions that occur within the prohibited time periods are not subject to review. Usually, the creditors who feel their interests have been adversely affected by preferential treatment of other creditors are the complaining parties.

For example: Cash sales of assets, for full consideration are valid. Payment of phone, electric and utility bills in the ordinary course of business is not subject to attack. Satisfying domestic obligations such as alimony, support and maintenance are excluded from the insider preference.

In *In re: Jet Florida System, Inc., f/k/a Air Florida System, Inc., 105 B.R. 137 (S.D. Fla 1989),* within 90 days of beginning the debtor's reorganization cases, the net amount of $13,575 was paid to satisfy a prior debt owed by Air Florida to COPA at a time when the payor was insolvent. In voiding the payment as a preferential transfer and entering judgment in its amount against COPA, the court stated:

117

"The Payments enabled COPA to receive more than it would have received if (a) the Debtor's cases were liquidation cases under Chapter 7 of the Bankruptcy Code; (b) the Payments had not been made; and (c) COPA received payment of the Air Florida debts to it to the extent provided by the Bankruptcy Code."

In *In re:Tabala, 11 B.R. 405 (S.D.N.Y. 1981)*, the trustee and an unsecured creditor sought to invalidate a gift conveyance of the debtors' residence to their three daughters approximately 17 months before they filed a voluntary petition under Chapter 7. Since the transfer occurred more than one year before filing, the trustee did not invoke the "insider transfer" rule; instead the New York Debtor and Creditor Law's six-year limitations period was used.

In addition to creditors holding secured claims when the house was transferred to the daughters without consideration, there was an unsecured creditor, Carvel Corporation who had a claim for $4,852.92 for merchandise sold the debtors in their operation of a Carvel ice cream business, and it joined the trustee in bringing this action.

"Now, there is a rule of long standing in New York courts that a voluntary conveyance made when the grantor is indebted is presumptively fraudulent. We think this means that, if one indebted makes such a transfer, it is presumed, in the absence of some proof to the contrary, that he was then insolvent . . . It imposes on the volunteer transferee of one who has creditors the duty of going forward with proof to show solvency of the transferor in order to prevent the conveyance from being set aside."

"The trustee in bankruptcy is entitled to an order declaring the debtor's fraudulent transfer of their residence null and void as against the trustee so that the property so transferred passes to the estate."

In *In re: Woodfield, 978 F.2d 516 (9ᵗʰ Cir. 1992)*, the debtors, as partners, operated two Wendy's franchised restaurants in Washington and Oregon. Within 10 days of their Chapter 7 filing, they formed a new corporation (QFI) in which they each held a 50% ownership interest, and transferred to it all franchise operating rights, equipment, fixtures, inventory and restaurant supplies from their Wendy's restaurants, receiving stock of QFI in exchange.

Prior to the bankruptcy filing the debtors somehow ascertained that Bettis would be their trustee, discussed these transactions in full with him and his counsel claiming they were without value due to existing defaults with Wendy's. After the Chapter 7 filing, Bettis then filed a "no asset" report at the creditor's meeting.

An unsecured creditor (EVA) objected to discharge of the bankrupts claiming they had "fraudulently misrepresented the true value of their assets and had transferred the operation of the two Wendy's to a new corporation in recognition of a value in the franchises in excess of what they had disclosed," and successfully demanded turnover of the properties and voidance of the transfers.

"To deny a discharge under this section, the court must find that the Debtors harbored actual intent to hinder, delay or defraud a creditor or officer of the estate. The existence of this intent is a finding of fact reviewable for clear error. We may infer the intent from the circumstances surrounding the transaction."

"Certain 'badges of fraud' strongly suggest that a transaction's purpose is to defraud creditors unless some other convincing explanation appears. These factors, not all of which need be present, include 1) a close relationship between the transferor and the transferee; 2) that the transfer was in anticipation of a pending suit; 3) that the transferor Debtor was insolvent or in poor financial condition at the time; 4) that all or substantially all of the Debtor's property was transferred; 5) that the transfer so completely depleted the Debtor's assets that the creditor has been hindered or delayed in recovering any part of the judgment; and 6) that the Debtor received inadequate consideration for the transfer."

Chapter 11 – Reorganization

In reorganization proceedings the debtor's existing business is not ended and assets are not liquidated. Rather, the objective is to give the debtor a reasonable period of time to re-structure its finances and eliminate its business problems.

The debtor stays in business, continues to operate under court protection, retains all its assets, and makes equitable settlements with creditors, who may not interfere while a plan of reorganization is being created. Chapter 11 is a potent negotiating tactic when dealing with company creditors pressing for payment.

If successful, the debtor comes out of Chapter 11 as a re-capitalized and more financially stable company, for the mutual benefit of all. If however, the debtor is unable to properly reorganize, the proceedings are converted into a Chapter 7, and liquidation occurs.

Many of the largest companies in the world of business have experienced temporary financial problems and reorganized under Chapter 11 proceedings, including Chrysler Corp., K-Mart, Dow-Corning, Macy's and many U.S. airlines.

1. Chapter 11 Basics
- Usually for corporations, but also for other entities and individuals, and may be voluntary or involuntary

- Includes small businesses whose debts do not exceed $2million

- Similar administrative procedures to Chapter 7 for filing petition, federal jurisdiction, automatic stay, order of relief, first meeting of creditors, and court ordered lifting of stay for petitioning creditor(s)

- Debtor usually continues to manage the business (debtor in possession) and has similar duties to a trustee

- Post-filing unsecured good-faith creditors, and secured creditors share 1st priority repayment as administrative expenses

- Separate trustee may be appointed by court or elected by creditors to oversee or manage the business if deemed necessary

- Creditor's committee of seven largest unsecured claims, secured creditors and equity security holders is usually appointed

- Plan of reorganization should be filed within 120 days after filing (New Act sets maximum time of 18 months.)
- Creditor approval of the plan should be within 180 days after filing (New Act sets maximum time of 20 months.)

- Court extensions of plan filing and creditor approval may be granted

- Plan divides creditor's claims and shareholder's interests into separate classes and specifies how they will be treated

2. Approval of the plan of reorganization is the key to a Chapter 11 proceeding. It must realistically present a viable new capital structure for the debtor that will enable it to continue business operations and at the same time fairly treat its existing creditors.

Since different creditors have differing agendas, no plan would ever be unanimously approved by all, but the beauty of reorganization proceedings is that plan "confirmation" can be accomplished in various ways:

Voluntary Acceptance Method – affirmative vote is required of at least ½ in number and at least 2/3 in amount of the allowed claims of each class. If the remaining creditors are "not – impaired" they are legally bound by the accepted plan even if they voted against it.

The impairment test requires that they not be discriminated against such as equivalent creditors of the same class being paid more. The plan must leave basically unchanged their legal, equitable and contractual rights.

Cram Down Method – when the acceptance method may not be used due to "impairment" of dissenting creditors, the Court can legally require them to participation in the reorganization plan, so long as it does not discriminate unfairly and is considered to be "fair and equitable" under the Act's guidelines.

3. Confirmation of the plan – the Court must approve the proposed plan in order for it to be legally binding on all parties. It will do so if it is satisfied that (1) the plan is proposed in good faith, (2) it has a good chance for success so that the debtor will not likely need further court protection, and (3) creditors will receive not less than they would have in a Chapter 7 liquidation.

Once confirmed, the plan legally binds the debtor and all creditors. A final court order is entered closing the proceedings. The debtor is legally discharged from any claims that arose before its Chapter 11 filing that were not included in the plan of reorganization.

Chapter 13 – Consumer Adjustment of Debts

This section of the Act provides a form of reorganization relief for individual consumers who are having problems paying their debts as they come due. It is faster, less expensive and simpler in procedures than Chapter 11, and does not have the adverse financial and credit impact of liquidation under Chapter 7. Creditors also favor it, because they normally recover a much higher percentage of their outstanding claims.

Here are the basics:
- Voluntary filings by insolvent individual consumers who seek to reduce their debts, extend time for payment, or otherwise reorganize their finances

- Unsecured debts do not exceed $307,675)

- Secured debts do not exceed $922,975)

- Regular income is available from salary, commissions, social security, pension or other benefits

- Administrative procedures similar to Chapter 7, including filing of financial schedules, automatic stay, appointment of Trustee, and meeting of creditors

The debtor must file the proposed plan for payment within 15 days of filing. It cannot exceed 3-year payment duration. (* Note: Five years under the 2005 Act)

The debtor begins making payments to the Trustee within 30 days and continues to do so. If the plan is denied by the Court, the monies paid are returned to the debtor less administrative expenses.

If the plan is confirmed by the Court, payments continue to be made to the Trustee who remits them to the creditor(s). The Trustee is compensated by receiving 10% of the debts paid under the plan.

Confirmation of the plan will be made if it is proposed in good-faith, the amount to be paid to creditors is not less than they would receive in Chapter 7 proceedings, the debtor is financially able to make the suggested payments, and although unsecured creditor's need not vote to approve the plan – any objecting creditors will be paid in full – or all of the debtor's disposable income for the next three (five in new Act) years is applied to plan payments. Once the plan is confirmed, the debtor and all creditors are legally bound.

After all the debtor's required payments under the plan are made, the Court will enter an Order of Discharge, closing the proceedings. Even if payments are not completed, the Court, in its discretion, may grant a "Hardship Discharge", if the debtor's problems were caused by unforeseen difficulties such as job downsizing, illness or accident, other outside no-fault events – and creditors have already received as much as they would have been paid in a Chapter 7 liquidation.

(Note: Debtors under the new Act are testing the loophole of how long must payments have been made before being allowed to request a "Hardship Discharge.")

The Order of Discharge has the legal effect of releasing the debtor from any unpaid debts that were covered by the plan. It can be revoked within one year if obtained by fraud. Most of the same categories on non-dischargeable debts under Chapter 7 also apply to these proceedings.

But an advantage exists to the debtor since there is no time prohibition on re-filing such as exists in Chapter 7. Successive petitions for Chapter 13 relief can be filed if 100% of unsecured claims were paid, or at least 70% were paid using the debtor's best efforts.

THE 2005 ACT'S MAIN CHANGES

Under the new Act, which formally took effect October 20, 2005 (six months from signing), fewer debtors are allowed to file for Chapter 7 debt discharge and instead will have to complete repayment plans under Chapter 13. There will be less debt discharges and more repayment plans.

The main changes are summarized:

- To qualify for Chapter 7 debtors must qualify their income under a complicated "means" income test that asks: Is your family income less than your state's median level? If yes, Chapter 7 is allowed. If not, can you afford to pay $10,000 of debt over the next five years?

If you can pay, Chapter 13 is required. If you can't, another question is asked. Can you pay at least $100 monthly for 5 years? If yes, only Chapter 13 is allowed. If no, Chapter 7 is allowed.

- To qualify for Chapter 7 or 13 debtors must file prior year's income tax returns and pay any balances due.

- Debtors may tithe up to 15% of income to charity. This is a loophole that may allow income reduction to permitted Chapter 7 filing levels.

- Chapter 13 filers will pay amounts over 5 years (3 years previously) based on IRS living standards, rather than what the debtor suggests as being reasonable.

- Individual Chapter 7 debtors have to pay for and complete an approved credit counseling course within 6 months of filing for protection, and an approved money management course to receive a discharge.

- Child support and alimony have Chapter 7 1st priority repayment.

- Effective *immediately* on Act signing, Chapter 7 filers may only exempt up to $125,000 of real estate homestead property if acquired within 40 months before filing, limiting the "millionaire's exemption" previously available in Florida, Texas, South Dakota, Idaho and Kansas. State homestead exemptions are otherwise only available if debtor has lived there at least 2 years before filing. Homestead exempt goods are limited to one of each item, with value cap of $500.

- Refiling time for Chapter 7 is extended from 6 years to 8 years.

- Attorneys for debtor's may be personally fined for inaccurate filing information in schedules of assets and liabilities under a zero-tolerance policy for acting without "substantial justification."

- New Chapter 13 debtors will have to repay the full balance of auto loans, instead of fair market value. Since cars can depreciate as much as 50% after three years, fair market value is often much lower than the unpaid loan balance.

- Time for voiding Chapter 7 fraudulent transfers is extended to 2 years.

- Experts have noted an unintended flaw in the effect of the new Act's moving debtors from Chapter 7 debt discharges to Chapter 13 payment plans. Since Congress failed to raise or eliminate Chapter 13 debt eligibility ceilings, debtors whose income is too high to qualify for Chapter 7 may also be denied access to Chapter 13. For these debtors, there is no Bankruptcy relief.)

CASE RESEARCH CYBERCISES

The following recent appellate cases relate to the material in this section, illustrate the types of disputes that may occur, and demonstrate how they are judicially decided. Notice how the court opinions follow a predictable format – (1) the facts creating the dispute are summarized, (2) the rules of law that apply to the legal issues presented are set forth, based upon the prior cases or statutes of the state in which the lawsuit is decided, or the cases/laws of other states if this is a case of first impression, (3) the majority opinion applies the case facts to the applicable law in order to do their reasoning as to which party should win, and (4) the decision is rendered as affirming, reversing, or remanding for a new trial the decision of the lower trial court. For each one of the listed cases, do the following:

1. Locate the case by name or citation, using an Internet research site like Lexis-Nexis, Westlaw, or any other site providing court case transcripts. (Print out a copy of the entire case, or highlight and print relevant excerpts)
2. Briefly summarize the dispute and the legal claims of both sides.
3. Who won at the trial court level? Who won/wins at the appellate level?
4. Who won if there was a third level of Supreme Court review?
5. What rules of law govern this dispute? Majority/minority views?
6. What reasoning was used in the majority/minority opinions?
7. Do you agree or disagree with the final decision? Explain why.
8. What business law time bomb(s) were involved? Discuss.
9. How could the time bomb(s) have been defused? Discuss.
10. Try to replay the case's facts to achieve a successful result for the loser.

Bankruptcy Cases after the 2005 Act:
1. *In re Diagostino 06*-10384 – case ruled religious tithes were not an allowable necessary expense, and were disallowed in a Chapter 13 filing. This was based on the Act's wording that deductions must "provide for the health and welfare of the debtors or are for the production of income."

2. *In re Rotunda 06-60054* – case allowed payment to creditors in a Chapter 13 filing of $1,200 per month less than they would have received under the old law. This resulted from using IRS higher expense standards instead of debtor's lower expenses in economically hard-pressed upstate New York where living costs are less than median.

3. *In re Cortez 05-10459* – case involved a Chapter 7 filing by unemployed debtor whose monthly expenses exceeded his income. But four days after filing he was hired for a new job that paid enough to disqualify him. He was not allowed to stay in Chapter 7 because "post-petition events are to be taken into account in ruling on whether to dismiss a bankruptcy petition."

VI. BUSINESS ETHICS

"Ethics and science have their own domains,
Which touch but do not interpenetrate.
The one shows us to what goal we should aspire,
The other, given the goal, teaches us how to attain it."
Poincare

"Beauty is in the eye of the beholder.
Margaret Wolfe Hungerford

Webster's Dictionary defines an *oxymoron* as "a figure of speech in which contradictory ideas or terms are combined (e.g. sweet sorrow)." To this we might add "jumbo shrimp", "military intelligence", and especially "business ethics."

The question of whether or not a particular act or non-act is "ethical" or "moral" and therefore in compliance with a proper standard of conduct cannot be definitively answered since we are dealing with opinions about which reasonable people may differ, rather than facts. Our pronouncements of good or bad change from moment to moment, depending upon a multitude of subjective and objective factors including but not limited to the following:

- one's personal background, education, upbringing, experience - philosophy, psychology, theology, and
- the changing external forces shaping one's life such as societal values, laws, politics, and experiential learning.

Behavior acted out based upon a moving party's beliefs will of necessity change as those underlying beliefs are modified. And the shifting sands of personal and business life in our modern society are characterized by periods of sudden and dramatic change. Companies may continually weave their way between the ethical polarities of good and bad as they complete business transactions, being viewed as hero or villain at any given point in time.

When commercial transactions ripen into a dispute and the parties decide to seek a judicial remedy, the decision-maker is faced with a similar dilemma. Most business disputes are evaluated using the "objective standard" of *reasonableness* by asking, "What would a hypothetical reasonable person do under the same or similar circumstances?"

Large corporations are financially powerful, politically influential, and often insulated from popular opinion. While they often have a positive influence in the benefits they create through employment, products and services, tax revenues, education, and philanthropy - they sometimes overstep the boundaries of permissible conduct in their quest for profitability. There are numerous historical examples including:

- **Automobile manufacturing and engineering defects**
- **Drug products with dangerous side-effects**
- **Toxic industrial chemical leaks affecting land and water supplies**
- **Oil spills and natural gas leaks**
- **Tainted foods and other consumables**
- **Anti-competitive trade practices by large retailers**
- **Securities and financial business frauds**
- **Tobacco, alcohol and firearms injuries**

We also live in an age of more corporate accountability, courtesy of financial scandals that seem to appear daily, and have run the gamut from Savings & Loan bank failures, the Enron bankruptcy, scenes of handcuffed corporate millionaires, bursting of financial bubbles, Bernard Madoff, s Ponzi schemes, and the like.

The legal system, like the world of nature, abhors a vacuum. Abuses of power and flagrant misconduct that boils to the surface of media attention generates public outrage that often results in legislation and litigation to prevent the now-prohibited conduct from being repeated in the future.

One of the most effective ways to make sure companies do business in a proper manner is the ethical oversight furnished by federal and state "whistle-blower" laws that provide protection against retaliation and compensation for employees of companies who report unlawful business practices, especially attempts to defraud local, state or federal governmental customers.

Another example of such legislation is the Sarbanes-Oxley Act of 2002 (SOA), also known as the "Public Company Accounting Reform and Investor Protection Act." Its main purpose is to improve accuracy and reliability of corporate financial reports and protect the public through management accountability by regulating:

- **Corporate governance**
- **Financial disclosure**
- **Public accounting**

The Act was a direct legislative response to the widespread corporate fraud and accounting and legal complicity uncovered in early 2002 in the Enron, WorldCom and Tyco scandals and subsequent bankruptcies.

Our judicial system has its own unique deterrents to corporate wrongdoing:

1) Punitive damages are awarded to financially punish a defendant and set an example for others, so that similar actions will not occur in the future. They may be awarded if the plaintiff proves that the defendant's conduct was willful, malicious, reckless and outrageous – in reckless disregard for the rights of others.

They were originally limited only by the upper limits of the defendant's net worth. As the size of these awards escalated to huge amounts in various cases where the defendant's conduct was particularly objectionable, the tort reform movement came into existence to try and put limits on punitive damages. In many states they are now limited to a specified multiple of compensatory damages suffered. The U.S. Supreme Court has suggested in its *State Farm v. Campbell* decision that punitive damages should usually not exceed nine times actual damages.

2) Class action lawsuits may be certified in situations where a large group of plaintiffs have claims arising from the same event or act of alleged misconduct. The relatively small amounts of their individual damages would make it cost-prohibitive to file separate lawsuits, and difficult to get quality legal representation. But if one class of hundreds or thousands of persons "similarly situated" is allowed to be the collective plaintiff, the economies of scale and bargaining power change dramatically. Lawyers hired on a contingent-fee basis flock to these types of cases, since liability is often admitted or easily proved, and the only real issue is the dollar amount of damages to be awarded. Tort reformers also have targeted class actions in their efforts to reduce the size of court judgments.

3) Contingent fee hiring of lawyers allows persons to hire lawyers who may not otherwise be able to afford them and pay for representation on the standard flat-fee or hourly rate basis. The usual contingent fee arrangement is no-win / no-pay. The lawyer fronts all or most of the out-of-pocket expenses of court costs and litigation expenses, sometimes running into the thousands of dollars. If the case is won, the lawyer usually receives a percentage of recovery between one-fourth and one-third, with the client receiving the remainder.

So where does that leave us regarding ethics in the commercial marketplace? Are businesses ethically self-regulated by current laws? Should companies have affirmative duties to conduct their business in a socially responsible manner? How can this be done and still achieve financial profitability? And what does the term "socially responsible" really mean?

Is it really possible to reach a consensus as to what conduct is ethical and what conduct is not? Probably not, other than to note that these difficult questions arise each time an important decision is made in one's personal or business life.

The questions are probably best answered on an individual / transactional basis by educating ourselves as to the issues involved through examining (a) historical theories of ethics, (b) real-life examples of the ethical implications of doing business, (c) self-tests to filter business decisions through a critical lens of ethical conduct, and (d) crisis management planning at the corporate level.

A. SOME THEORIES OF ETHICS

1. **Ethical egoism** – decisions as to right and wrong are based upon what promotes one's own long-term self-interest. The focus is internal and subjective – "my way or the highway." Even though society may benefit from such acts such as the recall of a defective product, its real motivation is personal gain – improved public relations, fending off lawsuits or legislation, blunting stockholder dissent, and related ways to achieve one's personal view of proper conduct.

2. **Ethical fundamentalism** – decisions as to right and wrong are based upon outside sources of authority. These sources can range from the different personal teachings of individuals (e.g. Albert Schweitzer, Mother Teresa, Adolph Hitler and Karl Marx), gurus and religious figures (e.g. Paramahansa Yogananda, Dalai Lama, Billy Graham and Pat Robertson), and universally known written works (e.g. Bible, Koran, Torah, and Book of Miracles). The focus is external and objectified; what is "reasonable" is defined by how conduct is portrayed in the particular sources relied upon.

3. **Ethical experientialism** – decisions as to right and wrong, whether initially influenced by one's emphasis on internal or external sources, are ultimately determined by the life experiences encountered by the decision-maker. This is a philosophical middle ground between egoism and fundamentalism that seeks input from both in reaching a final decision, but is not mutually exclusive.

4. **Utilitarianism** – moral authority is determined by the consequences of one's actions. Jeremy Bentham and John Stuart Mill expressed this theory of ethics as requiring choice of a course of action that provides the greatest good to society. Individual benefits are secondary to societal results. Mathematically speaking, an act is morally right if its net benefits to society exceed its costs. Applied literally, this could read, "The end justifies the means," and could be a way to rationalize improper acts that lead to a satisfactory result, like vigilantism.

5. **Ethical deontology** – moral duties owed by persons are based upon universal rules, the most universal of which is Immanuel Kant's suggested categorical imperative commonly known as The Golden Rule: "do unto others as you would have them do unto you."

   Almost every organized religion has the Rule at its base in one form or another. Even the Hippies of the 1960's social revolution incorporated it into their lexicon as creating good karma or bad karma by each conscious act.

It also can be viewed as the circle of life – "there is a destiny that connects us, none go their way alone, all that we bring into the lives of others comes back into our own."

Here are some other similar religious prescriptions for ethical interpersonal and business relationships:

- Judaism - "Thou shalt love thy neighbor as thyself."

- Christianity - "Therefore all things whatsoever ye would that men should do to you, do ye even so to them."

- Islam – "No one of you is a believer until he loves for his brother what he loves for himself."

- Hinduism – Good people proceed while considering that what is best for others is best for themselves."

- Buddhism – Hurt not others with that which pains yourself."

- Confucianism – What you do not want done to yourself, do not do to others."

6. Corporate business responsibility – whether or not a company's conduct is described as good or bad may depend on its internal philosophy of doing business as set forth by its board of directors and carried out on a daily basis by its officers and employees. The three general polarities of corporate social responsibility are:

- Maximize profits for the shareholder-owners of the company. So long as laws are not broken along the way, no duty exists to assist society other than the residual benefits received through the company's direct profit-oriented acts.

- Profits are desired as a primary focus, but there is a corresponding moral minimum duty to either avoid or financially correct social harms that occur. This duty "not to harm" helps to balance the excesses of the profit-only way of doing business.

- Corporations must be good citizens. They have an affirmative duty to make society a better place by "doing good." This corporate citizenship theory would prevent a company from producing toxic chemicals, selling armaments or engaging in environmentally destructive activities. It would also involve contributing a portion of business profits to good causes.

129

Critics of increasing corporate social responsibility and broadening the ethical duties owed by businesses to their consuming public make a number of arguments:

- **Inept Custodian:** Corporate executives lack the expertise to make non-economic decisions. If they are permitted to do so, society will be materialized rather than moralized.

- **Hand-of-Government:** Governmental regulation is required to keep in check the natural inclination of companies to financially enrich themselves at the expense of society.

- **Invisible Hand:** Contrary to the need for public oversight of business, the profit-making focus of corporations will itself result in the greatest good for society.

Those who favor broadening corporate duties of social responsibility suggest that it is a fair exchange for legally allowing the corporate form of business, complete with its legal entity status, insulated personal liability of shareholders, and other legal advantages of doing business in that form. In return, society has the right to expect corporations not to harm to society, to be accountable for their conduct if they do harm, and to point their activities in the direction of promoting the common good.

As a practical matter, notice how almost any corporate decision you can think of could arguably involve some or all of these theories of ethics at any point of the business transactional process.

B. ETHICS, OR THE LACK THEREOF, IN ACTION

Large corporations are wealthy and powerful. Their business management choices in the area of ethical behavior constantly present themselves. They do many positive things to help society. Mistakes of judgment will occur from time to time due to ignorance or bad luck because, after all, business managers are human beings.

But sometimes they are not inadvertent, and (as seen in the first five examples of corporate lack of business ethics), may have been repeated, covered up, or are a part of a calculated intentional course of unethical conduct that suggests an arrogant disregard of the rights of others.

Though a company so inclined to unethical conduct may get away with it for a period of time, ultimately the legal system steps in and the guilty are punished and substantial monies are awarded. This is the common pattern of most of the well-known instances of questionable corporate conduct. What follows are six of the most famous or infamous, depending on one's ethical perspective.

1. McDonald's Sale of Scalding Coffee

When the news of the "hot coffee" case appeared in visual and print media as a short headline that read, *Customer spill burns woman, Jury awards $29 million,* the general consensus was that this was just another frivolous lawsuit.

Most agreed it was evidence the legal system was out of control. But as in most of these situations when all facts were disclosed, the truth was quite different. Here's what really happened:

In 1992, Stella Liebeck, a 79-year old retired sales clerk, was a passenger in a car driven by her grandson, and ordered 49-cent cup of coffee at a McDonald's drive-through in Albuquerque, New Mexico. As she placed the cup between her knees and removed the lid to add cream and sugar, the entire contents of scalding hot coffee spilled out on her lap. The sweatpants she was wearing absorbed the coffee and held it next to her skin. She suffered third-degree burns on her groin, inner thighs and buttocks.

She was hospitalized for eight days, during which time she underwent skin grafting and removal of dead tissue. The burns left her scarred and disabled for more than two years. She notified McDonald's of her injuries and asked that it pay her medical bills that totaled $11,000. It countered with an offer of $600. She then decided to sue, claiming McDonald's was negligent in selling such super-heated coffee to the public and failing to warn of its known dangers. She sought to settle her claim at that point for $20,000 but that offer was refused.

During discovery it was revealed that McDonald's held the temperature of its coffee at 180-190 degrees, based on a consultant's advice that it would maintain optimum taste although that temperature produced third degree burns in less than three seconds exposure. Other establishments in the area sold their coffee at least 20 degrees cooler, and it was also determined that coffee served at home is usually 135-140 degrees. It was also revealed that the company had received more than 700 coffee claims of burns from scalding coffee, including some to the third degree, during the prior ten years. Many of these claims were settled, amounting to more than $500,000.

Prior to the trial plaintiff offered to settle for $300,000 and the judge ordered both sides into a mediated settlement conference, where the mediator who was a retired judge recommended that McDonald's settle for $225,000. McDonald's refused all settlement offers.

The trial lasted seven days. McDonald's own testimony was very damaging to its case Its quality assurance manager testified that even though the company knew a burn hazard to throat and mouth existed with coffee served at 140 degrees or above, the company actively enforced its requirement that the coffee be held in the serving pot at 180 – 185 degrees.

A company executive testified that the company knew its coffee sometimes caused serious burns, but hadn't seen the need to reduce the temperature, consult burn experts to remedy the situation, or warn customers.

A company human factors engineer testified that the number of hot-coffee burns was "statistically insignificant" compared to the billion cups of coffee sold annually, even after he was shown graphic photographs of the plaintiff's burns.

The jury awarded Mrs. Liebeck $200,000 compensatory damages, reduced to $160,000 because she was found to be 20% at fault in the coffee spill. The jury also awarded her $2.7 million in punitive damages, equaling two days of company sales, finding that the company's conduct was willful, wanton, reckless and malicious.

After the trial the judge reduced punitive damages to $480,000, or three times the compensatory damages. After this remititur, the parties entered into a post-verdict private settlement. Post-verdict investigation disclosed that coffee temperatures at local McDonald's had dropped to 158 degrees.

Jurors polled after the case said that although at the beginning they considered it just a nuisance claim for a coffee spill, they changed their minds when hearing the testimony. One juror remarked that the conduct of the company demonstrated "a callous disregard for the safety of the people."

Question: You are the new CEO of McDonald's and have an opportunity to turn back the clock and properly handle this matter. What management errors were made, what ethical aspects should have been considered, and how would you have done things differently?

2.   Ford's Exploding Pinto Automobile

In 1965, Ralph Nader was a young lawyer working for General Motors Corp. who discovered a company cover-up of defects in the Chevrolet Corvair. He became the first high profile whistle blower when he reported the problems in his book *Unsafe at Any Speed.* That brought public attention to the issue of automobile safety and resulted in Congress beginning to actively regulate the industry.

At the same time, in the late 1960's, Lee Iacocca was president of Ford Motor Company, had successfully created and marketed the Ford Mustang, and now sought a repeat performance. Since consumer demand for sub-compacts was rapidly increasing, he championed the new Ford Pinto. "The Pinto was not to weigh an ounce over 2,000 pounds and not cost a cent over $2,000." The company was anxious to get it to market.

But there was a problem. During design and early production, crash tests revealed a serious defect in the fuel tank that caused it to rupture and burst into flames in moderate-speed rear end collisions that exceeded 25 miles per hour. Nevertheless, with much sales and marketing fanfare the car went into full production.

As accidents happened and Pinto gas tanks exploded, word began to spread that these were not just isolated incidents and a real problem existed. But the company made no official statements and did not order a product recall. When Congress considered regulations on auto fuel tanks, company lobbyists were at the forefront of a successful effort to delay governmental regulations for another eight years.

Whether or not Chairman Iacocca was personally aware of the defective design is fairly debatable. What is clear however is the fact that any delay in bringing the Pinto to market was out of the question. Executives and managers at all levels did not dare to raise the subject, and there was a massive cover-up that lasted until 1978 when Ford finally agreed to recall 1.5 million vehicles.

The impetus for the recall came from a combination of factors. In 1974, the Center for Auto Safety started to receive reports from attorneys of deaths and serious injuries in Pinto gas tank explosions and petitioned the National Highway Traffic Safety Administration to order a recall. It refused, and did nothing until 1977. In that year an investigative story exposing the hazard was published in Mother Jones News Magazine, using documents found in the Center's files.

The story cited internal Ford documents that proved it knew of the weakness in the fuel tank before the car was placed on the market, but an internal cost-benefit study suggested to management it would be cheaper to cover up the problem and pay death and injury claims than order a recall and modify the fuel tanks. According to Ford's estimates the unsafe tanks would cause 180 burn deaths, 180 serious burn injuries, and 2,100 burned vehicles each year. It calculated that it would have to pay $200,000 per death, $67,000 per injury, and $700 per vehicle, for a total of $49.5 million. However the cost of saving lives was higher, $11 per vehicle for alterations which added up to $137 million per year, so the cover-up continued.

Shortly after publication of the article, national publicity was focused on the California case of *Grimshaw v. Ford,* on which the movie "Class Action" with Gene Hackman was later based. In it the jury awarded Richard Grimshaw $125 million in punitive damages for injuries he sustained while a passenger in a 1971 Pinto, which was struck by another car at an impact speed of 28 MPH and burst into flames. Although the award was later reduced to $3.5 million by the trial judge, the jury's reason for the large award (the largest in history at the time) was that Ford had marketed the Pinto knowing that injuries and deaths were inevitable. The award of $125 million was equivalent to the profit Ford had made on the Pinto since its introduction.

With the publication of the Mother Jones article and the publicity surrounding the *Grimshaw* case, the Center for Auto Safety re-submitted its petition for a defects investigation to the NHTSA and a formal defect administration case file was opened. Based upon crash tests performed which verified its preliminary findings of serious gas tank defects, and the tremendous publicity being generated, Ford agreed to recall all 1971-1976 Pintos.

Between the time that recall notices were mailed and parts were available at dealers to modify the defective fuel tanks, six more people died in Pinto fires after a rear impact. This caused an Indiana grand jury to take the unusual step of returning indictments against Ford Motor Company for criminal negligence, but a jury found the company innocent of the criminal charges. Even so, it suggested a possible additional remedy to be used in the future in cases involved extreme corporate misconduct.

Question: You are the new CEO of Ford Motor Company and have an opportunity to turn back the clock and properly handle this matter. What management errors were made, what ethical aspects should have been considered, and how would you have done things differently?

3. A.H. Robin's Defective Dalkon Shield

A.H. Robins was a small family-owned Virginia pharmaceutical firm in the 1960's. Some of their popular products were Chap Stick lip balm, Sergeant's flea and tick collars and Robitussin cough medicine. Then it heard about a new intrauterine device known as the Dalkon shield that was being tested at the Johns Hopkins Hospital birth-control clinic by the clinic director, Dr. Hugh Davis. The device was a plastic, nickel-sized, crablike instrument to be inserted into a woman's uterus as a way to prevent pregnancy.

Dr. Davis had reported in the February, 1970 issue of the *American Journal of Obstetrics and Gynecology* that use of the Dalkon Shield reduced the rate of pregnancy to 1.1%, a similar result to using the birth-control pill. His article did not disclose, however, that he was past-owner of the Dalkon Corporation that manufactured the IUD device.

By mid-1970, A.H. Robins sensed a business opportunity, acquired legal rights to the Dalkon Shield, and hired Dr. Davis as a consultant. Within two weeks of the purchase, it began to hear of potential difficulties for use of the product since its tail shield design, unlike that of other IUD's on the market, was open at one end and the exposed nylon filaments could potentially attract bacteria and cause infection. It essentially ignored the warnings.

The company made some minor design changes, conducted no more research on the possible problem, and rushed to bring their product to market, launching a massive marketing campaign that included reprints of the Davis study.

Rigorous testing of the device and approval by the Food and Drug Administration was not required before release because it was classified as a medical device rather than a drug. Within one year, the Dalkon Shield had captured 60% of the IUD market.

As sales and profits increased, more news of adverse results appeared. It was reported that the pregnancy rate for the device was closer to 4.3% than the 1.1% advertised. In addition, some users were developing pelvic inflammatory disease infections and others were being hospitalized for perforated uteruses. If a pregnancy did occur, users complained of ectopic pregnancy, septic abortions, and premature labor and delivery. Some users became sterile and some died from using the Dalkon Shield.

Finally, in 1973 the FDA ordered the company to stop selling the product due to health concerns. It promptly withdrew the device from the U.S. market, but waited another year before banning international sales.

Lawsuits were also being filed against the company for damages suffered by users. Between 1974 – 1979 the company refused to cooperate, denied liability, and essentially played hardball, finally settling many cases for an average of $11,000 each. But then a Colorado jury awarded an injured user $6.8 million in damages, including a large punitive component, and the financial handwriting was on the wall. By 1984 the company had paid out $314 million in 8,300 lawsuits, still faced 3,800 pending suits, and new cases were being filed against it daily.

The trial judge in one of the pending cases summoned the top A.H. Robins executives, including its CEO, severely criticized them for their lack of cooperation and hard approach with their injured customers, and demanded they take some type of protective action on behalf of the many women who still wore the Dalkon Shield.

Finally, in October, 1984 the company launched an advertising campaign telling users that it would pay for removal of their Dalkon Shields. It also established a litigation reserve fund of $615 million to pay for pending and future claims, which was the largest of its kind for liability concerning use of a medical device. But the company never issued a formal recall of the product and continued to claim that the Dalkon Shield was not defective or dangerous.

By August, 1985 it was obvious the company's litigation cost estimates were too low. The sum of $530 million had already been lost by A.H. Robins and its insurance company Aetna Life & Casualty in 9,500 completed lawsuits, there were an additional 5,200 cases pending, and new cases were being filed at the rate of 400 per month. The company also had been sued by its own shareholders for its actions that resulted in the severe diminution of the company's value, and settled those claims for $6.9 million. With no prospects for financial recovery the company filed for Chapter 11 bankruptcy, automatically stopping all pending litigation, preventing new suits, and limiting amounts of compensation to be paid to injured users of the Dalkon Shield.

(A Historical note: A.H. Robin's financial meltdown and subsequent Chapter 11 filing was similar to Johns-Manville's asbestos insulation, Dow Chemical's Agent Orange herbicide, and Corning Glass's silicone breast implants.)

Question: You are the new CEO of A.H. Robins Co. and have an opportunity to turn back the clock and properly handle this matter. What management errors were made, what ethical aspects should have been considered, and how would you have done things differently?

4. Occidental Petroleum's Toxic Love Canal

Love Canal is a residential neighborhood in Niagara Falls, New York. Its name came from the last name of William Love who owned the land in the 1890's. He began construction of a canal to divert water from the upper Niagara River for an electric power plant, but the economic depression left only one mile of the canal dug.

The land was sold at public auction in 1920 for unpaid taxes to the City of Niagara Falls, who began using it as a petroleum chemical waste disposal site. Later the U.S. government began using the same site to bury waste from its military chemical experiments. In 1942 Hooker Chemical Co., a subsidiary of Occidental Petroleum, bought the land and used it for burial of more than 20,000 tons of its own toxic chemicals. When the site was filled to capacity in 1952, it was closed for further waste disposal and the canal was back-filled.

The time of closure coincided with the housing demands of the expanding Baby Boom generation of the 1950's. The City of Niagara Falls needed to expand to satisfy these residential needs, and sought to buy the portion of the land not previously used for waste disposal and use it to build an elementary school. But Hooker Chemical wanted to only sell the entire property and the parties ultimately agreed on its sale to the Niagara Falls Board of Education for $1 dollar, with the sales agreement containing a warning clause that explained the dangers of building on the site, and an exculpatory release of the seller from liability.

The school was opened in 1955, and in 1957, the City sold the land to private developers for a 16-acre rectangular housing development and constructed sewers on land adjacent to the landfill site. The new owners of the land were not warned about its dangers. After the houses were built and sold to individual owners, a number of them began to complain about strange odors and foreign substances oozing into their basements. City inspectors were brought in to investigate, but nothing further was done to solve the problems.

By 1977 the residents of the neighborhood where the school was located had an unusually high incidence of cancer and their children had a similarly alarming level of birth defects. The Love Canal Homeowner's Association actively investigated and discovered the chemically dug canal and learned of the origins of the toxic dump site.

Complaints were made to government officials but they refused to intervene. Hooker Chemical also denied liability, claiming that any toxic chemicals had come from areas other than their disposal site, but agreed to demolish the school that was on their former property.

The homeowners felt trapped because they had no public agency to defend them and their sickness levels increased since they could not sell their properties and move away. By 1978 the Love Canal had become a national media event. Responding to the overwhelming evidence of a severe problem and massive cover-up by local governmental officials and the corporate property owner, and activist activity that included taking two EPA representatives hostage, President Jimmy Carter used disaster relief authority to declare a federal emergency. But he claimed there were not enough federal funds available to move affected residents away from the hazardous area without congressional action.

After extensive geological tests conclusively established that the underground toxic chemicals had leached into household basements, polluted household air, and were the cause of the severe health problems, and public outrage continued to escalate, the Environmental Protection Agency filed suit in 1979 against Occidental Petroleum. Bills were finally passed by Congress to allow the Federal Government to fund initial cleanup efforts, evacuation and relocation of almost 900 Love Canal residents, reimbursing them for the cost of their now abandoned homes.

As a result of the pending litigation and the attendant publicity about the dangers of other toxic dumpsites that existed in various locations around the country, Congress created the Superfund Law in 1980. It provided federal funds for cleanup of the most hazardous toxic waste sites around the country and required waste dumpers to pay the costs. The federal judge hearing the case against Occidental declared it to be a "responsible party" under the Superfund Law.

After passage of the Law, the federal government worked in tandem with the State of New York to clean up the Love Canal site. Dioxin was removed from creeks and sewers adjacent to the Love Canal so fish would not be contaminated, and a leachate collection system was put into operation to prevent contaminated groundwater from spreading outward from the Canal.

In 1988 the state and federal governments declared that most of the area was again suitable for residential use, and the Love Canal Revitalization Authority began selling 200 abandoned homes north of the canal to new families. The FHA provided mortgage insurance for the re-inhabited homes.

Finally in December of 1995, the Justice Department and the EPA succeeded in negotiating a settlement with Occidental under which it would repay the federal government all of the $101 million it spent on cleanup, $28 million in interest, an additional $102 million would be paid to the EPA Superfund, and $27 million paid to the Federal Emergency Management Agency (FEMA) for its funding of the cleanup and relocation prior to enactment of the Superfund Law.

Question: You are the new CEO of Occidental Petroleum Company and have an opportunity to turn the clock back and properly handle this matter. What management errors were made, what ethical aspects should have been considered, and how would you have done things differently?

5. Exxon's Alaska Oil Spill

In March 23, 1989 the Exxon Valdez, a supertanker owned by Exxon Corporation and carrying more than 53 million gallons of crude oil (1,260,000 barrels), left the trans-Alaska pipeline terminal in Valdez, Alaska heading for Long Beach, California. The run was a standard route, having been traversed by various oil tankers thousands of times in the twelve years since 1977, when the oil pipeline opened.

The ship's captain was Joe Hazelwood, who had a known history of alcohol abuse, had lost his automobile license for drunk driving, and later admitted to having has several drinks on the fateful evening of March 23, 1989. Icebergs had been encountered in the shipping lanes, so around midnight when the Captain retired to his quarters, he turned the ship over to his third mate who was not certified to take the tanker into those waters, and ordered the helmsman to steer around the icebergs and then return to the shipping lanes.

The mate steered the ship too far south, and as it entered Prince William Sound it crashed into Bligh Reef at a speed of 12 knots and ran aground, rupturing 8 of its 11 cargo tanks and spilling 11 million gallons of crude oil (260,000 barrels) into the pristine landscape. It was at the time the biggest environmental disaster in U.S. history.

The response to the disaster was far from satisfactory. The Alyeska Service Company, a consortium of seven oil companies led by Exxon, was primarily responsible for quick response. When its ranking executive was called within one-half hour of the spill in the early hours of the morning he sent a subordinate to check out the situation and went back to sleep. The required disaster contingency plan Alyeska had previously submitted to the Alaskan government stipulated that any disaster site could be reached with necessary equipment within five hours. In fact, the first Alyeska barge did not reach the spill site until fourteen hours after the spill, was unprepared to deal with a disaster of such magnitude, and didn't scoop up floating oil in the first two days before it reached the shoreline.

In addition, Exxon officials at the urging of their counsel refused to comment on the incident for almost one week at which time its CEO refused to acknowledge the extent of the problem and didn't even visit the scene of the accident for three weeks after the spill. Initially Exxon blamed state and federal officials for delays in containing the oil spill which had spread into a 12 square mile slick in the first two days.

The spill ultimately grew to 100 square miles, and eventually soaked over 1,400 miles of coastline, killing untold birds, fish and wildlife and destroying unique habitat. Then when asked how it would pay for the massive cleanup costs a company spokesperson said it would raise gas prices. The public was further upset when the company claimed it was misquoted and blamed the media.

Finally the company launched a massive newspaper ad campaign ten days after the spill apologizing for it but still refusing to accept any responsibility. The public was unimpressed and remained outraged as the facts about the incident became public knowledge.

Eventually Exxon put together a full response team and worked continuously for six months to remedy the oil spill as best they could, employing more than 12,000 local residents who could no longer fish because of the spill. It then left the scene, claiming it had done all it could and had met its social responsibilities. The State of Alaska and the Federal government filed civil and criminal lawsuits against Exxon and its principals that were finally settled in 1991 as follows:

- Civil charges: Exxon agreed to pay the State of Alaska and the U.S. $900 million over a ten-year period for restoration.

- Criminal charges: Exxon would pay a fine of $250 million. Two restitution funds of $50 million each were established, one state and one federal. $125 million of the balance was forgiven, over strong objection of many Alaskans, due to Exxon's "cooperation" during the cleanup and upgraded safety procedures to prevent a reoccurrence. The remaining funds were divided between the Victims of Crime fund and the North American Wetlands Conservation fund.

In 1994 a federal jury awarded $287 million in compensatory damages to 15,000 fishermen and also returned a $5 billion punitive damages verdict against Exxon. (The punitive award was overturned by an appellate court in 2001.) Captain Hazelwood was assessed $5,000 in punitive damages by the jury, acquitted of operating the ship while drunk, but convicted of a misdemeanor offense of illegally discharging oil. He was also required to spend 1,000 hours of community service picking up garbage along Anchorage area highways. The Exxon Valdez was renamed the SeaRiver Mediterranean and is still carrying oil around the world, but is forever barred from entering Alaskan waters again.

There were some positive results of the disaster, other than the monetary awards. It resulted in Congress passing the Oil Pollution Act in 1990. It strengthened safety standards and emergency-response planning requirements, as well as imposing tighter environmental regulations on tanker ships that included the requirement that they must be built with double hulls to protect against leakage. The actual cleanup experience also produced a workable step-by-step procedure for future cleanups.

The massive publicity that surrounded the incident highlighted its cause as well as the less than cooperative early efforts of Exxon officials to realize its magnitude and offer needed assistance. This also resulted in a group called the Coalition for Environmentally Responsible Economies (CERES) creating a set of ten corporate commitments to help companies behave in a more socially responsible manner called the *Valdez Principles*. Many of the largest companies in the world have adopted them in principle, although whether or not they are applied on a day-day basis is still an open question. The ten points are as follows:

1. Protection of the Biosphere
2. Sustainable use of Natural Resources
3. Reduction and Disposal of Waste
4. Wise Use of Energy
5. Risk Reduction
6. Marketing of Safe Products and Services
7. Damage Compensation
8. Disclosure
9. Environmental Directors and Managers
10. Assessment and Annual Audit

Question: You are the new CEO of Exxon Corporation and have an opportunity to turn back the clock and properly handle this matter. What management errors were made, what ethical aspects should have been considered, and how would you have done things differently?

Note: The BP oil spill that occurred in early 2010 has become the largest and most severe natural disaster in U.S. history. All the issues of the Exxon Valdez oil spill are being revisited as are the larger questions of the adverse effects of our country's continued dependence on oil.

These first five examples of ethical predicaments have a number of common aspects. The companies were actively involved in either causing the problems, covering them up, failing to be cooperative, adopting postures of dirty tricks, playing hardball to resist prompt and proper resolution, trying to obscure the real facts, and generally behaving in what could be described as an unethical manner. When faced with no other alternatives due to relentless media, legislative or judicial pressure they ultimately were brought to a point of accountability for their misconduct at a cost of millions to billions of dollars to their stockholders.

At the same time, as occurs in most instances of massive corporate misconduct, when the smoke clears and the guilty are punished society eventually benefits because corrective laws are passed and judicial decisions are rendered in response to the situations so that we are better equipped to deal with situations like this in the future.

Our legal system does not usually act in an anticipatory or preventive law manner. Rather, it treats problems after they arise instead of before, and uses the past as prologue for the future.

For our final real-world study, here is a famous incident of product tampering that shows us how a large company can behave properly and do the right thing when faced with a potentially disastrous situation. It is a positive example of socially responsible corporate behavior.

6. Johnson & Johnson's Tylenol Murders

In the fall of 1982 seven people in Chicago died after ingesting an Extra-Strength Tylenol capsule that had been laced with cyanide. The Tylenol bottles had been purchased at different store locations. Initially the incidents were thought to be isolated and the causes of death were listed as unknown. But in a short time public officials were able to link them together, and media attention was focused on the deaths.

Law enforcement and company officials were able to confirm that no tampering could have occurred in the production plants due to their strict quality control procedures and the fact that the poisoned capsules were from four different manufacturing lots. Since the tainted capsules only showed up in the Chicago area, it was determined that the perpetrator bought some bottles of the product, tampered with their contents by inserting cyanide into some capsules, and then placed the tainted bottles back on the shelves of five different randomly selected local stores.

A national and local panic was imminent as three major television networks reported the deaths on their evening news broadcasts, and police drove through Chicago broadcasting Tylenol warnings on loudspeakers. A Chicago hospital received 700 telephone calls about Tylenol in one day. Many people in cities across the country complained of various symptoms and were admitted to hospitals on a general suspicion of cyanide poisoning.

Company officials at Johnson & Johnson's McNeil Consumer Products subsidiary immediately burst into action together with the parent company's CEO who demanded quick action in accordance with the company's 1940's social consciousness credo which puts customers first and stockholders last.

A massive and costly three-phase campaign was launched by the company to protect the public from product tampering and, at the same time, protect the company's reputation with the consuming public and its most profitable product which was Tylenol.

(1) The first phase was the actual handling of the immediate crisis. Along with the nationwide alert, Johnson & Johnson established working relationships with the Chicago police, the FBI, and the Food and Drug Administration to assure a continuing active participation in the criminal investigation. The company also immediately put up a $100,000 reward for the killer.

(2) The second phase, upon which the company's future hinged, was its public relations plan. The company immediately alerted consumers across the nation and worldwide, via the media, not to consume any type of Tylenol product until the extent of the tampering was determined. All production and advertising of Tylenol was stopped, and all Tylenol capsules were recalled from the market within one week of the incidents. This recall involved more than 31 million bottles of Tylenol with a retail value of over $100 million. The company also offered to exchange all Tylenol capsules already purchased, estimated at several million bottles, for new bottles of Tylenol in tablet form.

The company went even further in addressing attention to the general problem of product tampering by developing at its own cost a revolutionary new triple-tamper-resistant package, the first of its kind in the industry.

(3) The third phase was a comeback plan to bring the company in general and Tylenol in particular back to its former market-leading position. Directly following the incident the company's stock fell sharply as its market share of the non-prescription pain-reliever market dropped from 35% to 8%. An extensive marketing and advertising campaign was now focused on restoring public confidence in the following areas:

- Reintroduction of Tylenol capsules with the new triple-seal packaging
- Providing discount coupons for all Tylenol products through print media and toll-free telephone
- Launching new consumer ad campaigns
- Instituting retailer stock and shelf-level discounts
- Having company personnel make presentations to the medical community

The efforts by Johnson & Johnson were successful. Media articles about the Poisonings, the company's response, and its new packaging applauded its efforts, in a sense providing free advertising. From the inception of the crisis, the company had decided to fully cooperate with the press, radio and television. As the situation unfolded, the media then was able to do much of the company's work in rebuilding itself. The major news services estimated that the story was given the widest U.S. news coverage since the Kennedy assassination.

The company was also praised for resisting the temptation to disclaim responsibility because of its non-fault in this incident of a criminal outsider doing product tampering. Many other large companies have not behaved in such an ethical manner, including our first five "ethics in action" examples in this section.

The event also resulted in federal legislation that responded to the problems that arose and sought to prevent them in the future. In May, 1983, Congress passed the "Tylenol Bill," making malicious tampering with consumer products a federal offense. In 1989 the Food and Drug Administration established a uniform national requirement for tamper-resistant packaging of over-the-counter products.

When the smoke cleared, the company had regained their former market position and surpassed it. Tylenol is currently the number one over-the-counter analgesic in the country.

What about apprehending the poisoner? No one was ever charged with the Tylenol murders. But the main suspect, James Lewis, was convicted of attempting to extort $1 million from Johnson & Johnson by sending its McNeil Products subsidiary a ransom demand that threatened more deaths if payment was not made. He received a 20-year sentence and was released in October, 1995 after serving 13 years.

Question: you are the new CEO of Johnson & Johnson and have an opportunity to turn back the clock. Is there anything you would have done differently in dealing with this incident?

C. ETHICAL SELF – TESTS

The Center for Business Ethics at Bentley College suggests these six questions be asked before the decision-making process is completed in pending transactions:

1. Is it right?
2. Is it fair?
3. Does it harm anyone?
4. What if it is reported on the front page of your local newspaper?
5. How would you explain it to your wife, son or daughter?
6. Is there any intuitive internal resistance to it?

Classical ethical self-tests suggested by various experts in the field include:

1. The Test of Reciprocity – ethical conduct to others brings it back to you. This is the equivalent of the Golden Rule as a theory of ethics.

2. The Test of Common Sense – think about the consequences of your actions before you act. If a contemplated act doesn't make sense, reconsider or restructure it.

3. The Test of Communication – discuss the situation with people whose opinions you respect on both sides of the issue before making a final decision.

4. The Test of Image – consider whether the proposed decision is compatible with your best view of yourself. If it isn't you, don't do it.

5. The Test of Fallout – what will be the ripple-effect of the contemplated decision? View it like throwing a pebble into a still forest pool. The ripples first cycle outward and then return back to the point of impact.

In the final analysis, parties are guided in their decision-making process by a multitude of factors that are easier to identify after the transaction is completed and its full impact felt than before it has been made. What is your own self-monitoring ethical decision-making process?

D. DEVELOPING CORPORATE CRISIS MANAGEMENT

Whether or not a company can withstand a crisis is usually dependant on how it responds when the crisis arises. Once a crisis occurs, the company becomes an immediate target of the media, especially in this age of instant communication. The public's perception is usually that involved companies try to obscure the truth and avoid responsibility for their acts or failures to act. Silence and denials at the corporate level only confirm this perception. Because of this basic skepticism in believing in the good intentions of corporations involved in crisis situations, and the assumption that there are misdeeds or cover-ups, positive response-time is accelerated and a workable crisis plan is essential.

Here are some of the suggested steps in preventive crisis management:

1. Establish an advance Crisis Management Team within the company composed of a cross-section including expertise in areas of public relations, management, security, personnel, financial, legal and internal industry specialists.

2. Develop an advance Crisis Response Plan based upon a worst-case scenario so that all potential problem areas can be considered and planned for. These would include everything from the death or resignation of the CEO to allegations that company products or services are killing people.

The plan should include the who, what, when, where and how of dealing with a crisis. It should also produce in advance many of the possible materials necessary if a crisis occurs, including press releases, company statements, fact sheets, background information, scientific reports and communication flow-charts. In addition, the plan should be regularly updated and practiced with crisis simulations.

3. Practice information gathering through using available technology, including on-line discussion groups, off-line focus and discussion groups, communications through cell phones, e-mail and wireless technology, and media outlets and news clipping services

Question: You are the CEO of Any Company, Inc. and have decided to establish an ethical risk-management department in your company. What quidelines and procedures would you suggest be implemented?

144

VII. LEGAL TRENDS UPDATED

"The future is now."
George Allen

"All the ages are linked together by a chain
of causes and effects which unite
the existing state of the world with all that has gone before."
Anne-Robert-Jacques-Turgot

"The only reason people want to be masters of the future
is to change the past."
Milan Kundera

We initially explored "Legal Trends Facing Business Managers" in Chapter 7 of the main text, and discussed some areas of business law that appeared to be in transition.

The law never really stands still. It may only give that impression from time to time since the gears of change usually grind slowly. And then sometimes there are sudden bursts of change energy that literally take our breath away.

What may have been declared as "final" legal precedents at a given point in time may then be modified by virtue of new court decisions from various judicial levels until a Supreme Court pronouncement puts the subject apparently to rest – until the Court changes its own prior decision as times and society change and new topical disputes are brought before it for consideration. The same process holds true for constitutional amendments, legislative enactments, regulatory rules, and local ordinances.

The scales of justice are continually being balanced by the diligent efforts of plaintiffs to locate, develop and legally test new causes of action, and the equally diligent efforts of defendants to resist.

And there may also be instances where the process of legal change comes full circle, back to where it started in the first place. Indeed, it may truly be said, "the only constant in law (and life) is change."

Let's attempt to predict future Legal Trends for the basic text and supplement material. Here are 25 category guesses, listed in no particular order other than their journey from the author's mind to his computer keyboard:

1. Requiring losing civil litigants to pay attorneys fees of the winner.

2. Capping attorney's contingent fees to a stated maximum percentage of successful awards.

145

3. Setting definitive limits on punitive damage recoveries as to specified types of lawsuits and percentage relationship to actual damages.

4. Increased use of alternate dispute resolution remedies in lieu of litigation.

5. Examination of possible limitations in civil cases on the right to trial by jury and appeal of adverse judgments.

6. Consideration of modifying the rule prohibiting the state from appealling adverse criminal verdicts.

7. Clarifying the doing business and contacts tests of in personam jurisdiction to clarify legal application for suits against non-residents.

8. Codifying state laws to achieve more uniformity and predictability.

9. Reducing (or increasing) use of civil procedures such as summary judgment and directed verdict that remove cases from juries.

10. Expanding (or limiting) the fairness doctrine of promissory estoppel.

11. Eliminating the mailbox (effective when sent) rule of contract acceptance.

12. Restructuring the pre-existing duty rule of contract consideration.

13. Changing majority vs. minority rules for enforcing minor's contracts.

14. Unifying state statutory penalties for usurious loans.

15. Clarifying rules for garage sale purchases and unconscionable contracts.

16. Removing undue influence presumptions in voluntary gifting cases.

17. Increasing the Statute of Fraud's sale of goods $500 limit to $5,000.

18. Adopting "first to notify" as the U.S. contract Rule of Law for multiple assignments or successive.

19. Reducing the right of sellers of goods to disclaim their warranties.

20. Unifying state statutes of limitation for commercial lawsuits.

21. Creating clearer guidelines for allowance of class action lawsuits.

22. Setting definitive legal rules for social host alcohol liability.

23. Creating and enforcing new laws and improving existing laws for Cyberlaw, E-Commerce and Internet technology such as:
- Electronic agreement signing and contract document transmittal
- Paperless filing of lawsuits and document transmittal
- Social networking site usage and security
- Digital Rights Management for electronic communication
- E-Reader technology and licensing of creative works
- Cell phone, Wi-Fi, and related communication issues
- Regulation of Online Gaming sites
- Protection against Internet pornography
- Hacking, identity theft and related online e-retrieval issues
- Spam and related mass advertising issues
- Liability of internet service providers for unlawful postings
- Domain name registration and Cybersquatting

24. Major legal issues involving Criminal Law:
- Capital punishment
- Police questioning and confessions of suspects
- Criminal penalties and sentencing guidelines
- 4th Amendment search and seizure
- 5th Amendment privilege against self-incrimination
- 6th Amendment right to effective counsel
- Parole and Pardon rules and procedures
- DNA innocence projects and related financial assistance
- Payment of reparations to victims of crime
- Decriminalization of certain drug offenses

25. Tort reform in civil damages and mass tort litigation

There are also major Social Legal Trends impacting our society that may result in dramatic legal changes in certain areas:
- Abortion
- Immigration
- Health care reform
- Bank and Securities reform
- Women's Rights and The Glass Ceiling
- Separation of Church and State
- Gay, Lesbian, and Transgender rights
- Assisted Suicide
- Tobacco and Alcohol litigation
- Gun rights and litigation
- Stem cells, genetics, and biotech research
- Tribal gaming and legal rights of native peoples
- Legal rights of the elderly and disabled

- Workplace discrimination - whistle blower lawsuits
- Environmentalism – pollution, global warming, toxic dumps, oil spills
- Uses of nuclear and other alternate energy sources
- Political and Corporate finance reform
- Regulation of vitamins and supplements as drugs
- Commercialization of internet usage
- Expansion of consumer protection laws
- Growth of private philanthropy

Now you have the opportunity, as the course ends, to present your personal vision of legal trends. This is your own subjective opinion, based on whatever factors are important to you in reaching your conclusions. Pretend you have a magic crystal ball that can foretell the future. There are no wrong answers here.

1) Discuss 5 areas of civil law you would retain as is, and explain why.
2) Discuss 5 areas of civil law you would not retain, and explain your changes.
3) Discuss 5 areas of criminal law you would retain and 5 areas you would change.
4) Rank the top 3 civil law changes in order of importance and explain why.
5) Rank the top 3 criminal law changes in order of importance and explain why.

FINAL NOTES

VIII. APPENDIX OF CHAPTER CASE DIGESTS

PREVENTATIVE LAW

CASE 1 – TIME BOMB OF BUSINESS TAKEOVER

Successor Corporation Assumes Product Liability Risks if Same Business Continued	
Description	South Carolina high court held that when a corporation buys another business in bankruptcy, and then continues the same business, product liability actions that date back to the original business will be imposed on the successor corporation.
Topic	Business Organization
Key Words	Corporation; Successor; Liability
CASE SUMMARY	
Facts	Simmons was injured at a construction site when an elevated work platform collapsed. Mark Industries produced and sold the lift in 1990. BPS sold the lift to the end user, which provided it for use on the construction site. Mark went bankrupt in 1991. Terex bought its assets at auction free and clear of all security interests, claims and liens, as approved by the bankruptcy court. Terex continued to produce the lifts that Mark had been making and sold them under the same name. Simmons sued Terex for product liability for defects in the lift. The federal district court asked the South Carolina supreme court if, under South Carolina law, successor liability could apply to Terex
Decision	Answer. A company that purchased the assets of an unrelated company at a bankruptcy sale, approved by the federal bankruptcy court, was liable under a theory of successor liability in product liability suits involving the lift. Such liability could exist because there was an agreement to assume such liability, or, as here. Terex, the successor, was a mere continuation of the manufacturer, Mark. Simmons' suit may proceed.
Citation	*Simmons v. Mark Lift Industries., 622 S.E.2d 213 (Sup. Ct., S.C., 2005)*

CASE 2 – TIME BOMB OF NOT USING A LAWYER

Why You Hire a Lawyer to Transfer Property Properly	
Description	Wyoming high court interpreted two deeds executed by parents in favor of their children. It was likely that one kind of tenancy was intended, but one deed was not clear and the default rule of law would automatically apply a presumption of joint tenancy.
Topic	Real and Personal Property
Key Words	Tenants in Common; Joint Tenants; Deed; Quiet Title
CASE SUMMARY	
Facts	Mike and Dorothy Thomas (grantors) transferred real estate to John Thomas and Margaret Dickson, their only children "as tenants by the entireties with right of survivorship, and not as tenants in common," by a deed filed with the county clerk. They also transferred a second piece of property to John and Margaret by a warranty deed filed with the county clerk. Years later, a dispute arose among John's heirs and Margaret as to the form of ownership of the two properties. John's heirs claimed both properties were owned as tenants in common; Margaret claimed they were owned as joint tenants. The district court held that the properties were owned as tenants in common. Margaret appealed.
Decision	Affirmed in part, reversed in part. The grantors, acting without legal advice, attempted to create a tenancy by the entireties in John and Margaret, but the transfer stated "with right of survivorship, and not as tenants in common." Grantors clearly did not want them to be tenants in common, so the intent was clear and created a joint tenancy in the first property, which they referred to as tenants by the entireties. The second property made no such declaration as it simply transferred ownership to John and Margaret, which created a tenancy in common.
Citation	*Estate of Thomas*, 199 P.3d 1090 (Sup. Ct., Wyo., 2009)

CASE 3 – TIME BOMB OF APPEAL

<table>
<tr><td colspan="2">Prison Sentence Too Light; Be Careful What You Ask For</td></tr>
<tr><td>Description</td><td>Appeals court held that the district court improperly deviated from the federal Sentencing Guidelines by imposing a sentence that was too light. The defendants appeal is rejected and the court will re-sentence the defendant in compliance with the Guidelines.</td></tr>
<tr><td>Topic</td><td>Criminal Law</td></tr>
<tr><td>Key Words</td><td>Sentencing Guidelines; Tax Evasion</td></tr>
<tr><td colspan="2">CASE SUMMARY</td></tr>
<tr><td>Facts</td><td>Roush was convicted of income tax evasion for failure to report millions of dollars in income from the receipt of millions of shares of stock that he received from a complicated securities fraud. Given his criminal acts, under the Sentencing Guidelines he should have received a prison term of 37 to 46 months. The trial court judge imposed a term of 27 months, stating that the shorter sentence would be more fair. Roush appealed the conviction, contending various defects in the prosecution.</td></tr>
<tr><td>Decision</td><td>Remanded for re-sentencing. The conviction stands with some minor problems in calculating the total income that was not reported. However, the judge deviated from the Sentencing Guidelines. Courts may deviate from the Guidelines if they articulate fact-specific reasons to justify the deviation. This did not happen here. The judge only expressed concern with fairness for the sentence given the size of the tax evasion. There was insufficient elaboration that could substantiate a reduction in the sentence below what is required by the Guidelines. The case is remanded for re-sentencing consistent with the Guidelines.</td></tr>
<tr><td>Citation</td><td>U.S. v. Roush, ---F.3d--- (2006 WL 2806701, 5th Cir., 2006)</td></tr>
</table>

CASE 4 – TIME BOMB OF CONTRACT DRAFTING

Full Policy Value in Force for Policy Cancelled after Short Time	
Description	**Appeals court held that the full limit of a policy would apply to damages sustained by a policy holder even though the policy was cancelled after three months. The policy did not state that coverage limits would be prorated, so full coverage was in effect.**
Topic	**Insurance**
Key Words	**Umbrella Policy; Cancellation; Prorated limits**
CASE SUMMARY	
Facts	**Insurer issued a comprehensive general liability (CGL) or umbrella policy to Georgia-Pacific (GP) designed to protect GP from claims by third parties. The policy, issued in 1967, has a $10 million annual aggregate limit of liability as well as a $10 million per occurrence limit. Three months later, GP cancelled the policy in favor of a policy issued by another company. Decades later, GP presented OneBeacon, successor to the company that issued the policy for three months in 1967, with a demand for $10 million for asbestos liability losses dating back to that time. OneBeacon maintained that its liability was capped at $2.5 million since the policy was in effect for only one-quarter of the year. The district court held for GP, holding that the policy did not say benefits would be prorated for part years. OneBeacon appealed.**
Decision	Affirmed. The cancellation of the umbrella liability policy before the end of the policy period, and the refund of the premium for the remainder of the year did not permit the insurer to prorate the limits of the policy. The cancellation clause stated that "all other terms and conditions remain unchanged" in the event of cancellation, hence the full annual value of the policy was in effect during the three months the policy was in force.
Citation	*OneBeacon Insurance Co. v. Georgia-Pacific Corp.*, 474 F.3d 6 (1st Cir., 2007)

REMEDIES

CASE 1 – ALTERNATE DISPUTE RESOLUTION

Res Judicata Applies to Matter Decided in Arbitration	
Description	Appeals court held that a matter resolved by arbitration has been settled, so the doctrine of *res judicata* applied. A party that previously submitted the dispute to arbitration for an award cannot later join a class action against the same defendant.
Topic	Alternate Dispute Resolution
Key Words	Arbitration; Award; *Res Judicata*; Investors
CASE SUMMARY	
Facts	The Aucoins had a brokerage account with an investment company. The account contract had a uniform arbitration clause that required disputes to go before the Financial Industry Regulatory Authority (FINRA). After some years, the Aucoins filed for arbitration, claiming negligence and other improprieties in the management of their account. The arbitration panel agreed with the brokerage firm that the account was not improperly handled and noted that no money had been lost. While that was in process, a class action suit was filed against the brokerage firm for improper management of accounts. The Aucoins filed to join the class for that litigation. The request was denied by the court as it held that the decision of the arbitration panel regarding their account was *res judicata* as to their claim. The Aucoins appealed.
Decision	Affirmed. The doctrine of *res judicata* applies to arbitration awards with respect to the issues presented to arbitration and decided in arbitration. Although the award in arbitration was not confirmed by a court, the procedures of arbitration were fair and a final award was issued. Judicial confirmation of awards is not required for the matter to have been legally resolved. Since the issue raised in the class litigation raises the same issues raised by the Aucoins in arbitration, they may not join the class as that would allow them a chance to litigate a matter already settled.
Citation	*Aucoin v. Gauthier*, ---So.3d--- (2010 WL 502793, Ct. App., La., 2010)

CASE 2 – MEASURE OF DAMAGES

Lost Profits Proper Damages for Violation of Non-Compete Agreement	
Description	Utah high court held that if a non-compete agreement is violated, the proper measure of damages is lost profits, not the remedy of restitution or unjust enrichment.
Topic	Contracts
Key Words	Non-Compete Agreement; Breach; Damages
CASE SUMMARY	
Facts	Mantz worked for TruGreen, quit, and went to work for Mower Brothers, a competing lawn care company. Other TruGreen employees followed Mantz to Mower. The employees had signed non-compete and non-solicitation agreements with TruGreen. It sued Mower, Mantz and others for violating the agreements they had also signed. The federal district court certified a question to the Utah high court, asking it what the proper measure of damages is in such a case.
Decision	Question answered. The purpose of contract damages is to compensate the non-breaching party for actual injury sustained, so that the non-breaching party may be restored, as nearly as possible, to the position it was in prior to the injury. The proper measure of damages for breach of a covenant not to compete is the non-breaching party's lost profits proven to a reasonable estimate of damages; however, the non-breaching party may use profits of the defendant if shown to correspond in whole or in part with the loss of the non-breaching party. Restitution and unjust enrichment are remedies found in quantum meruit and are not appropriate in cases regarding a breach of a non-competition agreement, as they are used only when no express contract is present.
Citation	*TruGreen Companies v. Mower Brothers, Inc.*, ---P.3d--- (2008 WL 4977320, Sup. Ct., Utah, 2008)

JURISDICTION

CASE 1 – SERVICE OF PROCESS

Service of Process Must Be Shown to Be Proper for Trial to Proceed	
Description	Appeals court held that a trial verdict for the plaintiff could not stand because when the defendant challenged the adequacy of service of process, competent evidence was not provided to show that service had met state law requirements.
Topic	Court Procedure
Key Words	Service of Process; Adequacy; Hearsay
CASE SUMMARY	
Facts	Burden sued Copco for injuries sustained in an auto accident. Copco defended that there was inadequate service. Oregon law allows a defendant to be served by delivering a true copy of the summons and complaint to any person 14 years of age or older residing in the dwelling or usual place or residence of the person to be served. Copco contended that never occurred. The trial court held for plaintiff. Defendant appealed.
Decision	Reversed. Sufficient service of process was not shown by competent evidence. When service is questioned, competent service must be shown. The plaintiff only offered an unsworn statement from the process server stating that service had been completed properly. That is hearsay, not competent evidence, so the presumption is that adequate service never occurred. The matter may not proceed unless proper service can be established.
Citation	*Burden v. Copco Refrigeration,*--- P.3d --- (2004 WL 1058814, Ct. App., Ore., 2004)

CASE 2 – NONRESIDENT JURISDICTION

<table>
<tr><td colspan="2" align="center">Nevada Casino's Efforts to Attract California Patrons Gives California Courts Jurisdiction</td></tr>
<tr><td>Descriptio n</td><td>Appeals courts held that California courts have personal jurisdiction over Nevada hotels and casinos sued by a California resident. The casinos direct advertising efforts at California residents and accept their business, so the state of California has a significant interest in their business dealings.</td></tr>
<tr><td>Topic</td><td>Court Procedure</td></tr>
<tr><td>Key Words</td><td>Personal Jurisdiction; Nonresident; Business Activities</td></tr>
<tr><td colspan="2" align="center">CASE SUMMARY</td></tr>
<tr><td>Facts</td><td>Snowney, a California resident, sued Harrah's and other Nevada casino operators in a class action suit claiming unfair competition, breach of contract, and false advertising. He brought suit in California state court. The trial court dismissed the suit for lack for personal jurisdiction. Snowney appealed.</td></tr>
<tr><td>Decision</td><td>Reversed. In determining whether the exercise of jurisdiction over a nonresident would be fair and reasonable, a court must consider 1) the burden on the defendant of defending an action in the forum; 2) the forum state's interest in adjudicating the dispute; 3) the plaintiff's interest in obtaining relief; 4) judicial economy; and 5) the states' shared interest in furthering fundamental substantive social policies. The hotels and casinos purposefully directed advertising at California residents; they also conducted business with some residents by an interactive web site. They solicited and received the patronage of California residents. These activities created sufficient connections for California courts to have personal jurisdiction over the hotels and casinos.</td></tr>
<tr><td>Citation</td><td>Snowney v. Harrah's Entertainment, 11 Cal.Rptr.3d 35 (Ct. App., Calif., 2004)</td></tr>
</table>

CASE 3 – THE UNIFORM COMMERCIAL CODE

Sale of Unfinished Goods Is Sale of Goods, Not Service, under the UCC	
Description	Appeals court held that the UCC governed a contract, not the common law, as the primary value in the contract was the provision of unfinished goods to be used by the buyer in its production. That is a sale of goods, not a service.
Topic	Sales
Key Words	Goods; Services; Statute of Frauds
CASE SUMMARY	
Facts	Attwood operated a foundry and produced rough castings of propellers used by PowerTech in making small steel boat propellers that used a unique "segmented blade" tooling technique. PowerTech sued Attwood for breach of contract. Attwood contended that the UCC governed the agreement and that its statute of frauds barred recovery because the contract lacked a written quantity term or a written specification that the buyer will purchases exclusively from the seller. The district court held for PowerTech, awarding over $7 million in damages. It held that the contract was for both goods and services and that services dominated the contract. Therefore, it fell under the common law, so the statute of frauds from § 2.201 of the USS did not apply. Attwood appealed.
Decision	Reversed and rendered. The contract to produce custom designed propeller castings was a contract for the sale of goods within the meaning of the UCC even though the castings were turned into finished goods by PowerTech. Unfinished products are goods under the UCC. This is not a service. The contract specifically referred to the propellers as a "product" and to the "production" of the propellers. Furthermore, the contract lacked any promise as to the quantity to be purchased even though it said the buyer would set a minimum order level that was suitable to both parties. Hence, the contract lacked consideration and mutuality. Since the UCC applies, its statute of limitations applies.
Citation	*Propulsion Technologies, Inc. v. Attwood Corp.*, 369 F.3d 896 (5th Cir., 2004)

CASE 4 – LONG ARM JURISDICTION

	Lebanese Bank Activity in U.S. Inadequate to Establish Jurisdiction in U.S. Court
Description	Federal court dismissed suits brought against Lebanese banks accused of providing financial services for a terrorist organization in Lebanon that assisted in that organization killing and injuring people in Israel. Federal and state requirements for long-arm jurisdiction were not met.
Topic	Court Procedure
Key Words	Jurisdiction; Long-Arm; Alien Tort Claims Act; Foreign Banks
	CASE SUMMARY
Facts	Hizbullah is a terrorist organization based in Lebanon. From its bases there, it fired rockets into Israel. Fifty-seven Israeli citizens who were injured in attacks, or are survivors of family members killed in attacks, brought suit in U.S. federal court, under the Alien Tort Claims Act, against five foreign banks, claiming that the banks assisted in terrorist activity by knowingly providing financial services to Hizbullah, which constituted aiding and abetting organizations to commit crimes against humanity. The banks, which are located in Lebanon, are connected to the international banking system. They moved to have the suit dismissed.
Decision	Motion granted. U.S. courts do not have jurisdiction over foreign banks under the New York long-arm statute nor under federal long-arm jurisdiction rules regarding foreign defendants. There was no substantial relationship between the foreign banks and operations in New York that would allow jurisdiction. For a claim to arise from a business transaction in New York, there must be a substantial relationship between transactions occurring within the state and the cause of action sued upon. Adequate evidence was not provided to establish such relationships.
Citation	*Tamam v. Fransabank SAL*, ---F.Supp.2d--- (2010 WL 21088, S.D., N.Y., 2010)

CASE 5 – DOING BUSINESS JURISDICTION

	No Jurisdiction Based on Website and Sporadic Activity in a State	
Description	Florida appeals court held that a foreign corporation could not sue a New York university in Florida court for an alleged tort. None of the activities occurred in Florida, and the university's activities in Florida, including a website and alumni association, were not sufficient contact to form personal jurisdiction.	
Topic	Court Procedure	
Key Words	"Doing Business;" Personal Jurisdiction; Interference with Contractual Relationship	
CASE SUMMARY		
Facts	Ocean World, a foreign corporation, operates Ocean World Adventure Park in the Dominican Republic (DR). It contracted with Briggs to buy 12 dolphins from Taiji, Japan for delivery in the DR. The DR denied a permit to import the dolphins. Ocean World sued various defendants for intentional interference with a contract or business relationship. Among the defendants was Columbia University of New York City. Suit was filed in Florida, contending that Columbia was "doing business" in Florida through its alumni association, interactive internet classrooms, and a website providing online courses for students to obtain degrees and professional certificates. Columbia also owns property in Florida. Ocean World contends that Columbia encouraged the DR to refuse to allow the dolphins to be imported, which was interference with a business relationship. Reiss and Columbia moved for dismissal for lack of jurisdiction in Florida courts. The trial court refused. They appealed.	
Decision	Reversed and remanded. Florida courts do not have jurisdiction over the defendants. None of the alleged tortious acts occurred in Florida, as would be required for personal jurisdiction. The facts that Columbia has alumni associations in Florida and offers internet lectures and owns property in the state do not amount to continuous and systematic general business contacts with Florida to warrant exercise of personal jurisdiction. The existence of a website that may be visible in every location does not make the owner of the website subject to jurisdiction in every location.	
Citation	*Trustees of Columbia University v. Ocean World*, S.A., ---So.3d--- (2009 WL 1212229, Ct. App., Fla., 2009)	

CASE 6 – REMOVAL JURISDICTION

All Parts of Class Action Test Must Be Met for Removal to Federal Court	
Description	Appeals court held that a federal district court properly refused to remove a class action suit from state court to federal court. Federal law allows removal if the amount in controversy exceeds $5 million. Defendant failed to show that much was likely to be at stake, so the suit will be heard in state court.
Topic	Court Procedure
Key Words	Class Action; Class Action Fairness Act; Amount in Controversy
CASE SUMMARY	
Facts	Amoche and others sued GTL, an insurance company, in New Hampshire state court, alleging that GTL owed refunds for a part of their credit insurance premiums. Amoche sought to represent a class of New Hampshire consumers who were due similar refunds under the terms of their policies. GTL filed a notice of removal, claiming federal jurisdiction under the Class Action Fairness Act (CAFA). The federal district court granted the plaintiffs' motion to remand the case to state court. GTL appealed.
Decision	Affirmed. CAFA provides for removal to federal court of state class actions that satisfy the statute's diversity and class size requirements and have more than $5million in controversy. The defendant, GTL, has the burden of showing federal jurisdiction. Here, there was diversity of citizenship and a class of adequate size, but GTL could not show with "reasonable probability" that the amount in controversy exceeded $5 million. The trial court properly reviewed the evidence by both parties as to the amount in controversy and found the $5 million requirement unlikely to hold.
Citation	*Amoche v. Guarantee Trust Life Insurance Co.*, 556 F.3d 41 (1st Cir., 2009)

CASE 7 – FORUN NON CONVENIENS

Trial to Be Moved Due to Factors Favoring Alternative Venue	
Description	Appeals court held that defendant's request to change venue from one federal court to another would be granted since all factors favored the other location; there was no tie to the venue where the case was filed except that the plaintiff chose that court.
Topic	Court Procedure
Key Words	Venue; Transfer; Factors; Interests
CASE SUMMARY	
Facts	A Volkswagen (VW) on a highway in Dallas was struck from behind and propelled into a truck parked on the side of a freeway. One person in the VW was injured and one was killed. The survivor sued VW, contending that design defects in the car caused the injury and death. The survivor filed sued in federal court in Marshall, Texas, which is 155 miles east of Dallas. VW moved to transfer venue to federal court in Dallas, contending that the VW was bought in Dallas, the accident occurred there, Dallas residents witnessed the accident, Dallas police responded to the accident, medical care was given in Dallas, the driver who struck the VW is in Dallas, and no party related to the litigation lives in Marshall. The district court refused to move the case. VW appealed.
Decision	Transfer of case ordered. Under the forum non conveniens doctrine, a court may decline jurisdiction if the case more conveniently could be tried in another forum. A transfer of venue must be in the interest of justice. The party seeing to transfer venue must show good cause. Factors relating to private interests are: 1) the relative ease of access to sources of proof; 2) the availability of compulsory process to secure the attendance of witnesses; 3) the cost of attendance for willing witnesses; and 4) all other practical problems. Factors relating to public interests are: 1) the administrative difficulties flowing from court congestion; 2) local interests in having local interests decided at home; 3) the familiarity of the forum with the law that will govern the case; and 4) the avoidance of unnecessary problems of conflict of laws. Some of these factors are not relevant here; the ones that are weigh in favor of moving to Dallas. The only reason the case was in court in Marshall was because plaintiff decided to file there; there was no other factor favoring that location.
Citation	*In re: Volkswagen of America*, 545 F.3d 304 (5th Cir., 2008)

TYPES OF CONTRACTS

CASE 1 - UNILATERAL PROMISES

Unilateral Contract Became Enforceable When Performed	
Description	Texas high court held that a promise by an employee to employees that they would be cut in on profits when the business was sold in the future, if they remained with the company, was a unilateral promise that was performed upon by the employees who remained with the company until it was sold.
Topic	Contracts
Key Words	Unilateral Contract; Enforceability; Employment-at-Will
CASE SUMMARY	
Facts	AES was formed in 1996 and hired employees that year. At a meeting in 1997, they expressed concern to an executive that the company was not likely to survive as they used outdated equipment and worked long hours. The executive told the employees that they should stay with the company because it was likely the firm would merge with another company and, if it did, the original eight employees would be rewarded with five percent of the value of the sale or merger of AES. In 2001, AES was bought by another company. Seven of the eight original employees were still with the firm and requested their five percent of the sale price. The company refused to pay, contending that the employees were at-will and there was no enforceable contract. The alleged agreement was illusory and, in any case, it violated the statute of frauds because it took more than one year to come into effect. The employees sued for breach of contract. The trial and appeals court agreed with AES; the employees appealed.
Decision	Reversed and remanded. The employees who remained with the company from 1997 forward performed on the unilateral contract, thereby making it enforceable. A unilateral contract is created by the promisor promising a benefit if the promise performs, and the contract becomes enforceable when the promisee performs. Even if the promise by AES to pay the employees five percent of the sale revenues was illusory, the at-will employees, by staying at AES until it was acquired by another company, performed on the unilateral contract, thereby making it enforceable.
Citation	*Vanegas v. American Energy Services*, ---S.W.3d--- (2009 WL 4877734, Sup. Ct., Texas, 2009)

CASE 2 – IMPLIED CONTRACT

Implied Contract Exists Once Original Contract Expired and Parties Continued to Deal	
Description	Appeals court held that upon the expiration of a contract between a city and a company that supplied water services, the company could not deny that an implied contract now governed the relationship since it continued to provide services for financial benefit.
Topic	Contracts
Key Words	Implied Contract; Franchise; Mutual Benefit; Cancelation
C A S E S U M M A R Y	
Facts	In 1988, the City of Las Cruces granted a franchise to Moongate to operate a water distribution system in the city. The contract specified Moongate's rights and obligations. Moongate paid a fee to the city based on the number of customers served. The franchise expired in 2002. Before the contract came to an end, the city told Moongate that because of uncertainty created by litigation with another water company over the water service area to be served, it would delay negotiating a new contract until the litigation was settled so the city would know for sure the boundaries of water operations. The city told Moongate the parties would continue to operate on a month-by-month basis until a new long-term franchise agreement could be drafted. Moongate filed a motion for a declaratory judgment that the contract had expired and it no longer had an obligation to continue water operations. The district court agreed with Moongate, ruling that the contract had expired. The city appealed.
Decision	Reversed and remanded. The franchise contract had expired, but since Moongate continued to operate after it expired, and the city continued to allow it to operate, there existed an implied contract. The terms of the expired agreement would continue to govern the relationship between the parties. Both parties received a financial benefit from the continued existence of the relationship. Hence, the agreement will continue in effect until the parties negotiate a new agreement or agree to cancel the existing implied contract. The relationship is impacted by the obligations of the parties in the provision of an essential utility to the city residents.
Citation	*Moongate Water Co. v. City of Las Cruces*, ---P.3d--- (2009 WL 3444780, Ct. App., N.M., 2009)

CASE 3 – PROMISSORY ESTOPPEL

<table>
<tr>
<td colspan="2" align="center">Promissory Estoppel Applied to Promise to Give Land to a Daughter for Building a House</td>
</tr>
<tr>
<td>Description</td>
<td>Maine high court held that promissory estoppel would apply to a promise made by parents to their daughter that they would give her some of their land if she built a house on their property. The fact that she built the house is evidence that she expected to receive a deed to the land.</td>
</tr>
<tr>
<td>Topic</td>
<td>Contracts</td>
</tr>
<tr>
<td>Key Words</td>
<td>Promise; Breach of Contract; Property; Promissory Estoppel</td>
</tr>
<tr>
<td colspan="2" align="center">CASE SUMMARY</td>
</tr>
<tr>
<td>Facts</td>
<td>The Dows are the parents of Teresa Harvey. The Dows own 125 acres of land. Teresa claimed the family had always discussed that she and her brother could each have a home on the property, and the Dows promised to transfer ownership of some land to her at some point in the future. Teresa and her husband put a mobile home on the land and later, with her parent's permission, built a garage. Teresa's husband was killed in an accident, and she used insurance proceeds to build a permanent home. She said the Dows encourage this and said they would transfer the deed to her later. She built a $200,000 home for herself and lent her brother $25,000. Relations among the family members began to sour. Teresa asked her parents for a deed to the property. They refused and she sued for breach of contract, requesting the court to compel conveyance of property to her. The Dows contended that they had made her no promise, and she had no right to any land. The trial court held that there was no enforceable promise. Teresa appealed.</td>
</tr>
<tr>
<td>Decision</td>
<td>Vacated and remanded. General promises by the Dows to convey land the Teresa as a gift or inheritance would not, alone, support a claim of promissory estoppel. It applies to promises that are otherwise unenforceable, and is invoked to enforce such promises so as to avoid injustice. A promise by the Dows to deed land to Teresa for her house could be fairly implied, as necessary for promissory estoppel, when coupled with the permission to build the house. Such a promise need not be express, but may be implied by the actions of the parties.</td>
</tr>
<tr>
<td>Citation</td>
<td>Harvey v. Dow, 962 A.2d 322 (Sup. Ct., Maine, 2008)</td>
</tr>
</table>

ILLEGAL CONTRACTS

CASE 1 – USURY

Payday Loans Violate State Usury Limits	
Description	Arkansas high court struck down a state statute that allowed payday loans by calling a loan a service rather than a loan and the interest charged a service fee rather than interest. These were loans in reality, and the interest rate charged was higher than permitted by the usury provision in the state constitution.
Topic	Consumer Protection
Key Words	Payday Loans; Usury; Constitutionality
CASE SUMMARY	
Facts	The Arkansas constitution limits interest rates that may be charged on loans. This restriction on interest rates, a usury law, was claimed to apply to payday loans. The legislature enacted the Check-Cashers Act. It applied primarily to payday loans. In those transactions, the consumer writes a check, the amount of which includes the cash to be advanced to the customer, plus a service fee. The check is dated in the future (payday) and the lender does not cash the check until that date. The Check-Cashers Act stated that such cash advances were not loans, so were not subject to the usury limit. The service fee was claimed not to be the same as interest on a loan. The constitutionality of the act was challenged. The lower court upheld the Act; plaintiffs appealed.
Decision	Reversed and remanded. The Check-Cashers Act is unconstitutional. The reality of the cash-advance transaction, regardless of what it is called, is that it is a loan with interest charged. The borrower is loaned money that is repaid later. The service fee is the same as interest charged by a lender. Hence, the usury limit applies and the legislature cannot assert that payday loans are not subject to the limit. The constitution limits the annual interest rate on consumer loans to 17%; in some cases the service fees on the payday loans amounted to an annual interest rate of 500%, a clear violation of the usury limit.
Citation	*McGhee v. Arkansas State Board of Collection Agencies*, ---S.W.3d--- (2008 WL 4823540, Sup. Ct., Ark., 2008)

CASE 2 – EMPLOYEE NON COMPETITION

Covenant Not to Compete for Two Years Held Enforceable	
Description	Appeals court held that a two-year restriction on working in competition with a former employer was reasonable given the special knowledge held by the former employee and the investment the former employer had made in providing specialized training for the employee.
Topic	Employment Law
Key Words	Covenant Not to Compete; Enforcement
CASE SUMMARY	
Facts	Zambelli Fireworks is one of the largest fireworks companies in the U.S. Pyrotecnico F/X is a direct competitor. Wood works in the industry as a pyrotechnician and choreographer, executing fireworks displays in combination with music. He began work for Zambelli in 2001. His employment contract contained a two-year non-compete provision that also restricted the use of trade secrets. At Zambelli, he developed his skills and was privy to many of the inner workings of Zambelli's business. In 2008, Wood was offered a new contract with expanded responsibilities. Not caring for company management, Wood contacted Pyrotecnico about employment and the parties came to an agreement. Knowing of the agreement at Zambelli, Pyrotecnico offered to pay Wood's salary for two years in case he was not allowed to work and also offered to cover litigation expenses. Wood quit Zambelli and went to work for Pyrotecnico and avoided using information covered by the non-compete agreement. Zambelli sued Wood and Pyrotecnico to enforce the non-compete agreement. The district court upheld the agreement and outlined the work areas in which Wood could not perform for two years. Wood and Pyrotecnico appealed.
Decision	Affirmed. Although restrictive covenants are a disfavored restraint on trade under Pennsylvania law, they are enforceable in equity when they are incident to the employment relationship between the parties, the restrictions imposed by the covenant are reasonably necessary for the protection of the employer, and the restrictions imposed are reasonably limited in time and place. Zambelli has a legitimate business interest in protecting its customer goodwill and in the specialized training, knowledge, and skill acquired by an employee at the employer's expense.
Citation	*Zambelli Fireworks v. Wood*, 592 F.3d 412 (3rd Cir., 2010)

CASE 3 – CAN'T ASSIGN NONCOMPETE

Employee's Noncompetition Agreement May Not Be Assigned without Consent	
Description	Nevada high court held that a noncompetition covenant in an employment contract could not be assigned to another company without permission of the employee.
Topic	Contracts
Key Words	Assignment; Noncompetition Agreement; Employment
CASE SUMMARY	
Facts	Burkhardt works for Traffic Control Services, a company that sells and rents trenching equipment to contractors in the Las Vegas area. Previously, Burkhardt worked for NES. As a condition of employment with NES, he was paid $10,000 to sign a noncompetition covenant. They provided that if he left NES he would not work for a competitor firm in the area for one year and that he would protect confidential company information. Later, NES was sold to United Rentals. Burkhardt refused to sign a new noncompetition covenant with United and left to work for Traffic. United sued Burkhardt and Traffic for violating the noncompetition covenant. The district court agreed and ordered the agreement to be enforced for one year. Burkhardt and Traffic appealed.
Decision	Reversed. An employee's covenant not to compete is personal in nature and is unassignable absent the employee's express consent or an express clause permitting assignment that has been negotiated at arm's length with the employee and supported by additional and separate consideration. Post-employment covenants are reviewed with greater care than are similar covenants incident to the sale of a business because the loss of a person's livelihood is a very serious matter.
Citation	*Traffic Control Services v. United Rentals Northwest*, 87 P.3d 1054 (Sup. Ct., Nev., 2004)

CASE 4 – ARBITRATION UNCONSCIONABILITY

	Arbitration Requirement Fails for Unconscionability
Description	California appeals court struck down a mandatory arbitration clause in a travel company contract as unconscionable on procedural and substantive grounds. Travelers had no choice in the matter and liability was too greatly restricted, so the clause was oppressive.
Topic	Alternate Dispute Resolution
Key Words	Arbitration, Mediation, Unconscionability; Oppression
	CASE SUMMARY
Facts	Lhotka went on a mountain climbing trip sponsored by GeoEx. The contract for the trip contained a dispute resolution clause that stated that in event of a dispute the parties could first go to mediation. If that did not resolve the matter, it would go to binding arbitration at the American Arbitration Association under California law. It stated that the maximum liability would be the cost of the trip purchased. Signing the dispute resolution agreement was mandatory if one wanted to go on the trip. Lhotka died of an altitude-related illness while on the trip. His mother sued GeoEx in California state court for wrongful death. GeoEx moved to compel arbitration. The trial court denied the motion. GeoEx appealed.
Decision	Affirmed. The agreement to arbitrate is unconscionable and, therefore, unenforceable. The trial court properly declined to enforce the entire arbitration clause. The arbitration agreement fails on both procedural and substantive grounds. The procedural element of unconscionability requires oppression. That occurs where a contract involves lack of negotiation and meaningful choice or when the unconscionable provision is hidden within a long, tedious form unlikely to be read. Substantive unconscionability exists when a contract provision reallocates risk in an objectively unreasonable or unexpected manner. GeoEx travelers had no opportunity to bargain and liability was greatly limited within the arbitration clause.
Citation	*Lhotka v. Geographic Expeditions*, ---Cal.Rptr.3d--- (2010 WL 325491, Ct. App., Calif., 2010)

CASE 5 – ADHESION CONTRACTS

Home Inspector's Contract Limiting Liability Stricken as Unconscionable	
Description	Appeals court held that a home inspector's contract that limited liability to a trivial sum, regardless of the basis of liability, was a contract of adhesion that was unconscionable and could not be enforced.
Topic	Contracts
Key Words	Unconscionability; Adhesion; Liability; Bargaining Position
C A S E S U M M A R Y	
Facts	A couple bought a home. They hired CAL to perform a home inspection. The inspection agreement states that CAL's liability for any matter related to the inspection cannot exceed 50 percent of the inspection fee. Since the fee was $385, liability was limited to $192.50. The inspection stated there were no problems with the home. After the couple moved in, they noticed a roof leak. A roofer said that the roof was defective because it had no flashing, something that should have been noticed by the inspector. The repair would cost between $8,000 and $10,000. The buyers sued CAL for breach of contract, fraud, negligence, and breach of warranty. CAL moved for a declaration that the limit of its liability was $192.50. The trial court held for CAL. The buyers appealed.
Decision	Reversed. The contract limiting the inspector's liability to half the fee was a contract of adhesion. There were no negotiations. The contract was presented to the buyer on a standard, pre-printed form prepared by the inspector on a take-it-or-leave-it basis, without any opportunity for modification of terms. Since the inspector was an expert and the consumer had no experience in the area, there was grossly unequal bargaining status. Such exculpation clauses are particularly disfavored in contracts for professional services. The damage limit was so small as to effectively eliminate responsibility for the inspector, which is contrary to state public policy of encouraging reliable home inspections and to hold professionals to industry standards.
Citation	*Lucier v. Williams*, --- A.2d --- (2004 WL 257036, App. Div., N.J., 2004)

EXCUSES FOR NON-PERFORMANCE

CASE 1 – CONDITION PRECEDENT

Failure of Condition Precedent Means No Contract Existed	
Description	Montana high court held that due to the failure of a condition precedent, no contract was formed. Because the contract was not formed, the arbitration clause in the contract could not be enforced.
Topic	Contracts
Key Words	Condition Precedent; Formation; Arbitration
CASE SUMMARY	
Facts	The Thompsons intended to buy a new pickup from Lithia Dodge. The retail installment contract with Lithia listed the annual interest rate as 3.9 percent. It stated that the contract was not binding until financing was completed. The contract also stated that any dispute must be resolved by arbitration. A week later, Lithia's finance manager said the 3.9 percent rate had not been accepted and they would have to sign a contract for 4.9 percent financing. They refused to pay the higher rate and a dispute followed. The Thompsons sued Lithia, as it demanded the pickup back and had already sold the vehicle the Thompsons traded in. The trial court held that because of the arbitration clause, the matter had to go to arbitration; the Thompsons appealed.
Decision	Reversed and remanded. Approval of 3.9 percent financing for the purchase of the pickup was a condition precedent to forming a contract between Lithia and the Thompsons. The order form said the dealer would not be obligated to sell until the financing had been approved by a bank or finance company. That did not happen so the condition precedent was not fulfilled. There was no agreement, so no contract. Hence, the arbitration clause is not binding, as it was part of the contract. The case may proceed to trial.
Citation	*Thompson v. Lithia Chrysler Jeep Dodge of Great Falls*, 185 P.3d 332 (Sup. Ct., Mt., 2008)

CASE 2 – FORCE MAJEURE

Geological Problem in Mining Not Sufficient to Invoke Force Majeure Clause	
Description	Appeals court held that a mining company breached its contract to supply coal to a utility when it quit delivery due to a geological problem that caused problems in mining. The mining company did not properly inform the utility of the nature of the problem, forcing it to pay a higher price for new supplies.
Topic	Contracts
Key Words	Breach; Force Majeure; Damages
CASE SUMMARY	
Facts	C.W. Mining (CW) signed an agreement in 2003 to provide Aquila, an electric power company, with 1.5 million tons of coal during 2004-06 with an option for Aquila to extend the contract through 2008. The contract contained a force majeure clause. It stated that if invoked, the party doing so would immediately inform the other party of the problem and obligations would be suspended until the problem was overcome and, if the problem continued for more than six months, the contract could be terminated. CW had many problems: a long strike, roof collapses and mine closures, unexpectedly muddy conditions, and unusual "hot spots" were hit when mining. CW invoked the force majeure clause due to the strike, which slowed its deliveries. Aquila accepted the smaller-than-expected coal deliveries and told CW it expected the quantities to be made up. Later, CW cancelled the contract, invoking the force majeure clause. Aquila then contracted with another company for coal, paying a higher price. It sued CW for breach. The trial court rejected the defense of force majeure and awarded Aquila damages of $24 million. CW appealed.
Decision	Affirmed. Aquila was not notified that the hot spots were a significant problem; in fact they had been told the opposite. The fact that a problem existed, and had been noted, is not sufficient to justify invoking the force majeure clause. Aquila did not waive its rights under the contract when it accepted lower-than-expected coal deliveries due to the strike. The labor dispute was a separate matter from the geological problem. As the price Aquila had to pay a new provider was shown to be the market price at that time, it had the right to the damages that were awarded to cover the higher cost suffered due to breach by CW.
Citation	*Aquila, Inc. v. C.W. Mining*, 545 F.3d 1258 (10th Cir., 2008)

171

RIGHTS OF THIRD PARTIES

CASE 1 – INTENDED BENEFICIARIES

Trustee Beneficiaries Can Intervene in Trust When Interest Becomes Known	
Description	Montana high court held that beneficiaries of a trust, who had been ignorant of their interest for years by the trustee, could now sue the trustee for an accounting of the handling of the trust in prior decades.
Topic	Wills, Estates, and Trusts
Key Words	Trust, Beneficiary, Accounting, Trial
CASE SUMMARY	
Facts	Zona and Rose are two beneficiaries of a trust created by their grandfather, Dunham, in a will written in 1966. Wells Fargo Bank was named as trustee. Dunham named his only child, Mary, to receive fixed income from the trust during her life, and then his four granddaughters, including Zona and Rose, were to become vested remainder beneficiaries upon Mary's death. The granddaughters were unaware that they were beneficiaries of the trust as neither Mary nor the bank told them of their interest. At Mary's instructions, the bank kept funds in the trust invested only in bonds. Over the decades, earnings were lower than they would have been had some of the trust been in stocks. Eventually, before Mary's death, Zona and Rose came to realize that they may have an interest in the trust and hired a lawyer to investigate. They sued the bank for mishandling the trust. Had 40 percent of the trust been invested in stocks, the trust would have been worth $10 million rather than $3 million. The bank protested that Zona and Rose had no right to intervene at this point in prior handling of the trust. The trial court held that they did have the right to bring suit as beneficiaries of the trust. The bank appealed.
Decision	Affirmed and remanded. The beneficiaries did not know of their interest in the trust earlier, so did not participate in supervision or control of the trust for many years. The trustee may have misrepresented or misadvised Zona and Rose about their rights and interest in the trust. They have the right to intervene at this point. The statute of limitations does not apply because they were unaware of their interests during the time they claim the trust was mishandled.
Citation	*In the Matter of Trust B*, 184 P.3d 296 (Sup. Ct., Mont., 2008

CASE 2 – AUTOMATIC ASSIGNMENT

Guaranty on Notes Transfer by Operation of Law	
Description	Appeals court held that, although the sale of notes from the original lender to a later holder did not specifically also transfer the guaranty on the notes that the maker of the notes had signed, the guaranty transferred by operation of law, so the maker owed the current holder due to default on the notes.
Topic	Negotiable Instruments/Commercial Paper
Key Words	Note; Default; Guaranty; Holder; Operation of Law
CASE SUMMARY	
Facts	The maker executed three promissory notes in favor of Allegiant Bank to borrow over $2 million for property purchases. The maker executed three deeds of trust in favor of Allegiant and its assignees, naming the maker's interest in the property and its improvements as collateral. Also, the maker signed a guaranty on the notes. Allegiant assigned the deeds of trust to the holder and made the notes payable to the holder rather than Allegiant, but did not expressly transfer the guaranty. When the maker failed to make payments, the holder issued a notice of default. When the maker failed to pay, the holder sold the property at a foreclosure sale to the highest bidder, Eureka. Eureka transferred the deeds to Battlefield Properties. The holder Battlefield then sued the maker and the guarantor to recover the remaining balance due, as the sale price did not cover the obligation in the notes. The court granted summary judgment to the holder. The maker and guarantor appealed.
Decision	Affirmed. The guaranty transferred by operation of law to the holder, Battlefield, as assignee of the original holder. The holder therefore had standing to sue the guarantor. It is true that the agreement between Allegiant and later holders did not expressly transfer the guaranty, but it transferred by operation of law along with the principal obligation in the underlying promissory notes. There was no showing of a wrongful foreclosure on the property or improper sale, so the maker, who is also the guarantor, owes the holder for the balance due on the notes.
Citation	*American First Federal v. Battlefield Center*, ---S.W3d--- (2009 WL 112439, Ct. App., Mo., 2009)

SPECIAL SALES RULES

CASE 1 - IMPERFECT TITLE

Good Faith Buyer of Vehicle Obtained by Swindle Gets Good Title	
Description	Colorado high court held that when a seller accepts a bad check for a vehicle, which is then sold to an innocent buyer, the innocent buyer can keep the vehicle. One of the two injured parties must suffer a loss. It falls on the one best able to prevent the loss.
Topic	Negotiable Instruments/Commercial Paper
Key Words	Bad Check; Good Faith Purchaser; Stolen Property; Recovery
CASE SUMMARY	
Facts	SW Legal turned his car over to a buyer who presented what appeared to be a valid cashier's check but, ten days later, turned out to be counterfeit. The police could not locate the car, but SW Legal located it two years later. The car had been resold to Roberts by the passer of the bad check. SW Legal sued Roberts to recover the car under UCC 4-405. The trial court held that 4-405 does not apply to situations like this. Instead the court applied UCC 2-403. Roberts, as a good faith purchaser for value, could retain ownership of the car. SW Legal appealed.
Decision	Affirmed. Roberts, as a good faith purchaser for value, obtained good title to the car under 2-403. A good faith purchase from a dishonest non-merchant seller can occur. SW Legal voluntarily parted with the car as a result of a criminal act. But Roberts was a bona fide purchaser who obtained good title. One of two innocent parties must suffer because of the wrongdoing of a third person. The loss must fall on the party who by his conduct created the circumstances which enabled the third party to perpetuate the wrong. SW Legal failed to confirm the validity of the check before releasing the car and title to the fraudulent buyer.
Citation	*SW Legal v. Roberts,* 143 P.3d 1037 (Sup. Ct., Colo., 2006)

CASE 2 – BREACH OF WARRANTY

<table>
<tr>
<td colspan="2">Breach of Warranty for Selling Goods Subject to Claim of Trademark Infringement</td>
</tr>
<tr>
<td>Description</td>
<td>Appeals court held that the supplier of goods breached an implied warranty under the UCC that goods would be free of rightful claims of infringement by another party. Although the claim in this case failed, it was not a frivolous claim, so the seller breached its warranty to the buyer.</td>
</tr>
<tr>
<td>Topic</td>
<td>Sales</td>
</tr>
<tr>
<td>Key Words</td>
<td>Warranty; Infringement; Trademark</td>
</tr>
<tr>
<td colspan="2" align="center">C A S E   S U M M A R Y</td>
</tr>
<tr>
<td>Facts</td>
<td>Olaes sold PacSun 16,000 t-shirts with a graphic design for "Hot Sauce Monkey." Another company, SNCL, sued PacSun for trademark infringement, contending that some of the graphics infringed on graphics SNCL used on shirts. The district court found that there was insufficient copying for there to be infringement, and the parties settled out of court. PacSun then sued Olaes for breach of warranty under Section 2-312 of the UCC which states that goods must be delivered "free of the rightful claim of any third person by way of infringement or the like." The trial court held for Olaes because no infringement was found to exist in the suit brought by SNCL. PacSun appealed.</td>
</tr>
<tr>
<td>Decision</td>
<td>Reversed. A "rightful claim" for infringement covered by the UCC means a nonfrivolous claim that has a significant and an adverse effect on the buyer's ability to make use of the good. It does not require that the plaintiff claiming infringement must prevail in litigation. The claim made by SNCL was not frivolous. Some elements of infringement were found to exist, but not enough to allow SNCL to prevail at trial. Since there was an infringement issue that was found to justify a trial, PacSun was forced to bear the cost of the litigation and Olaes did breach its implied warranty under the UCC that the goods would not expose the buyer, PacSun, to such claims.</td>
</tr>
<tr>
<td>Citation</td>
<td>Pacific Sunwear of California v. Olaes Enterprises, ---Cal.Rptr.3d--- (2008 WL 4509090, Ct. App., Calif., 2008)</td>
</tr>
</table>

CASE 3 – STRICT LIABILITY

Consumer-Expectation Test Is from Perspective of User for Strict Liability in Illinois	
Description	Illinois high court held that in a strict liability claim for design defect, the consumer-expectation test would apply from the perspective of the purchaser, not a child who may happen to grab the product. The jury may also employ the risk-utility test.
Topic	**Torts**
Key Words	Product Liability; Design Defect; Risk-Utility Test; Consumer-Expectation Test
CASE SUMMARY	
Facts	Calles lived with her four young daughters. One night, she ran an errand to the store, leaving the girls alone. A three-year old started a fire using an "Aim-N-Flame" lighter (the kind about a foot long with a handle and a trigger to start a flame). One child died in the fire. Calles sued Scripto, the distributor of the lighter for defective design in that it did not contain a child-resistant device to reduce the risk. Scripto defended that the product is for adults, so it does not have a duty to make it child proof and the dangers were open and obvious. After complicated proceedings, the matter went to the Illinois high court.
Decision	Illinois uses both the consumer-expectation test and the risk-utility test in design defect cases. The consumer-expectation test is from the point of view of the adult mother as a purchaser, not from the viewpoint of a three-year-old child. Hence, it is not the basis of strict liability for design defect. The factors to be considered in the risk-utility test include: 1) its utility to a user, 2) safety aspects, 3) substitutes that could meet the need and not be as unsafe, 4) ability to reduce unsafe characteristics without reducing usefulness or making too expensive, 5) users ability to avoid danger by using care, 6) users likely awareness of dangers inherent in the product, and 7) feasibility for the maker to spread losses by having a price that could cover liability insurance. The jury will consider such factors when considering the sensibility of a child-resistant design.
Citation	*Calles v. Scripto-Tokai Corp.*, ---N.E.2d--- (2007 WL 495315, Sup. Ct., Ill., 2007)

	Email Describing Terms of Agreement Can Satisfy Statute of Frauds
Description	Appeals court held that oral discussions that were summarized in an email could satisfy the statute of frauds requirement that key terms of an agreement must be in writing to be enforceable. If plaintiff can show at trial that such was the case, then there was an enforceable contract.
Topic	Contracts
Key Words	Agreement; Writing; Statute of Frauds; Email
CASE SUMMARY	
Facts	Lamle owned a game, Farook. Mattel was interested in distribution rights. They signed an agreement that Mattel had exclusive rights to negotiate with Lamle from March 18 until June 15 for $25,000, but there was no distribution contract unless it was in writing. On June 11 the parties reached an agreement. Mattel asked Lamle to draft a formal contract to memorialize 'The Deal.' On June 26, Mattel employee Bucher sent Lamle an email entitled "Farook Deal" that repeated the key terms of the June 11 meeting. It stated that the terms had been agreed to and ended "Best regards Mike Bucher." August 13, Mattel sent Lamle a fax saying it was "waiting for a draft licensing agreement." Lamle sent it on August 19. Mattel then decided it was not interested and told Lamle so in October. He sued for breach of contract. The district court dismissed the suit. Lamle appealed.
Decision	Vacated in part and remanded. Whether a contract is formed depends on the mutual assent of the parties as determined by the objective expressions of the parties. There is a question of fact here whether or not the parties entered into a contract. The initial written agreement may have been replaced by a later oral agreement, if they mutually intended. If that was the case, then the issue is if the parties reached a new written agreement for distribution rights. Under the statute of frauds, there must be a writing that contains the material terms of the agreement. The email sent by Bucher is a valid writing and signature that satisfies California's statute of frauds. The question to be determined at trial is if there was a binding oral agreement that was memorialized sufficiently in the email sent by Bucher.
Citation	*Lamle v. Mattel, Inc.*, 394 F.3d 1355 (Fed. Cir., 2005)

CYBERLAW

CASE 1 - MESSAGE BOARD IMMUNITY

Message Board Operator Not Liable for False Comments Posted by Users	
Description	Appeals court held that a company that claimed to be defamed and cyberstalked by users of a message board had no grounds for suit against the provider of the board. The Communications Decency Act specifically provided immunity for such operators.
Topic	Cyberlaw
Key Words	Defamation; Cyberstalking; Communications Decency Act; Provider; Message Board
CASE SUMMARY	
Facts	Universal Communication Systems (UCS) sued Lycos, the provider of assorted Internet message boards, including RagingBull.Com, which hosts a financially-oriented board that allows users to post comments about publicly-traded companies. Some postings were negative about UCS's financial condition. It sued Lycos and eight John Does, the posters of negative comments. It claimed cyberstalking under the Communications Decency Act (CDA) and defamation. The district court dismissed the suit. UCS appealed.
Decision	Affirmed. Under the CDA, an Internet message board operator is immune from liability for allegedly false and defamatory postings made by third party subscribers to the board. None of the alleged misinformation was generated by Lycos. Similarly, there is no claim for defamation of the company name or trademark. Congress intended such message board operators to be immune from liability for statements posted by users.
Citation	*Universal Communications Systems v. Lycos*, 478 F.3d 413 (1st Cir., 2007)

CASE 2 – ISP IMMUNITY- WEB POSTINGS

Web Users Who Republish False Information Not Liable	
Description	California high court held that under the Communication Decency Act an Internet provider or user cannot be held liable for the publication of defamatory material provided by another. There is no obligation to not post or pass on false material even if notified that it is potentially defamatory.
Topic	**Cyberlaw**
Key Words	Internet Providers; Communications Decency Act; Libel
CASE SUMMARY	
Facts	Doctors Barrett and Polevoy operate Web sites devoted to exposing health frauds. They sued Rosenthal, who directed the Humantics Foundation for Women and operated an Internet discussion group. They allege that Rosenthal committed libel by publishing defamatory statements in e-mails and Internet postings, impugning their character and competence and disparaging their efforts to combat health fraud. This publication continued even after they notified Rosenthal of the false and defamatory information. Rosenthal claimed protected speech. The district court dismissed the suit; the appeals court reversed. Rosenthal appealed.
Decision	Reversed. Although there were messages posted accusing the doctors of being quacks, of stalking women, and other falsehoods, the (CDA) Communications Decency Act states: "No provider or user of an interactive computer service shall be treated as the publisher or speaker of any information provided by another information content provider." This prohibits imposition of defamation liability on distributors as well as publishers. This promotes self-regulation of the Internet. This is unlike publishers of books or newspapers, who can be liable for common law defamation on the same basis as an author, but only if they knew or had reason to know of a publication's defamatory content. The CDA offers greater protection against defamation actions. A "user" in this case could be an individual alternative health proponent. They are free to repeat information even if they have been informed it is false. The CDA makes no distinction between active and passive users of the Internet.
Citation	*Barrett v. Rosenthal*, 146 P.3d 510 (Sup. Ct., Calif., 2006)

ISP Not Liable for Discriminatory Content in Ad Postings	
Description	Appeals court affirmed that craigslist is not liable for ads posted for rental property that contained possibly illegal discriminatory content. It is the carrier of the material, it is not responsible for screening it for compliance with the law.
Topic	Cyberlaw
Key Words	ISP; Discrimination; Liability; Craigslist; Housing
C A S E S U M M A R Y	
Facts	The Fair Housing Act prohibits discrimination on account of race, religion, sex or family status when selling or renting housing. As part of that restriction, it prohibits ads that indicate a preference based on race, color, religion, sex, handicap, family status or national origin. The law exempts single-family housing that is sold or rented by a person who does not own more than three such houses. The Chicago Lawyers' Committee for Civil Rights Under Law sued craigslist for posting discriminatory ads. Some ads stated "No Minorities" or "No Children." The district court held for cragislist. The Committee appealed.
Decision	Affirmed. Online services such as craigslist are somewhat like common carriers like the telephone or delivery services such as UPS. The telephone companies do not control the content of what is said on the phone. UPS does not control discriminatory words that may be in written materials it delivers. Craigslist would have a difficult time screening listings. If it banned certain words, such as black or white, it would affect many things besides reference to race. Hiring staff to read each posted ad would be very expensive and delay postings, as craigslist has more than 30 million postings monthly. The Committee objects to a statements such as "Catholic Church and beautiful Buddhist Temple within one block." The Committee claims that is discriminatory on religious grounds; craigslist sees that as useful information about the neighborhood near a residence. Section 230(c)(1) of the Communications Decency Act provides "No provider or user of an interactive computer service shall be treated as the publisher or speaker of any information provided by another information content provider." Craigslist is the publisher of information provided by others. It is just the messenger that may reveal a third party's plan to engage in unlawful discrimination.
Citation	*Chicago Lawyers' Comm. for Civil Rights Under Law, Inc. v. craigslist, Inc.*, ---F.3d--- (2008 WL 681168)

CASE 4 – ISP IMMUNITY – MYSPACE

MySpace Not Responsible for Assault by Users Who Came Into Contact with Each Other	
Description	Court dismissed a suit against MySpace by a minor girl who contended that she was lured into a sexual assault through MySpace. It is protected by the Communications Decency Act for liability as it is not an information content provider.
Topic	Cyberlaw
Key Words	Website Owner; Communications Decency Act; Liability; Assault
CASE SUMMARY	
Facts	Jane Doe, a 15-year-old girl alleged that she "was lured from her home and sexually assaulted by a sexual predator, who communicated with her and ultimately orchestrated his sexual assault of her through the MySpace.com website." Plaintiff contends that MySpace is liable for the assault and is not entitled to immunity under the Communications Decency Act (CDA) because it refused to employ reasonable safety measures on its website and that MySpace acted as an information content provider by creating and developing information that led to the injuries alleged. As such, MySpace should be liable for negligence, gross negligence, and strict product liability. MySpace moved to dismiss the complaint.
Decision	Motion granted. The CDA states that "No provider or user of an interactive computer service shall be treated as the publisher or speaker of any information provided by another information content provider." MySpace is not an information content provider; it is the provider of a forum on which users share information.
Citation	*Jane Doe IX v. MySpace, Inc.,* ---F.Supp.2d--- (2009 WL 1457170. E.D. Texas, 2009)

CASE 5 – LONG ARM JURISDICTION

Website Advertising Created Sufficient Basis for Long-Arm Jurisdiction	
Description	Appeals court held that a Tennessee resident who allegedly infringed a trademark of a Florida resident on a Tennessee website is subject to jurisdiction of courts in Florida for purposes of the trademark suit. The long-arm statute applies since the website was intended to help attract business in Florida.
Topic	Cyberlaw
Key Words	Website; Trademark; Infringement; Jurisdiction; Long-Arm Statute
CASE SUMMARY	
Facts	Carman Licciardello (Carman) has been a musician and entertainer for years. One year, Carman hired Lovelady as his personal manager and to manage concert tours in 80 cities, including several in Florida. That contracted ended in 2001. In 2006, Carman alleges that Lovelady posed a website that promoted Lovelady as a personal manager for music artists. The site used Carman's trademarked name and his picture, implying that Carman endorses Lovelady's skill as a manager. Carman sued Lovelady, who lives in Tennessee, for trademark infringement in federal court in Florida. The district court dismissed the action for lack of personal jurisdiction. Carman appealed.
Decision	Reversed and remanded. A federal district court in Florida may exercise personal jurisdiction over a nonresident defendant to the same extent that a Florida court may, so long as the exercise is consistent with federal due process. The website advertising Lovelady's services, which had been provided in Florida at various times, was accessible in Florida. That was sufficient contact to give jurisdiction over Lovelady under the Florida long-arm statute since the alleged infringement occurred within the state.
Citation	*Licciardello v. Lovelady*, 544 F.3d 1280 (11th Cir., 2008)

CASE 6 – EBAY SELLER CAN'T BE SUED IN BUYER'S STATE

No Personal Jurisdiction in State of Buyer Over Seller via eBay	
Description	Appeals court held that when a buyer of merchandise on eBay is in one state and the seller is in another state, the courts in the state of the buyer do not have personal jurisdiction over the seller in the event of a dispute about the deal.
Topic	Court Procedure
Key Words	Personal Jurisdiction; eBay; Breach of Contract; Fraud
CASE SUMMARY	
Facts	Boschetto, who lives in California, bought a 1964 Ford Galaxie 500XL that was advertised on eBay by a seller, Hansing, who lives in Wisconsin. He stated that the car was in excellent condition, classified as "R code." Boschetto paid $34,106 and had the car shipped to him. Then he discovered that it was not "R code" and had many problems. Hansing would not rescind the deal, so Boschetto sued him in federal court in California. Hansing moved to dismiss based on lack of personal jurisdiction. The court agreed and dismissed the suit. Boschetto appealed.
Decision	Affirmed. Due process requires that principles be applied to impose jurisdiction over a nonresident: 1) the defendant must purposefully direct his activities with the forum (California in this case) or resident so as to invoke the benefits and protections of its laws; 2) the claim must be one which arises out of or relates to defendant's forum-related activities, and 3) the exercise of jurisdiction must comport with fair play and substantial justice. Hansing did not purposefully avail himself of the privilege of doing business in California when he a sold one car to a buyer by an Internet auction site, and so was not subject to specific personal jurisdiction by courts in California. The fact that eBay is in interstate commerce does not change the result, as it is only a virtual forum for the exchange of goods, not a merchant selling the goods, a car in this case, in California.
Citation	*Boschetto v. Hansing*, 539 F.3d 1011 (9th Cir., 2008)

A. TORTS

CASE 1 – ELECTRONIC CONVERSION

	Theft of Electronic Files Is Common Law Conversion
Description	New York high court held that the doctrine of conversion applies to intangible goods such as electronic files on computers. The taking of such property will be treated the same at law as the taking of physical property.
Topic	**Cyberlaw**
Key Words	Tort; Conversion; Files
	CASE SUMMARY
Facts	Thyroff worked as an agent for Nationwide Mutual Insurance. Their agreement specified that Nationwide leased Thyroff's office computer hardware and software to facilitate sharing of customer information and other business data. He used it for the Nationwide business as well as for other personal and business correspondence. After several years, Nationwide terminated the agreement, as it had the right to do. The next day, Nationwide seized Thyroff's computer equipment and denied him access to all his records. He sued Nationwide in federal district court for conversion for taking his personal and business files not related to Nationwide. That court dismissed the suit for failure to state a cause of action. Thyroff appealed to the federal appeals court which held that New York law had not been resolved on that issue, so it asked the New York high court: is a claim for the conversion of electronic data cognizable under New York law?
Decision	Question answered. The common law cause of action of conversion applied to intangible electronic records that are stored on a computer and are indistinguishable from printed documents. Conversion is the unauthorized assumption and exercise of the right of ownership over goods belonging to another to the exclusion of the owner's rights. This applies to tangible and intangible goods. [Thyroff may now proceed against Nationwide in federal district court.]
Citation	*Thyroff v. Nationwide Mutual Insurance Co.*, 8 N.Y.3d 283, Ct. App., N.Y. (2007)

CASE 2 – FRAUD CONVERSION

	Innocent Recipient of Money Obtained by Fraud Liable for Conversion	
Description	Appeals court held that parents given large sums of money by their daughter who engaged in fraud to obtain the money were liable to the financial institutions that were the rightful owners of the money.	
Topic	Torts	
Key Words	Conversion; Bank; Fraud	
	CASE SUMMARY	
Facts	Davis and others conspired to obtain millions of dollars through fraudulent mortgage applications. A sham buyer would make an offer on multi-million dollar homes. The paperwork would be changed to a higher price than the price paid to the seller and the conspirators, who operated at every step of the transaction, would collect the difference. Davis collected $2.8 million as her share of the fraudulently obtained funds. She was sentenced to 12 years in prison and others were also convicted. While this was going on, Davis passed on large sums of money to her parents deposited in bank accounts held in trust for her. Lehman Brothers, the victim of the scam, and its insurer and title companies sued Davis' parents for conversion. The parents did not deny that they had the money, but contended they were innocent as they had no idea the funds were obtained by fraud. The trial court held that the parents were liable for conversion. They appealed.	
Decision	Affirmed. The crux of conversion is wrongful exercise of dominion or control over property of another without authorization and to the exclusion of the owner's rights in that property. Conversion does not require that defendant have an intent to harm the rightful owner, or know that the money belongs to another. The victim of the fraud has a superior right to the return of the money than the recipient has to keep it, even if the recipient had no knowledge of the fraud. The recipient of the gift, the parents, have benefited from an unearned windfall from a wrongdoer who had no right to confer the benefit, and has no greater right to keep money wrongfully obtained than if a pickpocket stole a watch and gave it as a gift to a friend.	
Citation	*Chicago Title Insurance Co. v. Ellis and MS Financial Services, ---A.2d--- (2009 WL 2145988, App. Div., N.J., 2009)*	

Family Members Who Lost Other Family Members in Air Crash Cannot Recover for Mental Distress	
Description	Trial court dismissed a claim for mental distress for members of a family who lost two family members in a house hit by a plane in an accident. Since the survivors did not witness the crash or suffer direct physical injury themselves, there is no mental distress claim.
Topic	**Torts**
Key Words	Mental Distress; Wrongful Death; Damages
CASE SUMMARY	
Facts	A mother and her son were killed when an American Airlines plane hit their house in New York. The father and surviving children, who were not home at the time of the accident, sued for mental distress. The airline moved to dismiss the claim.
Decision	Motion granted. Under New York law, the surviving family members cannot recover damages for alleged mental injuries. They did not observe the accident, they were not physically harmed themselves, and did not witness the deaths. They can recover for loss of support, loss of household services, and loss of parental care and guidance.
Citation	*Lawler v. American Airlines, Inc.,* ---F.Supp.2d--- (2006 WL 2742029, S.D.N.Y., 2006)

Pets Are Personal Property; Value Is Fair Market, But May Include Sentimental Value	
Description	Appeals court held that when a pet is killed, personal property has been lost. The owner may sue a negligent party for the fair market value of the pet, but that can include the sentimental value of the pet. There may be no recovery for emotional distress.
Topic	Real and Personal Property
Key Words	Professional Negligence; Pet; Damages
CASE SUMMARY	
Facts	Kaufman bought Salty, a macaw, in 1996. The bird was much enjoyed by Kaufman. In 2005, the bird had medical problems. Dr. Langhofer did surgery on Salty and she died. Kaufman sued Langhofer for professional negligence and wrongful death. He sought damages for emotional distress, loss of companionship, and other claims. The trial court allocated 30 percent of fault to the veterinarian and 70 percent to Kaufman and awarded no damages. Kaufman appealed.
Decision	Affirmed. Animals are personal property and damages for negligent injury or death for an animal are limited to the animal's fair market value. If goods have no clear market value, their actual worth to the owner is the test for determining damages. When goods have special value (sentimental value) to the owner, the owner may sue to recover that value and the jury may determine that value. However, a pet owner cannot recover damages for emotional distress and loss of companionship for a pet negligently killed or injured.
Citation	*Kaufman v. Langhofer*, ---P.3d--- (2009 WL 4980337, Ct. App., Ariz., 2009)

CASE 5 – INTERFERENCE WITH CONTRACT

Oklahoma Recognizes Tort of Interference with a Contract; Punitive Damages Possible	
Description	Oklahoma high court held that under state law a firm can be liable for the tort of interference with a contract if it intentionally and improperly interferes with a valid contract between other parties. Punitive damages may be imposed if the action was intentional.
Topic	Torts
Key Words	Interference with Contract
CASE SUMMARY	
Facts	Wilspec and DunAn both design, produce, and sell parts for air conditioning (AC) units. Wilspec entered into a three-year contract with DunAn, a Chinese corporation, for DunAn make certain parts for AC units sold in North America. The DunAn parts were to be sold under the Wilspec name, and Wilspec would be the exclusive distributor for the products in North America. Wilspec made AC parts for several AC manufacturers. Wilspec claims that while the contract was in force, DunAn intentionally interfered with Wilspec's contractual relations with its AC customers by soliciting the sale of products to Wilspec's customers in North America and by making disparaging remarks to Wilspec's customers about Wilspec's ability to perform. Wilspec sued DunAn in federal court. The contract was made under Oklahoma law. The federal court certified questions to the Oklahoma high court about the law in Oklahoma regarding intentional interference with a contract.
Decision	Questions answered. In Oklahoma, one who intentionally and improperly interferes with performance of a contract between another and a third party, by preventing the other from performing the contract or causing performance to be more expensive or burdensome, is subject to liability to the other for his pecuniary loss. For a plaintiff to seek punitive damages for tortious interference with a contract, the plaintiff must prove the defendant acted recklessly, intentionally, or maliciously by clear and convincing evidence.
Citation	*Wilspec Technologies, Inc. v. DunAn Holding Group Co.*, 204 P.3d 69 (Sup. Ct., Okla., 2009)

SPECIAL TORT RULES

CASE 1 – SOCIAL HOST ALCOHOL NON-LIABILITY
BEVERAGE BROUGHT BY MINOR

Social Hosts Not Liable for Minor's Drinking Alcohol Not Provided by Hosts	
Description	Wisconsin high court held that there could be no negligence action against parents who allowed high school students to have a party at their house were alcohol that was brought to the party by one of the students was consumed. Although a drunk student later caused an accident, negligence could not be imputed to the social hosts.
Topic	Torts
Key Words	Negligence; Social Host; Alcohol; Minors; Injury
C A S E S U M M A R Y	
Facts	Beth Carr, a high school student, attended a party on property owned by the Niesens. She consumed alcohol at the party and, when driving home, cross the line and hit an on-coming car, injuring four members of the Nichols family. They sued the Niesens for negligence as social hosts for allowing minors to consume alcohol on their property. The Niesens did not serve the alcohol but apparently were aware that some kids snuck it into the party. The Nichols contended that the Niesens violated their duty by failing to prevent the alcohol consumption. The district court dismissed the suit; the appeals court reversed. The Niesens appealed to the Wisconsin high court.
Decision	Reversed. The test of negligence is whether the conduct foreseeably creates an unreasonable risk to others. The plaintiff must set forth fact that the defendant had knowledge, or should have had knowledge, of a potential and unreasonable risk. On public policy grounds a claim for common-law negligence cannot be maintained against social hosts who were allegedly aware that minors were consuming alcohol on their property, but they did not provide the alcohol, and an alcohol-related accident occurred later. Allowing such recovery would have no sensible or just stopping point. Any expansion of liability for social hosts for such instances should come from the legislature, not the common law courts.
Citation	*Nichols v. Progressive Northern Insurance Co.*, 746 N.W.2d 220 (Sup. Ct., Wisc., 2008)

CASE 2 – SOCIAL HOST ALCOHOL NON-LIABILITY PARTY CRASHING MINOR

	Organizers of Party Where Alcohol Served to Minors Not Liable for Negligence
Description	Appeals court upheld dismissal of a suit brought by the mother of a student who died from a criminal assault when he was ejected from a beer party for high school students. While the assailant may be liable, the party organizers violated no duty of care to the student who crashed the party.
Topic	Torts
Key Words	Negligence; Third Parties; Alcohol; Duty
CASE SUMMARY	
Facts	A group of high school students in Seattle planned a keg party to celebrate graduation. Expecting about 100 participants, one of the students bought six kegs (about one gallon of beer per person) from a cousin who was a beer distributor. One person who showed up at the party was Glen Anderson. Some of the seniors confronted him as he was a junior, so was not invited to the party. One of the seniors, Murray, hit Anderson in the forehead with a beer mug. The wound appeared to be minor and was stitched up in an emergency room. Four months later, Anderson went into a coma, was in a vegetative state for four years, and died. The cause of death was determined to be the wound suffered at the keg party, and the death was ruled a homicide. Anderson's mother then sued Murray and other party organizers and the beer company. She contended that they should be held jointly and severally liable for the death. The trial court dismissed the suit with respect to the students who organized the party and confronted Anderson but did not strike him.
Decision	Affirmed. The students who did not hit Anderson were not liable for negligence. The students did not foresee the possibility of a criminal assault by Murray. There was nothing in his background to give the students warning that he might engage in such an assault. Even though the keg party violated the law regarding alcohol purchase and consumption by minors, the statute was not intended to protect against an event such as this one. The students who did not commit the assault owed no duty of care to Anderson.
Citation	*Cameron v. Murray*, P.3d (2009 WL 2488433, Ct. App., Wash., 2009)

CASE 3 – COMMERCIAL HOST ALCOHOL NON-LIABILITY INTOXICATED CUSTOMER

Neither Wholesaler or Retailer of Alcoholic Beverage Violated Duty to Drunk Patron Who Died

Description	Tennessee appeals court held that the heirs of a restaurant patron, who became drunk and later fell off a bridge and was killed, had no cause of action under the Dram Shop Act or common law against either the restaurant or the company that sold alcoholic beverages to the restaurant.
Topic	Torts
Key Words	Negligence; Wrongful Death; Dram Shop Act; Restaurant

CASE SUMMARY

Facts	M, a customer at Gondolier restaurant, was served alcoholic beverages and became intoxicated. Gondolier staff called for a taxi to take him home. The taxi driver agreed he was drunk, testified that M kept saying he did not want to go home, that he wanted to go back to the Gondolier. Several times he grabbed the steering wheel, causing the taxi driver nearly to lose control. The taxi driver pulled over and removed M from the cab. The driver called 911 to report that he left a very drunk man at the side of the road. Later, M's body was found. He had fallen off a bridge and was killed. His blood alcohol was very high. His heirs sued the Gondolier and the seller of alcoholic beverages to the Gondolier for negligence by violating the Tennessee Dram Shop Act, which imposes liability on servers of alcoholic beverages under certain conditions. The trial court granted defendants summary judgment. M's heirs appealed.
Decision	Affirmed. The Gondolier is relieved of liability. It fulfilled any duty it had to Montgomery by calling a taxi cab, seeing him to the cab, and paying his fare to go home. His subsequent behavior was not foreseeable. Hence, the Gondolier is not liable under either the Dram Shop Act or under the common law of negligence. The sellers of alcoholic beverages to the Gondolier are not liable under the Dram Shop Act, as it applies to retailers of alcoholic beverages, such as the Gondolier, not wholesalers to the retailers. Any liability for the alcoholic beverage wholesalers would be based on negligence, and that does not exist. Suppliers could not foresee Montgomery's behavior.
Citation	*Montgomery v. Kail Orexi, LLC*, ---S.W.3d--- (2009 WL 837711, Ct. App., Tenn., 2009)

CASE 4 – COMMERCIAL HOST ALCOHOL LIABILITY

NIGHTCLUB ASSAULT

Alcohol Seller May Be Liable for Injuries Caused by Third Party in Criminal Assault	
Description	Appeals court held that under Colorado statutory law regarding liability for the sellers of alcohol, a nightclub could be found liable for selling alcohol to a visibly intoxicated patron who then stabbed a person outside of the club.
Topic	Real and Personal Property
Key Words	Premises Liability; Alcohol; Vendor Liability; Criminal Assault
CASE SUMMARY	
Facts	Strauch, plaintiff, and his assailant, who did not know each other, both attended a New Year's Eve party at defendant's nightclub. The assailant bought the most expensive admission pass that allowed unlimited alcoholic drinks. After leaving the club about 1 a.m., Strauch was walking back to his hotel room. Assailant, who was drunk, stabbed Strauch with a knife. Strauch sued the nightclub for serving an intoxicated patron who then stabbed him. The Colorado legislature abolished common law tort actions regarding intoxicated patrons, but imposes limited liability upon alcohol vendors for injuries caused to third parties by intoxicated patrons. The district court dismissed the suit. Strauch appealed.
Decision	Reversed and remanded. Under Colorado law, to establish limited statutory liability of a licensed alcohol vendor, Strauch need not prove that the vendor should have foreseen the injuries caused by its visibly intoxicated patron. It suffices that the vendor's improper service of alcohol to a person who was visibly intoxicated caused the patron's intoxication and the person's intoxication caused the plaintiff's injuries.
Citation	*Struach v. Build It and They Will Drink, Inc.*, ---P.3d--- (2009 WL 3464129, Ct. App., Colo., 2009)

INTELLECTUAL PROPERTY RIGHTS

CASE 1 – TEST DESIGN PATENTS

	Test for Design Patent Infringement Simplified to Ordinary Observer Rule
Description	Federal Circuit abandoned a dual test for infringement of design patents that it had used for 24 years and returned to a one part test. Courts should look to see if an ordinary observer, familiar with the prior art, would see imitation.
Topic	Intellectual Property
Key Words	Patents, Design Patent, Test, Infringement
CASE SUMMARY	
Facts	EGI sued Swisa for infringing on EGI's design patent for a fingernail buffer that consists of a rectangular, hollow tube with a square cross-section and buffer surfaces on three of its four sides. The trial court upheld the design patent but found Swisa had not infringed with its nail buffer, which was similar but has buffer surfaces on all four sides. EGI appealed.
Decision	Affirmed. An ordinary observer familiar with prior art would not be deceived into believing that the Swisa buffer was the same as the patented EGI buffer. [Note: This case is important because it is a return to an old rule by the Federal Circuit regarding design patents. The test that is to be used is what an "ordinary observer" would recognize as infringing in two competing designs. Design patents generally cover the look and feel of a product, not detailed internal working mechanisms. For a number of years the court had also required the use of a "point of novelty" test. That made infringement more difficult to prove in design patent cases. The simpler rule means the focus is on what the product looks like to an "ordinary observer" who has some familiarity with the prior art. This is expected to result in stronger legal support for design patents.]
Citation	*Egyptian Goddess, Inc. v. Swisa, Inc.*, 543 F.3d 665 (Fed. Cir., 2008)

CASE 2 – COPYRIGHT PARODY EXCEPTION

Parody of Song Allows Use without Copyright Violation	
Description	Court dismissed a copyright infringement suit by the owner of a song that was used as the basis for a song on a television program. Since the new song was a parody of the original song, it is a transformation of the song that is protected under the fair use doctrine.
Topic	Intellectual Property
Key Words	Copyright; Song; Infringement; Fair Use; Parody; Transformative
CASE SUMMARY	
Facts	"When You Wish Upon a Star" was written for the Walt Disney film *Pinocchio*. Bourne owns the copyright for the song. A segment on "Family Guy," a Fox Network cartoon program, used the song as the basis for a song called "I Need a Jew." Fox agrees that it used the original song for the melody for its song. Bourne sued for copyright infringement for using the song without permission.
Decision	Judgment for defendants. Under the fair use doctrine, the song "I Need a Jew" could reasonably be perceived as commenting on the original song, "When You Wish Upon a Star." Hence, it was a parody. The parody was transformative in nature; the lyrics are almost completely different than the original song, but most listeners would know the basis of the music. Hence, the fair use doctrine applies as the parody did not infringe on the market for the original song.
Citation	*Bourne Co. v. Twentieth Century Fox Film Corp.*, ---F.Supp.2d--- (2009 WL 700400, S.D.N.Y., 2009)

CASE 3 – EMAGAZINE COPYRIGHT

Publisher of Magazine Has Right to Reproduce Old Issues Electronically	
Description	Appeals court held that the publisher of a magazine was privileged to reproduce the magazine in a digitized format that faithfully reproduced previous issues. This reproduction did not violate the copyrights of photographers who contributed photos to the original magazine.
Topic	**Intellectual Property**
Key Words	Copyright; Infringement; Magazine; Photographs; Privilege
CASE SUMMARY	
Facts	Greenberg provided photographs for four articles that appeared in different issues of the *National Geographic* magazine. Past issues of the magazine were digitized and sold on CD-ROM sets that showed all previous issues. Greenberg sued, contending republication of his photographs in that format without his permission was infringement. The jury found there to be willful infringement and awarded the maximum damages allowed, $100,000 per incident, for $400,000 total damages. The magazine appealed.
Decision	Reversed and remanded. The electronic reproduction of the magazine was privileged revision of the original works. Similarly, a computer program that allows a user to search the electronic collection of articles and photographs is privileged revision of the copyrighted works. The collection contained exact images of the original works; the publisher had the right to republish the magazine in this format.
Citation	*Greenberg v. National Geographic Society*, 488 F.3d 1331 (11th Cir., 2007)

CASE 4 – COPYRIGHTS – FILM STORY THEMES

Copying General Theme of Copyrighted Work Is Not Infringement	
Description	**Appeals court affirmed that there was no infringement when one film company developed a story similar to that contained in a script the company had a chance to review but did not use. Infringement requires copying of specific parts of material, not general themes and story lines.**
Topic	**Intellectual Property**
Key Words	**Copyright, Infringement, Similarity**
CASE SUMMARY	
Facts	**While O'Donnell was writing a screenplay, "The Funk Parlor," about a family-run funeral parlor, her script was shown to the head of programming at HBO. Soon after, HBO hired a writer to develop "Six Feet Under," a similar story. Both stories concern a family-run funeral parlor taken over by children of the deceased founder; assorted romances and business problems occur. O'Donnell sued HBO for copyright infringement. The district court held for defendants; O'Donnell appealed.**
Decision	Affirmed. A determination of substantial similarity requires detailed examination of the allegedly infringed and infringing works. Protectable expressions include the specific details of an author's rendering of ideas, but general scenes and plots-lines are not protectable under copyright law. Infringement requires copying of concrete elements that make up the total sequence of events and the relationships among the major characters. An impression that the stories are similar is not sufficient to find infringement.
Citation	*Funky Films, Inc. v. Time Warner Entertainment Co., 462 F.3d 1072 (9th Cir., 2006)*

CASE 5 – COPYRIGHT REGISTRATION

Copyright Must Be Registered Before Infringement Takes Place or No Damages	
Description	Appeals court held that under the Copyright Act, copyrighted material must be registered for there to be a claim for damages. If infringement begins before the copyright is registered, while the copyright may be valid, there are no damages for the infringement.
Topic	Intellectual Property
Key Words	Copyright; Registration; Logo; Infringement; Damages
CASE SUMMARY	
Facts	Bouchat sued the Baltimore Ravens NFL football team, contending the team copied his drawing that he submitted in a contest to pick a logo for the Ravens. A jury held that the Ravens had infringed Bouchat's copyright on the logo but no damages were awarded. Bouchat then sued several hundred companies that used the infringing logo when they marketed Ravens merchandise containing the logo under a license granted by the Ravens. In that case, the trial court held that the licensees had infringed Bouchat's copyright but denied damages. Bouchat appealed.
Decision	Affirmed. The claims Bouchat raised in the suit against the licensees come under the previous ruling. Since he received no damages in the original suit against the Ravens, the doctrine of claim preclusion applies to further suits, such as against the licensees. Since Bouchat failed to register his copyright before infringement bega,n he cannot pursue statutory damages under the Copyright Act. Bouchat registered his copyright on July 25, 1996, but infringement began the month before. That was why he received no damages for the infringement and cannot here either.
Citation	*Bouchat v. Bon-Ton Department Stores*, 506 F.3d 315 (4th Cir., 2007)

CASE 6 – TRADEMARK PARODY EXCEPTION

	Parody of Famous Mark Allowed
Description	Appeals court held that the maker of a dog chew toy that was a parody of expensive handbags make by Louis Vuitton did not infringe or dilute the original mark. Such parody is fair use.
Topic	Intellectual Property
Key Words	Trademark; Infringement; Dilution; Lanham Act; Confusion; Parody
	C A S E S U M M A R Y
Facts	Louis Vuitton makes expensive luggage, handbags, and accessories. It sued Haute Diggity Dog for making chew toys for dogs, including small handbags called "Chewy Vuiton." Vuitton sued for trademark infringement and trademark dilution in violation of the Lanham Act and the Trademark Dilution Revision Act. The district court held for Haute Diggity Dog; Vuitton appealed.
Decision	Affirmed. Chewy Vuiton was a successful parody of the Vuitton marks and trade dress. The toy was obviously irreverent and an intentional representation of the handbag, but there was no doubt that it was not an image of the mark created by the maker. To be a parody, for trademark purposes, the product must convey that it is the original but also that it is not the original, it is only a parody for amusement. There would be no confusion between genuine products and the chew toys. The Vuitton mark is strong; no one would think it was being used on the dog toys, so it does not violate the Lanham Act. Similarly, under the Trademark Dilution Revision Act, fair use by parody is allowed since it does not impair the distinctiveness of the famous mark.
Citation	*Louis Vuitton Malletier S.A. v. Haute Diggity Dog, LLC*, 507 F.3d 252 (4th Cir., 2007)

Descriptive Trademark without Secondary Meaning Cannot Be Enforced	
Description	Appeals court held that a trademark that had clear geographic meaning was, at best, a descriptive mark. As such, it receives no protection from infringement. To become enforceable, a descriptive mark must have secondary meaning that goes beyond its original meaning.
Topic	Intellectual Property
Key Words	Trademark; Generic; Descriptive; Secondary Meaning; Mark Cancellation
CASE SUMMARY	
Facts	Douglas, the founder of OBX-Stock, invented OBX as an abbreviation for the "Outer Banks" of North Carolina. OBX-Stock used the letters OBX on oval stickers for cars to indicate that the cars were from or had visited the Outer Banks. OBX was also applied to souvenirs and other items sold in stores at the Outer Banks. The company obtained trademark registration for OBX for use in connection with a wide range of goods and services. In practice, OBX is widely used by many businesses that advertise their Outer Banks location. Bicast began to sell stickers printed with "OB Xtreme." OBX-Stock sued Bicast for trademark infringement. The district court held for Bicast, finding that OBX was either a generic mark or a descriptive mark without secondary meaning and so was not valid. OBX-Stock appealed.
Decision	Affirmed. A generic mark can never be valid under any circumstance. A descriptive mark cannot be a valid trademark without evidence of secondary meaning. The secondary meaning in connection with geographically descriptive marks means that the mark no longer causes the public to associate the goods with the geographical location, but to associate the goods with a particular product or source of the product. OBX was adopted, promoted, and received as an abbreviation for "Outer Banks." As such, it is geographically descriptive. It did not have secondary meaning. The fact that the mark was registered does not make it more valid, so it cannot be enforced.
Citation	*OBX-Stock, Inc. v. Bicast, Inc.*, 558 F.3d 334 (4th Cir., 2009)

CASE 1 – APPARENT AUTHORITY – PERSONAL ERRAND

Ostensible Authority for Vehicle Use by Employee May Impose Liability on Employer	
Description	Appeals court held that an employer could be liable for injuries caused by an employee who caused an accident while using a company car to run an errand. While there was no express permission to use the vehicle for this purpose, the jury could find ostensible authority.
Topic	Agency
Key Words	Tort; Agent; Scope of Employment; Ostensible Authority
CASE SUMMARY	
Facts	Lewis, an employee of Roseville Toyota, was driving a Roseville car on a personal errand during his lunch break when he rear-ended another car that stopped for a red light. The occupants of the other car sued Lewis and Roseville for their injuries. The jury found Lewis to be negligent and that while he was not acting in the scope of his employment, he was using the car with permission of Roseville, which was found liable for $277,662 in damages. Roseville appealed.
Decision	Affirmed. The fact that a vehicle owner either failed to monitor or supervise the use of its vehicles is a factor in determining implied permission for someone to use the vehicle. Lewis testified that the employee who controlled keys to company cars said he could use the car to run an errand. This use may have been without express permission by the vehicle owner, but showed ostensible authority to use the vehicle. Ostensible authority is authority that the principal, either intentionally or by lack of ordinary care, causes or allows a third party to believe the agent possesses. The jury could reasonably infer here that the employee was acting with the permission of the employer.
Citation	*Taylor v. Roseville Toyota, Inc.*, 138 Cal.App.4th 994 (Ct. App., Calif., 2006)

CASE 2 – APPARENT AUTHORITY – CHARITY WORK

Tort Related to Charitable Activities While at Work Not Employer's Responsibility	
Description	Mississippi high court held that an employer is not liable on the theory of respondeat superior for a car accident caused by an employee who was engaged in charitable activities during work time. Those activities were not a central part of the work duties.
Topic	Agency
Key Words	Respondeat Superior; Scope of Employment; Indirect Benefits; Accident
CASE SUMMARY	
Facts	Thornton was manager of a branch of Commercial Bank. One afternoon, while delivering a United Way pledge solicitation package to a local business, Thornton hit a vehicle driven by Hearn. Hearn's infant child died in the accident. Hearn sued Thornton and the bank for wrongful death. The bank filed a motion for summary judgment, claiming Thornton was not acting within the scope of employment at the time of the accident. The court rejected the motion. The bank appealed.
Decision	Reversed and remanded. An indirect benefit to an employer is not the appropriate test for respondeat superior. The bank was not responsible under respondeat superior as there was no evidence that Thornton was employed to perform that kind of conduct (delivering the pledge package) nor was it enough to say that Thornton 's good deeds might have resulted in new customers for the bank. While there may be evidence that the bank encouraged Thornton 's participation in charitable activities, and benefited from them, far more was required to impute liability to the bank.
Citation	*Commercial Bank v. Hearn,* 923 So.2d 202 (Sup. Ct. , Miss. , 2006)

CASE 3 – DIRECT EMPLOYER LIABILITY
NEGLIGENT HIRING OF EMPLOYEE

Negligent Hiring and Negligent Retention of Employee Basis for Employer Liability	
Description	California appeals court held that tort liability based on negligent hiring and retention is a cause of action distinct from vicarious liability based on respondeat superior. The employer may face greater liability than would be the case based on vicarious liability alone.
Topic	Agency
Key Words	Vicarious Liability; Respondeat Superior; Negligent Hiring
CASE SUMMARY	
Facts	Carcamo was driving a truck for his employer, Sugar Transport. When Tagliaferri tried to pass Carcamo, the rear of her car hit Carcamo's front tire, causing Tagliaferri to lose control. Her car when over the median and landed on top of Diaz's car that was coming in the opposite direction. The jury awarded Diaz $22.5 million in damages; apportioned 45% of fault to Tagliaferri, 20% to Carcamo, and 35% to Sugar Transport. Sugar Transport was held vicariously liable for its negligent hiring and retention of Carcamo. Sugar Transport appealed, contending that while it is vicariously liable for Carcamo's driving on a theory of respondeat superior, there should have been no claim for negligent hiring and retention.
Decision	Affirmed. Negligent hiring and retention are theories of liability independent of vicarious liability. That is, the liability comes from hiring and retaining an employee who is incompetent or unfit. Not only is the employer responsible on the theory of vicarious liability for the accident caused by an employee, but because the employer had reason to believe that an undue risk of harm would exist because of the employment. Hence evidence about Carcamo's employment and driving history, which involved previous accidents, was relevant. It showed that Sugar Transport disregarded Carcamo's past record and the unreasonable danger to others exposed by his driving. Hence, the jury properly considered that evidence when apportioning fault for the accident.
Citation	*Diaz v. Carcamo*, ---Cal.Rptr.3d--- (2010 WL 654346, Ct. App., Calif., 2010)

CASE 4 – EMPLOYER NON-LIABILITY
INDEPENDENT CONTRACTOR

Employer Not Responsible for Underage Worker Employed by Independent Contractor	
Description	West Virginia high court held that the owner of a building who contracted for a new roof to be installed hired an independent contractor when a firm was employed to do the roofing work. The building owner did not control the work, so had no knowledge that one worker, who suffered a serious injury, was underage.
Topic	Agency
Key Words	Independent Contractor; Underage Worker; Inherently Dangerous
CASE SUMMARY	
Facts	Hensley did business under the name Royalty Builders. He hired 16-year-old Robert France to do roofing work for him during his spring break from high school. Southern Equipment (SE) needed a new metal roof on a building. It accepted a bit from Quality Metal Roof (QMR). That company supplied the materials to Royalty, which did the installation work. France, working with others on the roof, fell through the roof and suffered serious head injuries. France sued SE and QMR for failing to provide a safe work environment and for vicarious liability because they exposed him to the inherently dangerous job of roofing. He also sued them for negligence for hiring Royalty to do the job, because Royalty hired underage workers in violation of state and federal law. QMR settled with France for $875,000. SE refused to settle and was granted summary judgment. France appealed.
Decision	Affirmed. SE did not know that Royalty employed an underage worker and did not sanction that practice. Royalty was an independent contractor, and SE had the right to presume that the work would be performed properly. There can be an exception to the independent contractor defense when underage workers are employed, but that exception does not apply because SE had no way of knowing France was a member of the roofing crew. SE was not responsible for controlling the work environment in the roofing job, and the job is not "inherently dangerous" so as to require heightened awareness by SE of what was occurring on the job.
Citation	*France v. Southern Equipment Co.*, ---S.E.2d--- (2010 WL 334922, Sup. Ct., W.Va., 2010)

TRADE SECRETS
CASE 1 – LEGAL DEFINITION

Swimming Program May Be Protected Trade Secret	
Description	**A group of swim instructors left their employer who had developed a special swim program for infants. The former employees went into direct competition. An appeals court held it was to be determined at trial if the program was due trade secret protection.**
Topic	**Intellectual Property**
Key Words	**Trade Secret; Misappropriation; Swimming Instructions**
CASE SUMMARY	
Facts	**Barnett founded Infant Swimming Research (ISR) in 1966. It is described as a "scientific, behavioral approach to pediatric drowning prevention" utilizing a method known as "swim, float, swim" and containing nearly 2,000 "prompts and procedures" for teaching infants as young as six-months old how to survive in water. In a five-week course, ISR trains and certifies instructors who then teach survival skills to infants in private lessons, ten minutes a day, five days a week for three to four weeks. ISR instructors sign nondisclosure agreements and covenants not to compete. Several former ISR instructors started a competing firm, Infant Aquatic Survival that uses the ISR methods. Barnett sued the former employees for misappropriation of trade secrets. The district court dismissed the suit. Barnett appealed.**
Decision	Reversed. Factors considered to determine if a trade secret exists under Colorado law include: 1) the extent to which the information is known outside the business; 2) the extent to which information is known by those inside the business; 3) the precautions taken by the holder of the trade secret to guard secrecy of information; 4) the savings effected and the value to the holder in having information as against competitors; 5) the amount of effort or money expended in obtaining and developing the information; and 6) the amount of time and expense it would take for others to acquire and duplicate the information. It is an issue of material fact as to whether the swimming program qualified as a trade secret under Colorado law, even though some elements were in the public domain. The suit will proceed.
Citation	*Harvey Bennett, Inc. v. Shidler*, 338 F.3d 1125 (10th Cir., 2003)

CASE 2 – REVERSE ENGINEERING DEFENSE

	Protected Proprietary Process Not Trade Secret if Subject to Reverse Engineering
Description	**Mississippi high court held that while a company did make efforts to protect its bid process on steel fabrication jobs, and the process was valuable to the firm, a person skilled in the field could figure out the bid process, so it was not a trade secret.**
Topic	**Intellectual Property**
Key Words	**Trade Secrets; Proprietary Procedures**
	CASE SUMMARY
Facts	**GSI is a steel fabricator—a contractor that makes steel components for various construction projects. Scott Marshall used to work for GSI as an estimator—he determined how much GSI could bid on a project and still earn a profit. Scott asked his brother, Alan Marshall, to write a program to help him with estimates. Alan did so and was not paid for his work. Scott used the program while he worked at GSI. When Scott left GSI, he and Alan tried to market a new version of the program to sell to project estimators. GSI sued, contending that the key elements of the bid estimation process in the program were stolen from GSI by Scott, and so constituted a trade secret. The trial court enjoined the brothers from marketing the program; they appealed.**
Decision	Reversed. The process by which bids were estimated was easy to figure out by proper means and hence was not a trade secret. While the process has value to GSI, a person competent in the field could figure it out by reverse engineering . GSI provided evidence that it did protect the secrecy of its bid process, but the process is still not a trade secret. The fact that Marshall never signed a non-disclosure agreement is not relevant to the outcome, as he would have a duty not to use trade secret information in any event.
Citation	*Marshall v. Gipson Steel, Inc.*, 806 So.2d 266 (Sup. Ct., Miss., 2002)

CASE 1 – LIABILITY OF CORPORATE OFFICERS / DIRECTORS

Company Officer Personally Liable for Failure to Pay Company Taxes	
Description	Appeals court held that a company officer was personally liable for the taxes owed by a company he worked for. His defense that he was only an employee responding to orders from superiors did not hold, as he was an officer of the company responsible for payroll and taxes.
Topic	Agency
Key Words	Corporate Officer; Responsible Person; Taxes
C A S E S U M M A R Y	
Facts	Lubetzky joined MediaForum as an employee and was appointed treasurer and chief financial officer. He had check-signing authority and prepared payroll checks and tax returns. A year later, MediaForum, a subsidiary of a British company, was sold in pieces and Lubetzky served as president while the company was dissolved. The IRS sued Lubetzky for failure to pay federal withholding taxes for MediaForum for more than a year. The trial court held that Lubetzy was a responsible person, given his position in the corporation, and was personally liable for a $90,000 judgment for the unpaid taxes. He appealed.
Decision	Affirmed. Lubetzky's defense is that for most of his time at MediaForum he was under the control of the company president. He had told him that taxes had not been paid, but was told to wait. As such, he contends that he did not have sufficient authority, on behalf of the corporation, to pay taxes. That defense is not available. Under federal tax law, a person is personally liable for willfully failing to pay federal withholding taxes if the defendant knew that the taxes were due from his employer yet failed to pay the taxes. Lubetzky was an officer of the corporation with check writing authority, so he was a responsible person. Hence, he assumed personal liability for taxes due from MediaForum when he failed to pay the taxes.
Citation	*Lubetzky v. U.S.*, 393 F.3d 76 (1st Cir., 2004)

CASE 2 - PIERCING THE CORPORATE VEIL
PARENT - SUBSIDIARY

Court May Pierce Corporate Veil to Allow Recovery of Debt Under Certain Conditions	
Description	Appeals court held that a creditor could pierce the veil of a corporation to hold its parent liable for an unpaid debt because the corporation failed to follow the standards expected of a corporation to be treated as an entity.
Topic	Business Organization
Key Words	Corporations; Pierce the Veil; Parent Corporation; Fraud
CASE SUMMARY	
Facts	Plaintiff gave Karen Lynn, a corporation, a ten-year lease for retail space in Chicago. Later, Lynn was in default due to unpaid rent and the court issued a default judgment for $22,000. Plaintiff moved to enforce the judgment, but Lynn had insufficient assets. Plaintiff sued Lynn's parent corporation and the owners of that corporation, requesting the court to hold them liable for the debt. The trial court dismissed the suit. Plaintiff appealed.
Decision	Reversed. Karen Lynn never did anything other than sign the lease. It is owned by Fashion Enterprises, which owns other corporations that also have retail outlets. Karen Lynn only had sufficient capital in it to maintain a bank account. The corporation was dissolved once the default judgment was entered. Fashion Enterprises, its parent corporation, is owned by one person. "A corporate veil will be pierced where (1) there is such unity of interest and ownership that the separate personalities of the corporation and the individual are nonexistent, and (2) the circumstances are such that adherence to the fiction of a separate corporate existence would promote injustice or inequitable consequences." The court looks to evidence such as inadequate capitalization, failure to observe corporate formalities, insolvency of the debtor corporation, and absence of corporate records. Plaintiff may proceed against the parent corporation to recover the debt for unpaid rent.
Citation	*Miner v. Fashion Enterprises, Inc.*, --- N.E.2d --- (2003 WL 21659093, App. Ct., Ill., 2003)

CASE 3 – LIMITED LIABILITY OF CORPORATE MANAGERS
FOR UNPAID WAGES

Employing Corporation, Not Managers, Are Liable for Unpaid Wages of Employees	
Description	Nevada high court held that when a corporation went bankrupt, and failed to pay employees' wages, the employees could not sue the managers of the corporation for the wages, even though the managers owned the corporation.
Topic	Business Organization
Key Words	Employer; Manager; LLC; Liability; Unpaid Wages
CASE SUMMARY	
Facts	Former employees of the Castaways Hotel in Las Vegas sued to recover unpaid wages they lost when the hotel-casino filed for bankruptcy. They sued several former high-level mangers at Castaways. The managers were also the owners of Castaways, which was incorporated as an LLC. The former employees contend that under state law, the managers were liable for their wages. The federal district court dismissed the suit, concluding that, under Nevada law, the managers were not employers. Appellants appealed. The federal appeals court certified a question to the Nevada high court about the legal liability of managers and employers under Nevada law in such situations.
Decision	Question answered. Generally, a corporate officer is not considered the employer responsible for creating the contractual employment relationship and is not personally liable for a breach of that relationship. Under Nevada corporate law, individual liability does not extend to officers, directors, or stockholders of a corporation unless otherwise provided by specific statute. Individual management-level corporate employees cannot be held liable as "employers" for the unpaid wages of employees under Nevada's wage and hour laws. The employees' claim was against the corporation, the Castaways, as their employer, not against the manager-owners of the Castaways.
Citation	*Boucher v. Shaw*, 196 P.3d 959 (Sup. Ct., Nev., 2008)

CASE 4 – PIERCING THE VEIL FRAUD LIABILITY OF SHAREHOLDER

When Company Manager Engages in Fraud, Piercing the Corporate Veil May Occur	
Description	Appeals court held that where a company shareholder and manager personally misused down payments made by people who expected to have a home built, the manager could be personally liable for the fraud he helped to direct.
Topic	Business Organization
Key Words	LLC; Manager; Breach of Contract; Fraud; Liability; Pierce the Veil
CASE SUMMARY	
Facts	Two LLCs were formed to buy, finance, and develop a residential real estate subdivision. Longhi was a shareholder in one and an officer of both. He was an architect who met with customers at the development, helped them with designs, and served as liaison between customers and constructors. He was a friend of the Mazzonis and told them he could build them a house in the subdivision for half the normal price. Longhi said that because he was giving them a big discount, they had to make a $50,000 down payment. They did, but two years later, when nothing had happened, the Mazzonis requested their money back. About that time, Longhi was fired. In 1999, they sued one LLC for breach of contract and also sued Longhi, personally, for taking the $50,000 down payment. The trial court found Longhi personally liable under the doctrine of piercing the corporate veil. Longhi appealed.
Decision	Affirmed. To pierce the corporate veil, the plaintiff must show that a corporation is merely an instrumentality that has been misused by fraud or promotes injustice. The plaintiff must show: 1) undercapitalization, 2) absence of corporate records, 3) fraudulent representation by corporate shareholders or directors, 4) use of the corporation to promote fraud, injustice or illegal activities, 5) payment by the corporation of individual obligations, 6) comingling of assets and affairs, 7) failure to observe required corporate formalities, or 8) other acts or conduct ignoring, controlling, or manipulating the corporate form. The evidence shows it. Longhi, the manager, can be personally liable for the $50,000 down payment, as construction never began and the deed to the property was never executed.
Citation	*Longhi v. Mazzoni*, ---N.E.2d--- (2009 WL 3231456, Ct. App., Ind., 2009)

State Citizenship of Multi-State Business May Rely on Nerve Center Test	
Description	Appeals court held that, for purposes of jurisdiction, the citizenship of a business usually depends on its principal place of business. When the business has locations in many states, it is possible it is not a citizen of the state in which it does the most business volume. Rather the court looks to the nerve center of business operations to determine its home state.
Topic	Business Organization
Key Words	Principal Place of Business; Nerve Center Test; Class Action
CASE SUMMARY	
Facts	Davis, on behalf of himself and a class of California consumers, sued HSBC Bank Nevada and Best Buy Stores in court in California, claiming that defendants defrauded California customers by offering credit cards without adequately disclosing the annual fee customers would be charged. Defendants removed the action to federal court based on the Class Action Fairness Act (CAFA). Davis moved to remand the action to state court, invoking the local controversy exception in CAFA. The district court granted the motion to remand the case to state court and defendants appealed, contending the case should be in federal court.
Decision	Reversed and remanded. HSBC Bank Nevada is clearly a citizen of Nevada. The only question is whether Best Buy has its principal place of business in California. If not, then it is not a citizen of California and the local controversy rule does not apply and federal jurisdiction exists. Best Buy Company is headquartered in Minnesota. Best Buy Stores, L.P., is located in Virginia. A limited partnership or a corporation is a citizen of: 1) the state under whose laws it is organized or incorporated and 2) the state of its principal place of business. The principal place of business is the state containing "a substantial predominance of corporate operations." Best Buy has more stores, employees and sales in California than in any other state. However, this does not mean that a substantial predominance of its activities are in California. Like many companies, it is spread out in many states, so the "nerve center approach" is used, otherwise California would be the home state to many businesses. Just because Best Buy has more sales in California than in any other state does not make it a citizen of California under the nerve center test.
Citation	*Davis v. HSBC Bank Nevada*, 557 F.3d 1026 (9th Cir., 2009).

SECURITIES REGULATION

CASE 1 – IS IT A SECURITY?

	Foreign Currency Trading Pools Meet Howey Test for SEC Regulation
Description	**Appeals court upheld an injunction issued by a federal judge at the request of the SEC to prevent further operation of a foreign currency trading pool run out of Florida, with trades executed in the Bahamas. The operation met the criteria of the Howey test, so there was a security in the trading pool subject to SEC regulation.**
Topic	**Securities Law**
Key Words	**Howey Test; Investment Contracts**
CASE SUMMARY	
Facts	Unique Financial Concepts offered the sale of foreign currency options. The company advertised heavily, promising large returns. Customer agreements explained that investment money would be pooled together and that Unique had sole discretion over investments, although these terms were later dropped from customer agreements. Unique representatives advised investors as to which currencies to invest in. Trades were made via companies in the Bahamas. Of the $6.5 million invested in one year, only $2.5 million was sent to the Bahamas for currency trades. The rest of the money went to sales commissions, the heads of Unique, and overhead expenses. The SEC sought and obtained a preliminary injunction against Unique from further operations due to securities law violations. Unique appealed.
Decision	Affirmed. The Howey test was satisfied-there was a pooling of investors' money into a common enterprise with the expectation of profits. Unique asserted it was selling a "commodity pool" involving merging of client money to buy and sell assorted foreign currencies. The details of the operation are muddled, as the books were poorly kept, but it is clear that these were not individual client accounts entirely under the control of the individual investors. This is within the jurisdiction of the SEC and the CFTC.
Citation	*Securities and Exchange Comm. v. Unique Financial Concepts, Inc.*, 196 F.3d 1195 (11th Cir., 1999)

CASE 2 – PONZI SCHEME SECURITY

	Internet Stock Market Game Is Securities Fraud
Description	**Appeals court held that an Internet game offering shares of stock in virtual companies earning high rates of return was the sale of unregistered securities, since the terms of the deal meet the *Howey* test of an investment contract. The operation was a Ponzi scheme to be halted immediately with all assets frozen.**
Topic	**Securities Law**
Key Words	**Investment; *Howey* Test; Ponzi Schemes**
	CASE SUMMARY
Facts	**SG ran a "StockGeneration" website offering the chance to buy shares in "virtual companies" listed on SG's "virtual stock exchange." SG arbitrarily set the buy and sell prices of each stock in the imaginary companies biweekly and allowed investors to buy and sell any quantity at posted prices. Millions of dollars had been collected by SG, and participants had trouble redeeming their shares until SG suspended operations. The SEC sued, contending that the sale of shares in a company that was a "game without any risk" that had an average increase in value of 10% per month, was a sale of an unregistered security in violation of the Securities Exchange Act. The district court dismissed the complaint, holding that the shares were clearly marked and defined as a game lacking a business context. The SEC appealed.**
Decision	Reversed. Under the *Howey* test, these are investment contracts, given how they were marketed to the public. It does not matter if the promoter presents the enterprise as a serious commercial venture or calls it a game. The game was a Ponzi or pyramid scheme in which there was a pooling of assets from multiple investors in a manner that all share in profits and risks of the enterprise operated by third parties. An injunction against the operation is issued and assets of SG are to be frozen.
Citation	*SEC v. SG Ltd.*, 265 F.3d 42 (1st Cir., 2001)

CASE 3 – SECTION 16B INSIDER LIABILITY

Short-Swing Profits Earned by Insiders Must Be Disgorged	
Description	**Court held that insiders who held more than ten percent of the securities in a company had a duty to disgorge profits earned in short-swing transactions that occurred within six-month time periods by matching highest sale prices to lowest purchase prices.**
Topic	**Consumer Protection**
Key Words	**Section 16; Short-Wing Profits; Insiders; Disgorgement**
CASE SUMMARY	
Facts	**Two distinct groups of defendants were involved in a series of private placements of KFx securities that resulted in each group owning more than ten percent of the shared of KFx. As a result of holding more than ten percent of the stock, defendants were subject to insider restrictions on short-swing sale profits under Section 16 of the Securities Exchange Act. Segen sued in a shareholder derivate action on behalf of KFx shareholders, seeking disgorgement of $9 million in short-swing profits. The insiders moved for summary judgment.**
Decision	Motion granted. The defendants had already disgorged profits of $185,000 that they agreed could be found to be short-swing profits in violation of Section 16. The $9 million claimed by plaintiff is incorrect. To determine the maximum possible recovery in short-swing profits from insider's transactions, it is necessary to define the transactions subject to insider prohibitions, and then a date and time must be established for each purchase or sale to determine the price of the underlying security. Trades must be matched in a manner maximizing disgorgeable amounts, which is accomplished by matching highest sale prices with lowest purchase prices within six-month periods. Defendants have done so. No further disgorgement is due.
Citation	*Segen v. Westcliff Capital Management*, --- F.Supp.2d --- (2004 WL 78648, S.D., NY, 2004)

CASE 4 – MISAPPROPRIATION THEORY OF INSIDER TRADING
NON – LIABILITY OF OPPOSING SHAREHOLDER

Shareholder Breached No Duty By Selling Stock After Being Provided Non-Public Information	
Description	District court dismissed an SEC action against a shareholder of a private firm who was told, in confidence by the firm's CEO, of a planned public offering. As the shareholder opposed the offering, he sold his shares. That breached no duty and was not a basis for a claim of insider trading based on misappropriation of information.
Topic	Securities Law
Key Words	Insider Trading; Misappropriation of Information; Duty
CASE SUMMARY	
Facts	The SEC sued Mark Cuban, owner of the Dallas Mavericks, under the misappropriation theory of insider trading. The SEC alleged that after Cuban agreed to maintain the confidentiality of material, nonpublic information concerning a planned private investment, he sold his stock in the company without first disclosing That he intended to trade on this information, thereby avoiding substantial losses when the stock declined. Cuban owned 6.3% of Mamma.com when it was a private company and knew of the plan to go public. He opposed the PIPE because it would dilute the value of his shares. The CEO of Mamma.com claimed that Cuban promised he would not sell his shares before the public offering was announced, but he did. Cuban moved to dismiss the complaint.
Decision	Motion granted. The SEC did not adequately allege that Cuban entered into an agreement with Mamma.com that could support shareholder liability under the misappropriation theory of insider trading. The SEC merely alleged that Cuban agreed to keep confidential whatever information Mamma.com's CEO intended to share with him regarding the planned PIPE offering. The SEC did not allege that Cuban agreed to refrain from trading on information or otherwise use it for his own benefit. There was a unilateral expectation by the CEO that Cuban would not sell his shares; that is no basis for the SEC action as Cuban had the right to sell. Cuban did not share his information with third parties, so breached no duty to the corporation.
Citation	*SEC v. Cuban*, ---F.Supp.2d--- (2009 WL 2096166, N.D. Tex., 2009)

BANKRUPTCY

CASE 1 – CHAPTER 7 TO 13 CONVERSIONS

Bad Faith by Bankrupt Forfeits Right to Convert from Chapter 7 to Chapter 13	
Description	**Supreme Court held that when a Chapter 7 bankrupt was shown to have hidden assets, the bad faith behavior allows the court to prohibit the petitioner from converting to Chapter 13, which was a right otherwise.**
Topic	**Bankruptcy**
Key Words	**Chapter 7, Chapter 13, Conversion, Objection, Bad Faith**
CASE SUMMARY	
Facts	**Marrama filed a Chapter 7 petition, thereby creating an estate of all his property "wherever located and by whomever held." Citizens Bank is the principal creditor. Marrama made statements that were misleading. He transferred valuable property into a trust before filing. When that was discovered, the trustee moved to attach the property as part of the estate. Marrama then requested to covert to a Chapter 13 bankrupcty. The creditor and trustee objected as the conversion was made in bad faith and was an abuse of the process. The bankruptcy court and appeals courts agreed. Marrama appealed.**
Decision	Affirmed. The debtor forfeited his right to proceed under Chapter 13, by conversion from Chapter 7, by engaging in pre-petition bad faith conduct that established cause to warrant dismissal from Chapter 13, rendering him unqualified to be a debtor under Chapter 13. While there is a right of conversion from 7 to 13 under the code, that right is lost by bad faith conduct. Bankruptcy courts must have authority to prevent abuse of process.
Citation	*Marrama v. Citizens Bank of Massachusetts*, 127 S.Ct. 1105 (2007)

CASE 2 – ATTORNEY LEGAL ADVICE

	Speech Restrictions in 2005 Bankruptcy Reform Act Unconstitutional
Description	**Trial court held that bankruptcy attorneys many not be prevented from advising their bankruptcy clients to take financial actions that are legal under the bankruptcy law. Restriction on advice is unconstitutional under the free speech provisions of the First Amendment.**
Topic	**Bankruptcy**
Key Words	**BAPCPA; Constitutionality; Free Speech; Attorney and Client**
	CASE SUMMARY
Facts	**The Bankruptcy Abuse Prevention and Consumer Protection Act (BAPCPA) of 2005 contains provisions that apply to consumer bankruptcy attorneys and how they provide service to clients. Hersh, a Dallas attorney who counsels clients regarding federal bankruptcy law, sued the government, contending that the provision of the BAPCPA that prohibits attorneys from advising clients to incur additional debt in contemplation of bankruptcy is an unconstitutional restriction of speech.**
Decision	As defined by the BAPCPA, Hersh, as a bankruptcy attorney, is a "debt relief agency" subject to the statute. Congress clearly intended to have the statute apply to bankruptcy attorneys. The Act states that a debt relief agency may not "advise an assisted person or prospective assisted person to incur more debt in contemplation of such person filing a case under [the bankruptcy law]." That provision is facially unconstitutional. Content-based restrictions on speech are subject to strict review. Regulation of speech must be narrowly tailored to promote a compelling government interest. As drafted, the Act prohibits attorneys from advising clients to take actions that are lawful under the BAPCPA. The Act also prohibits attorneys from giving financially prudent advice.
Citation	*Hersh v. U.S.*, ---B.R.--- (2006 WL 2088270, N.D. Texas, 2006)

CASE 3 – CHAPTER 7 DISCHARGEABLE DEBTS

STUDENT LOANS – HARDSHIP TEST

No Partial Discharge of Student Loans Absent Hardship	
Description	Appeals court held that a bankruptcy court improperly allowed partial discharge of student loans. The debtor failed to show that she suffered hardship as she had non-essential expenses such as a cell phone and cable TV, and it was likely that her income would rise in the future.
Topic	Bankruptcy
Key Words	Chapter 7; Student Loans; Partial Discharge
CASE SUMMARY	
Facts	To help pay for college and graduate school, Miller took out student loans of almost $90,000. At the time she filed for bankruptcy she had paid only $368 toward the loans. Her income at the time she filed was $26,500 a year. The bankruptcy court granted Miller a partial discharge of the loans, dismissing $55,000 of what she owed. The Pennsylvania Higher Education Assistance Agency (PHEAA) appealed the discharge.
Decision	Reversed and remanded. A grant of partial discharge under the equity powers of the bankruptcy court, can be made only upon a showing of undue hardship with regard to the amount discharged. The factors taken into account are: 1) that the debtor cannot maintain, based on current income and expenses, a minimal standard of living for herself if forced to repay the loans, 2) that additional circumstances exist indicating that this condition is likely to persist, and 3) that the debtor has made good faith efforts to repay the loans. The discharge was improper here because Miller did not show undue hardship and did not show that her current income was likely to be the level that she would earn in the future. She made little effort to repay the loan while using non-essential services such as cell phone and cable television services, so partial discharge cannot be justified.
Citation	*Miller v. PHEAA*, 377 F.3d 616 (6th Cir., 2004)

CASE 4 – CHAPTER 7 INSIDER TRANSFER RULE

Former Bank Director Not Insider for Purposes of Preferential Transfer Issues	
Description	Appeals court held that a long retired director of a bank, accused to making preferential payments to the bank prior to filing bankruptcy, was not an insider, so there was no preferential treatment issue requiring the bank to repay the money to the bankruptcy trustee.
Topic	Bankruptcy Law
Key Words	Chapter 7; Preferential Transfers; Former Director
CASE SUMMARY	
Facts	Kunz filed Chapter 7 bankruptcy in 2002. Rupp was the court appointed trustee. Kunz had been involved in the formation of United Security Bank and had been a member of the board of directors until he resigned in 1990. He held the title "director emeritus" but had no authority and had not attended any board meetings, but received an annual payment of about $5,000 and is listed in bank materials. Prior to filing bankruptcy, Kunz had made payments to creditors United Bank, Comerica Bank and Wells Fargo Bank. The trustee contended that the payments to United were preferential relative to other creditors and sued to recover funds Kunz paid to United. After complicated proceedings, the matter was appealed.
Decision	Kunz's title of director emeritus of United did not make Kunz a director of the bank or an insider of the bank. As such, there is no preferential avoidance issue here, so United need not repay the money paid by Kunz prior to filing bankruptcy. Per se insiders are officers and directors. Other parties who may be classified as insiders are based on the professional or business relationship and requires a weighing of the evidence. Kunz was long removed from the control of United Bank business and was not an insider.
Citation	*In re Kunz*, 489 F.3d 1072 (10th Cir., 2007)

CASE 5 – CHAPTER 13 REPAYMENT FORMULA

	Current Income Most Relevant to Determining Bankruptcy Debt Repayment Plan
Description	Appeals court held that while the bankruptcy statute refers to using a six month average to calculate income to help determine repayment plan in Chapter 13, the court should look to the most relevant income due to changes in circumstances.
Topic	Bankruptcy Law
Key Words	Chapter 13; Income Measure

	CASE SUMMARY
Facts	Lanning, a single woman with no children, filed a Chapter 13 petition in October 2006 to address $36,793 in unsecured debt. Her annual gross income was $33,147 in 2004 and $56,516 in 2005. She took a buyout of $27,500 from her employer in May 2006. She then took another job that paid $1,922 monthly. Her expenses were listed as $1,773 monthly, leaving $149 monthly in "excess income." However, the formula used to calculate "current monthly income" is the average of income for the six months before filing bankruptcy. Using that method, her monthly income was $5,344, as it included the buyout. Using that formula on the bankruptcy form, her "excess income" to apply to debt was $1,115. Lanning proposed to pay $144 per month for 36 months ($5,184) to satisfy her total debt. The bankruptcy court, noting her current income of $1,922, accepted her plan. The trustee appealed. The district court affirmed. Trustee appealed.
Decision	Affirmed. When a Chapter 13 plan contemplates less than full repayment of all unsecured claims, the starting point for calculating the debtor's projected disposable income is presumed to be the debtor's current monthly income subject to a showing of a substantial change in circumstances. The statute refers to "projected disposable income to be received in the applicable commitment period beginning on the date that the first payment is due under the plan." While Lanning did have higher income prior to current employment, it is her current income that is most relevant to calculating income during the repayment period.
Citation	*In re Lanning*, ---F.3d--- (2008 WL 4879134, 10th Cir., 2008)

CASE 6 – PREFERENTIAL TRANSFER 90 DAY RULE

Bankrupts May Not Transfer Funds among Debtors 90 Days before Filing	
Description	Appeals court held that it was a preferential transfer for parties who filed bankruptcy to make transfers from one credit card to another within 90 days of filing. The debt transfer is an abuse of the bankruptcy process that the trustee has the right to reverse.
Topic	Bankruptcy
Key Words	Abuse; Preferential Transfers
CASE SUMMARY	
Facts	The Marshalls filed for Chapter 7 bankruptcy. Less than 90 days before they filed, they directed one credit card company to pay off another credit card company $17,000 through a balance transfer from one card to another. They had another credit card company pay off a $21,000 balance owed by a similar balance transfer to another card. The trustee filed an adversary complaint against the card company that received payments, contending that since they were made within 90 days of the bankruptcy filings they were preferential transfers that could adversely impact other creditors, which is abuse of the process. The bankruptcy court disagreed and upheld the funds transfer. The trustee appealed but the district court affirmed. The trustee appealed again.
Decision	Reversed and remanded. The trustee had the right to "avoid" the payoffs ordered by the Marshalls during the 90 days before filing. The ability to control debt on their cards made that an "interest of the debtor in property" subject to the rules regarding preferential treatment of creditors. The credit lines in the credit cards were in the control of the debtors. The funds involved in the estate would have been different had the transfers not been made, so the transfers will be reversed so as not to upset the rights and preferences of the creditors.
Citation	*In re Marshall*, 550 F.3d 1251 (10th Cir., 2008)

Repayment of Retirement Account Loan Not "Necessary Expense"	
Description	Appeals court affirmed that a debtor who filed for Chapter 7 bankruptcy would have to convert his filing to Chapter 13 as he engaged in abuse of the means test. The bankrupt could not deduct as a necessary expense the payments he was making to his retirement account to repay a loan he took from that account.
Topic	Bankruptcy
Key Words	Chapter 7; Abuse; Deductions; Retirement Fund Loan
CASE SUMMARY	
Facts	Egebjerg filed a voluntary Chapter 7 bankruptcy petition on December 31, 2006. He earned a gross income of $6,115.56 per month; was single and had no assets. He had unsecured consumer debt of $31,000. Two years before, he had taken a loan from his retirement plan. The plan automatically deducted $734 from his paycheck each month to repay the loan, which was scheduled to be repaid in September 2008. According to Egebjerg's schedule of necessary expenses, which included the retirement fund repayment, he was left with a monthly disposable income of $15. The trustee moved to dismiss the Chapter 7 petition, arguing that the retirement fund repayment was not a necessary expense. With that subtracted from his expenses, Egebjerg's filing was an abuse of the means test. The bankruptcy court agreed and ordered Egebjerg to convert his filing to Chapter 13. Under that, he could pay unsecured creditors $525 a month and could make smaller payments toward repaying his retirement fund. Egebjerg appealed.
Decision	Affirmed. Payments made on a loan from a debtor's retirement account cannot be deducted in performing a Chapter 7 means test. Such payments may not be classified as "other necessary expenses" and deducted from income. Contrary to Egebjerg's position, such payments do not fall under "special circumstances" that rebut the presumption of abuse. The Chapter 7 filing will be converted to Chapter 13.
Citation	*Egebjerg v. Anderson,* ---F.3d--- (2009 WL 2357706, 9th Cir., 2009)

221

BUSINESS ETHICS

CASE 1 – BROADCAST CENSORSHIP

	Punishing Broadcaster for One "Fleeting Expletive" Was Arbitrary and Capricious
Description	Appeals court vacated an agency finding of liability by a TV network fined for broadcasting the f-word. The agency showed no consistency in its application of its policy against obscene and indecent broadcasts.
Topic	**Administrative Law**
Key Words	Regulatory Policy; Arbitrary and Capricious; Broadcasting; Language; Indecency
	CASE SUMMARY
Facts	On a musical awards program, Bono said that the award was "f***ing brilliant." Fox Television was held liable by the Federal Communications Commission (FCC) for violating its policy against indecency and profanity for "fleeting expletives" on a broadcast. Fox appealed the decision.
Decision	Vacated and remanded. The FCC policy to punish "fleeting expletives" was arbitrary and capricious. For decades, while a broadcaster could have been punished under FCC rules against obscene or indecent broadcasts, no broadcaster had been punished as happened in the Fox case. The FCC's decision was devoid of any evidence to suggest that the incident that occurred warranted government intervention. The FCC did not provide any explanation of when the policy would be enforced and when it would not, and what the basis was for the policy. Agencies may change their policies, but must provide a reasoned analysis for departing from prior precedent.
Citation	*Fox Television Stations, Inc. v. Federal Communications Comm.*, 489 F.3d 444 (2nd Cir., 2007)

Giving Creditor Conflicting Rescission Forms Violates TILA	
Description	Appeals court held that for a mortgage company to give a creditor conflicting forms about the right to rescind violated the TILA rule of a clear and conspicuous disclosure statement that includes the right of rescission. That violation gave the consumer up to three years within which to rescind, rather then three days.
Topic	Consumer Protection
Key Words	Truth in Lending Act; Notice; Defect; Mortgage
CASE SUMMARY	
Facts	Handy obtained a new mortgage on her home from Anchor Mortgage. TILA requires that a creditor clearly disclose to a borrower her right to rescind the loan within three business days. If the creditor fails to do so, the right to rescind may be extended to three years. Two years after obtaining the mortgage, Handy sought to rescind the loan based on TILA disclosure defects. At closing, she was given two rescission forms, one form was proper; the other stated that if she rescinded, it would not cancel the loan. The trial court held for Anchor, ruling that the different forms were not significant, that Handy could have still rescinded within three days if she wanted to do so. Two years later made little sense. She appealed.
Decision	Reversed and remanded. Providing the borrower two rescission forms, one of which was inappropriate, violates the TILA requirement that the notice be clear and conspicuous. An ordinary consumer would be confused by the different forms; one of which stated that the loan was not rescinded in the event it was rescinded. That violation of TILA gave Handy up to three years in which to rescind the mortgage.
Citation	*Handy v. Anchor Mortgage Corp.,* 464 F.3d 760 (7th Cir., 2006)

LEGAL TRENDS UPDATED

CASE 1 – PRIVATE PURPOSE TAKING

Eminent Domain Power May Be Used for Private Development Purposes	
Description	Supreme Court held that a city has the right to use its powers of eminent domain to take property to be used for private economic development. So long as the city has participated in the planning and believes that it is in the public good for creating jobs and tax revenues, the action is constitutional.
Topic	Constitutional Law
Key Words	Eminent Domain; Public Use; Economic Development; Taking
CASE SUMMARY	
Facts	The City of New London approved an economic development plan to gain control of some land to be used in a new private development. Some property owners were not willing to sell their houses to the developer, so the city condemned their property. The owners sued, contending that the use of eminent domain by the city for a private developer was unconstitutional because it was not for public use. The Connecticut supreme court approved the taking; the property owners appealed.
Decision	Affirmed. The city's determination that the area was sufficiently distressed to justify a program of economic rejuvenation is entitled to deference. The city has developed the plan to help create new jobs and increase tax revenue. There will be a variety of commercial, residential, and recreational uses. The whole will be greater than the sum of the parts. Connecticut has a state statute that allows the use of eminent domain for such purposes. The state has determined that the private development plan has a public purpose, so it is not an unconstitutional taking. The court will not adopt a bright-line rule for such cases, as they must be reviewed case-by-case.
Citation	*Kelo v. City of New London, Conn.,* --- U.S.--- (2005 WL 1459118, Sup. Ct., 2005)

CASE 2 – VACANT LAND TAKING

Property Owners May Not Be Forced into Redevelopment	
Description	New Jersey high court held that a town violated the state constitution by planning to force property owners to sell their land for redevelopment. The owners had clear title and preferred the land be left vacant; as such it did not contribute blight, so could not be forced into development.
Topic	Constitutional Law
Key Words	Eminent Domain; Taking; Blighted Area; Redevelopment
CASE SUMMARY	
Facts	The Gallenthin family has owned a 63-acre piece of land in Paulsboro, New Jersey, since 1951. It is mostly vacant protected wetlands bordered by an industrial property, a river, and a street. The property was zoned as a marine industrial business park, which would permit commercial, light industrial, and other non-residential uses, but nothing had been placed on the property. A wild-growing reed is harvested from it, but that generates little income for the owners. The city hired a company to study how land in the town could be developed. The company recommended the Gallenthin parcel be tied into unused business property next to it to create a larger parcel for development. The BP and Dow companies were interested. The town declared that the Gallenthin property was "in need of redevelopment." That designation would allow eminent domain to be used. The Gallenthins objected, but the lower courts held for the town, finding that it followed proper process. The Gallenthins appealed.
Decision	Reversed. The statute that allowed redevelopment of land that was in a stagnant condition did not give the town authority to redevelop the land simply because it was not in its highest valued use. Although the Blighted Areas Clause of the New Jersey constitution undoubtedly enlarges the legislature's eminent domain power to take land for redevelopment purposes, the judiciary is the ultimate arbiter of constitutional issues. The concern with "stagnant" land is mostly about land tied up because of title problems. Blighted property generally means land that has deteriorated into a mess. The Gallenthin's property is neither. It is vacant land that they prefer to keep in that condition. The town cannot force redevelopment.
Citation	*Gallenthin Realty Development v. Borough of Paulsboro*, 924 A.2d 447 (Sup. Ct., N.J., 2007)

CASE 3 – EMINENT DOMAIN LOSS OF BUSINESS VALUE

No Compensation for Loss of Business Value Due to Eminent Domain Taking	
Description	Appeals court held that in the District of Columbia there is no recovery for the loss of business value that occurs when property is taken by eminent domain. The business owner receives the value of the property taken, but not damages for the loss of business.
Topic	Constitutional Law
Key Words	Eminent Domain; Business Losses; Damages
CASE SUMMARY	
Facts	Mamo owned a gas station for 20 years in the District of Columbia. The District took the land that had Mamo's business and specified that the value of the land was $680,000 for just compensation purposes under eminent domain. The company that supplied his gas, BP, then terminated his franchise because of the condemnation of the property. Mamo sued the District for the value of the franchise he lost, his leasehold interest, and goodwill. He demanded $500,000 payment for the value of his business beyond the value of the real property taken. The trial court dismissed his suit; he appealed.
Decision	Affirmed. Mamo was not entitled to compensation for business losses, goodwill, or other consequential damages under the Fifth Amendment. Since BP cancelled his franchise, it had no value. The taking of the property ended any leasehold interests. The District's compensation law did not authorize recovery of business loss or goodwill, so he has no claim.
Citation	*Mamo v. District of Columbia*, 934 A.2d 376 (Ct. App., D.C., 2007)

CASE 4 – FOREST FIRE NON-TAKING

<table>
<tr><td colspan="2" align="center">Government Not Liable for Taking of Property that Burned Due to Fire Suppression Policy</td></tr>
<tr><td>Description</td><td>Appeals court held that homeowners who claimed their homes were destroyed by a forest fire because of the Forest Service policy to let forest fires run their natural course rather than suppress fires, had no claim against the government for an uncompensated taking of property.</td></tr>
<tr><td>Topic</td><td>Constitutional Law</td></tr>
<tr><td>Key Words</td><td>Fifth Amendment; Taking; Forest Fire; Land Management Policies</td></tr>
<tr><td colspan="2" align="center">CASE SUMMARY</td></tr>
<tr><td>Facts</td><td>A deer hunter got lost in a national forest near San Diego. He lit a signal fire to attract rescuers. The fire spread, killing 15 people, burning 273,000 acres of land, and destroying more than 2,000 homes. Forest Service policy is to allow fires to run their natural course rather than suppress them. Cary and other property owners were among the affected homeowners. They sued the government, contending that the Forest Service policy of not containing forest fires resulted in an uncompensated taking, by inverse condemnation, of their property. The U.S. Court of Federal Claims granted the government's motion for judgment on the pleadings. Plaintiffs appealed.</td></tr>
<tr><td>Decision</td><td>Affirmed. The injuries suffered by the landowners were not the direct, natural or probable result of government acts, as required on a taking claim based on inverse condemnation. The destruction of their property did not provide any benefit for the government, so there was not a takings.</td></tr>
<tr><td>Citation</td><td>Cary v. U.S., 552 F.3d 1373 (Fed. Cir., 2009)</td></tr>
</table>

CASE 5 – CITY SOVEREIGN IMMUNITY

Sovereign Immunity Blocks Wrongful Death Suit for Improper Medical Procedure by EMT	
Description	Appeals court held that sovereign immunity protected the city and a city EMT from suit in a case where improper treatment in a call for help resulted in death.
Topic	Torts
Key Words	Wrongful Death; Negligence; EMT; Sovereign Immunity
CASE SUMMARY	
Facts	Sanford Richardson had trouble breathing. His wife called the St. Louis Fire Department which provided emergency medical services to the public. The emergency medical technician (EMT) who responded to the call placed a tube into his esophagus instead of his trachea, causing him to suffer anoxic brain injury that resulted in his death. His wife sued for wrongful death due to negligent training of personnel and for mistreatment by the EMT who inserted the breathing tube. The trial court dismissed the suit, holding that defendants were entitled to sovereign and official immunity. Plaintiff appealed.
Decision	Affirmed. Municipal corporations are entitled to sovereign immunity when engaged in governmental functions, but not when engaged in proprietary functions. The operation of a city-owned emergency medical service was a governmental function and, therefore, the city was entitled to sovereign immunity against plaintiff's wrongful death and negligence suit. Even though the city charged a fee for the service, the service provided a general public benefit and served the public health and welfare, so was not a proprietary service. Similarly, application of official immunity may be appropriate, on a case-by-case basis, to city-employed EMTs who allegedly acted negligently on the job. Official immunity shields public officials for alleged acts of negligence committed during the course of their official duties. That applies in the case of "discretionary acts" for which a public official exercised reason in determining how or whether an act should be done.
Citation	*Richardson v. City of St. Louis*, ---S.W.3d--- (2009 WL 3050917, Ct. App., Mo., 2009)

EPA Has Authority to Regulate Greenhouse Gases	
Description	Supreme Court held that the EPA, contrary to its position, has authority to regulate vehicle emissions that contribute to greenhouse gases that the Court recognized as contributing to global warming.
Topic	Environmental Law
Key Words	Clean Air Act; Greenhouse Gases; Auto Emissions
CASE SUMMARY	
Facts	Massachusetts and some other states petitioned the EPA to tighten the standards for vehicle emissions (specifically carbon dioxide, which is not regulated) that contribute to greenhouse gases. The EPA refused to regulate the emissions contending it did not have authority in the Clean Air Act (CAA) and that, even if it could, it would be unwise as Congress is considering regulatory options and possible international treaties. The appeals court agreed with the EPA; the states appealed.
Decision	Reversed and remanded. The states have standing to sue for review of the matter as their environment is affected by the regulation or lack of regulation. The CAA authorizes the EPA to regulate emission from new vehicles in the event it forms a judgment that such emissions contribute to climate change. The EPA can avoid taking regulatory action with respect to greenhouse gases only if it determines that the gases do not contribute to climate change or if it can provide a reasonable explanation as to why it cannot or will not exercise its discretion in the matter.
Citation	*Massachusetts v. EPA*, 128 S.Ct. 1438 (Sup. Ct., 2007)

CASE 7 – CRIMINAL LAW SENTENCING GUIDELINES

	Sentencing Guidelines Are Guidelines, Not Statutory Requirements
Description	Appeals court held that the Sentencing Guidelines are to give guidance to judges in sentencing, but, unless a statute requires a specific sentence be imposed, judges are not required to follow the sentences recommended by the Guidelines.
Topic	Criminal Law
Key Words	Sentencing Guidelines; Advisory Status
CASE SUMMARY	
Facts	Corner pleaded guilty to possession of more than five grams of crack cocaine with intent to distribute. He was sentenced to 188 months' imprisonment as a career offender under the Sentencing Guidelines. Corner appealed, raising the question of whether a district judge is entitled to disagree with the career-offending Guideline from the Sentencing Commission.
Decision	Vacated and remanded. The Supreme Court, in the 2005 Booker decision, held that the Sentencing Guidelines are advisory and that judges may vary from Guideline recommendations as long as they respect all statutory requirements. The Guidelines impose much longer sentences for possession of crack cocaine compared to equal quantities of powder cocaine. Since the difference in sentences is based on a Guideline from the Commission, not a statute passed by Congress, judges are at liberty to reject the Guideline, although they must act reasonably when using that power. Sentencing judges must implement statutes, whether or not the judges agree with them or not, but Sentencing Commission Guidelines are only a benchmark that judges may use for guidance. Corner will be resentenced.
Citation	*U.S. v. Corner*, ---F.3d--- (2010 WL 935754, 7th Cir., 2010)

CASE 8 – INSURED'S FAILURE TO COOPERATE

Insurer Need Not Make Payments When Insured Parties Fail to Cooperate

Description	Court held that when a home owner refuses to cooperate with the homeowner's insurance company in an investigation of a house likely burned by arson, the insurer has no duty to pay benefits due to a breach of contract, which requires cooperation under oath.
Topic	Insurance
Key Words	Homeowner; Breach of Contract; Loss; Fire; Cooperation

CASE SUMMARY

Facts	The Miles' home, insured by Great Northern, was substantially damaged by a fire. Miles was in bankruptcy. Authorities determined that the fire was intentionally set. While Miles was a "person of interest," no charges were filed against him. Great Northern would be liable under the policy unless the Miles set the fire. Miles told Great Northern that various people wanted "to destroy" him, but he would not provide the names. Mrs. Miles, relying on advice of her husband, an attorney, refused to answer questions posed to her by Great Northern. A sworn proof of loss had to be provided within 60 days, but the Miles did not provide it for five months. Great Northern denied the claim because the Miles had not cooperated in the investigation and had filed the proof of loss beyond the due date. The Miles then said they would cooperate more. Great Northern then agreed to pay the $800,000 mortgage on the house and paid the Miles $250,000 for living expenses, but denied a request for about $800,000 for lost personal property. Miles sued for breach of contract and other claims. Great Northern sued the Miles for unjust enrichment and breach of contract.
Decision	The motion by the Miles is denied. When an insurer investigates a claim of loss, the insured has a duty to cooperate by submitting to an examination under oath and producing documents relevant to the claimed loss. The insurer reasonably determined that the insureds had breached their duty to cooperate with the investigation into the fire. Great Northern was not obligated to reconsider claims made after the 60 day proof of loss period when the Miles decided to produce some documents. Correcting the breach of the duty to cooperate came after the required period.
Citation	*Miles v. Great Northern Insurance Co.*, ---F.Supp.2d--- (2009 WL 2998529, D. Mass., 2009)

CASE 9 – CERCLA SUPERFUND PROPERTY POLLUTION LIABILITY

Supreme Court Refines Terms of Possible Liability under Superfund	
Description	The Supreme Court held that a company that sold a chemical to another company is not liable for contamination at the property of the buyer who spilled some of the chemical. Knowledge that accidental spills may occur does not mean the seller was arranging for disposal of the chemical.
Topic	Intellectual Property
Key Words	CERCLA, Cleanup, Liability, Potentially Responsible Parties, Contribution
CASE SUMMARY	
Facts	In 1960, B&B, an agricultural chemical distributor, began operations on a piece of land owned by the company in Arvin, California. It later expanded operations onto an adjacent piece of land owned by two railroad companies. B&B used hazardous chemicals, including a pesticide D-D purchased from Shell Oil. Over time, these chemicals were spilled and contaminated the ground. After an examination of the site, the EPA ordered a cleanup and spent $8 million. It then sued Shell and the railroads to recover the costs. The district court and court of appeals found defendants liable for the costs. The railroads and Shell appealed to the Supreme Court.
Decision	Reversed and remanded. Shell is not liable as an "arranger" of the disposal of hazardous substances the Arvin facility. While the statute does not define the term, plain language would imply that an arranger takes intentional steps to dispose of a hazardous substance. The facts do not support that. Shell sold the pesticide to B&B for its resale. No doubt Shell knew that B&B might accidentally spill some of the chemical on its property, but it was not arranging to have the chemical disposed of. Mere knowledge that spills can occur does not impose liability. Given the costs of the cleanup and where they occurred, it is reasonable to hold the railroads liable for nine percent of the cost. Only a small portion of the cleanup was on railroad land. The railroads cannot be held potentially liable for the entire cost of the cleanup.
Citation	*Burlington Northern and Santa Fe Railway v. U.S.*, 129 S.Ct. 1870 (Sup. Ct., 2009)

CASE 10 – SEX DISCRIMINATION CUSTOMER LIABILITY

Sex Discrimination Applies to Business Relationships	
Description	New Jersey appeals court held that a woman who suffered the loss of a large sale contract with a customer, because she failed to submit to sexual demands, could pursue a claim of sex discrimination against the customer for tying the business relationship to sexual favors.
Topic	Employment Discrimination
Key Words	Sexual Harassment; Contract Termination
CASE SUMMARY	
Facts	Eileen Totorello owned J.T.'s Tire Service, a company that sold industrial tires. One customer was United Rental. J.T.'s began selling tires to its Piscataway, New Jersey branch in 1998. Totorello alleged that, beginning in 2005, the manager of that United branch, Hinkes, began to pressure her for sexual favors. He made it clear to her that he would quit buying tires from J.T.'s if she did not submit to his advances, which included kissing and groping her. His advances became more and more insistent. In 2007, when she flatly refused, he quit buying tires from J.T.'s. Sales had previously averaged $29,000 per month. Tororello sued United and Hinkes for violating the New Jersey Law Against Discrimination. The trial court dismissed the complaint, holding that the law did not apply to such situations. Totorello appealed.
Decision	Reversed and remanded. When harassment consists of sexual overtures and unwelcome touching or groping, it is presumed that the conduct was committed because of the victim's sex. Hence, Totorello has established, under the Law Against Discrimination, that harassment has occurred because of her sex. Demanding sexual favors as a condition of continuing business does state a claim for sex discrimination. Both Title VII and the New Jersey Law Against Discrimination prohibit sexual harassment in the employment context, which extends to such situations.
Citation	*J.T.'s Tire Service, Inc. v. United Rentals North America*, 985A.2d 211 (App. Div., N.J., 2010)

Punitive Damages without Compensatory Damages May Be Awarded	
Description	Appeals court held that where an employer allowed a racially hostile work environment to exist for years, there was no violation of due process for a jury to award plaintiffs punitive damages but no compensatory damages. The law does not require compensatory damages to exist to justify punitive damages.
Topic	Employment Discrimination
Key Words	Race Discrimination; Hostile Environment; Punitive Damages
CASE SUMMARY	
Facts	Eight African-American employees of Kansas City Southern Railway Company (KCS) sued the company for subjecting them to a hostile work environment. They alleged they encountered repeated instances of racially derogatory acts in KCS's diesel operation in Shreveport, Louisiana, including racial graffiti, a noose, racially derogatory comments and threats, spoken and written, and inferior shift assignments. The jury found that KCS created a hostile work environment and did not correct the problem. It awarded no compensatory damages, but awarded each plaintiff $125,000 in punitive damages. KCS appealed, contending such an award violated due process.
Decision	Affirmed. An independent award of punitive damages for a violation of Title VII, without compensatory damages, did not violate due process. There was evidence of multiple incidents of racially discriminatory behavior in the workplace over ten years, that supervisors knew of the discrimination, but did nothing to correct it. The employer failed to institute a meaningful policy against racial harassment.
Citation	*Abner v. Kansas City Southern Railroad Co.*, 513 F.3d 154 (5th Cir., 2008)